The **WIRE** Primers

A Guide to Modern Music

Edited by Rob Young

First published by Verso 2009
Copyright in the collection © *The Wire* 2009
Copyright within the contributions © The contributors 2009
Illustrations: Savage Pencil

The moral rights of the authors have been asserted

1 3 5 7 9 10 8 6 4 2

Verso
UK: 6 Meard Street, London W1F 0EG
US: 20 Jay Street, Suite 1010, Brooklyn, NY 11201
www.versobooks.com

Verso is the imprint of New Left Books

ISBN-13: 978-1-84467-427-5

British Library Cataloguing in Publication Data
A catalogue record for this book is available from the British Library

Library of Congress Cataloging-in-Publication Data
A catalog record for this book is available from the Library of Congress

Typeset using Executive (www.optimo.ch) and Arno Pro
by MJ Gavan, Truro, Cornwall
Printed in the United States by Maple Vail

Contents

About the Contributors

Mike Barnes is a writer and drummer, and the author of *Captain Beefheart: The Biography* (Omnibus Press). He lives in Hampshire.

Nick Cain contributes regularly to *The Wire*. He lives in London.

Philip Clark is a composer and writer for *The Wire*, *Gramophone* and other publications. He is currently writing a book on Dave Brubeck.

Louise Gray has written on music and visual art for *The Wire*, the *Guardian*, the *Independent on Sunday*, *Art Review* and many others. She is the music correspondent for *New Internationalist*, who published her *No-Nonsense Guide to World Music* in 2009.

David Keenan is a writer and critic, and the author of *England's Hidden Reverse* (SAF). He lives in Glasgow.

Art Lange has written about jazz and classical music for over 30 years. He teaches poetry at Columbia College, Chicago, and is co-editor (with Nathaniel Mackey) of *Moment's Notice: Jazz in Poetry & Prose* (Coffee House Press).

Stewart Lee has been a stand-up comedian since 1989. He has also written for the stage and television, and reviews music for the *Sunday Times* and other publications.

Alan Licht is a musician and the author of *Sound Art: Beyond Music, Between Categories* (Rizzoli). He lives in New York City.

Edwin Pouncey has written articles and reviews for a wide range of music and art magazines including: *Sounds*, *NME*, *Kerrang!*, *Top*, *Frieze*, *Juxtapoz* and *Mojo*. He is a regular contributor to *The Wire* and, as Savage Pencil, is the magazine's resident illustrator and cartoonist.

Ben Ratliff has been a jazz and pop critic at the *New York Times* since 1996 and is the author of *Coltrane: The Story of a Sound* (Faber & Faber). He lives in New York City.

Simon Reynolds's books include *Totally Wired*, *Bring the Noise*, *Rip It Up and Start Again* (all Faber & Faber) and *Energy Flash* (Picador).

Peter Shapiro is the author of *Turn the Beat Around: A Secret History of Disco* (Faber & Faber).

John Szwed is the author of *Space Is the Place: The Life and Times of Sun Ra* (Payback Press), *So What: The Life of Miles Davis* (Arrow) and *Global Jukebox*, a forthcoming biography of Alan Lomax (Arrow).

Derek Walmsley is *The Wire*'s Reviews Editor.

Barry Witherden has contributed to *The Wire* since 1986, as well as *Jazz Review, Jazz Journal, BBC Music, Gramophone, Music Week, Avant, The Guinness Who's Who of Jazz* and *The Rough Guide to Classical Music*.

Rob Young is *The Wire*'s Editor-at-Large. His books include *Warp* and *Rough Trade* (Black Dog Publishing) and *Electric Eden: Unearthing Britain's Visionary Music* (Faber & Faber, summer 2010).

Introduction
by Rob Young

A working title for this book was "How to Buy Modern Music". When *The Wire* magazine began a series of articles under the heading "The Primer" back in December 1996, with Barry Witherden's guide to the recordings of Karlheinz Stockhausen, the idea was to bolster the consumer confidence of anyone intrigued by the names that were frequently dropped in the pages of the magazine, and which seemed to play important and influential roles in the story of contemporary sound and music. The Primers were conceived as potted guides to the work and, by extension, to the lives of significant individual artists, groups or umbrella genres. Thirteen years and more than threescore Primers later, the feature is far from exhausted and remains one of the magazine's most popular regular sections.

The Wire Primers contains a selection of 19 of those articles, many of them specially updated, plus an additional three chapters written exclusively for this book. Taken together, the contents are designed to provide an overview of significant tendencies in modern music since the mid-twentieth century, while the selection favours artists whose catalogues possibly require an extra guiding hand. For instance, in the Jazz & Improvisation section, instead of, say, John Coltrane, whose

discography from 1963 until his death four years later is by now well annotated and universally accepted as essential, we have included more problematic figures such as Derek Bailey and Ornette Coleman, and their Primers function as reassessments of their work and careers in their own right.

The book's searchlight ranges far and wide, both geographically and historically: from countercultural Brazil in the late 1960s to the impoverished denizens of late 1970s downtown New York; from the studios of Radio France in the aftermath of World War II to the teenage bedrooms of twenty-first century dubstep producers. When placed together in a book like this, all manner of intriguing crosstalk occurs: the creative usage of turntables, from early adopters John Cage and Pierre Schaeffer via the dextrous hiphop pioneers Grandmaster Flash and Kool Herc and on to conceptual artists such as Christian Marclay and Philip Jeck; the politicised polystylism of Brazil's Tropicalistas and Nigeria's funk railroader Fela Kuti, all of whom butted up against authoritarianism in their respective developing nations; even the virtuoso playing of a squeaking door's hinges by two artists of wildly different origins, Pierre Henry and Sun Ra. It's a Primer's job to unpick and lay bare these tangled and occasionally esoteric histories and extend a friendly, critically engaged guiding hand. If you purchase just one album or download a single track as a result of reading this book, then it's succeeded. But that number, we suspect, will be far higher.

How to use this book

Each Primer includes a brief introduction, placing the subject in its historical and artistic context and providing any relevant background information. Each release is listed with the artist or group name (unless the same as the previous entry), album or track title, and record label and format information for the most recent edition available on CD. Release information changes over time, of course, but in almost every case we have restricted entries to those which it was still possible to buy as of the date of publication.

Where reissues are concerned, another line is included listing the label (if different from the CD version) and date of the recording's original release.

Occasionally – for instance, when dealing with unreleased material discovered after the fact – a third variable comes into play, when it is necessary to differentiate between original *recording* date; label and date of its subsequent first commercial release; and label/date of the current CD version.

Where a CD compiles numerous pieces from different periods or artists, the individual dates are supplied in the text itself. And in the Modern Composition section, dates when pieces were actually *written* (as opposed to recorded) are included within each entry.

Thanks to:

Tony Herrington at *The Wire* for initiating and developing the Primer series during his editorship of the magazine, and for steering the present book through to completion in numerous ways.

The Wire's current editorial team – Chris Bohn, Anne Hilde Neset and Derek Walmsley – all of whom have played a part in commissioning and editing the originals and/or revisions for this book.

Edwin Pouncey, aka Savage Pencil, for his magnificent series of illustrations which have accompanied every one of the magazine's Primers, as well as the jacket and interior of the present volume.

Nick Richardson for delving into *The Wire*'s archives and assistance with copy input.

Rowan Wilson at Verso for making the book a reality, and his colleagues Bob Bhamra and Mark Martin.

Julie McCarroll for US publicity.

Neil Taylor for representation.

Publishing history

Avant Rock

Captain Beefheart: *The Wire* 170 (April 1998)

The Fall: *The Wire* 266 (April 2006), revised and updated 2009

Noise: previously unpublished; exclusive to *The Wire Primers*

No Wave: *The Wire* 225 (November 2002)

Sonic Youth: *The Wire* 217 (March 2002), revised and updated 2009

Tropicália: *The Wire* 184 (June 1999), revised and updated 2009

Frank Zappa And The Mothers of Invention: previously unpublished; exclusive to *The Wire Primers*

Funk, Hiphop & Beyond

James Brown: *The Wire* 177 (November 1998)

Grime: *The Wire* 254 (April 2005)

Dubstep: *The Wire* 279 (May 2007), revised and updated 2009

Fela Kuti: *The Wire* 234 (August 2003)

Turntablism: *The Wire* 179 (January 1999)

Jazz & Improvisation

AMM: *The Wire* 271 (September 2006)

Derek Bailey: previously unpublished; exclusive to *The Wire Primers*

Ornette Coleman: *The Wire* 181 (March 1999), revised and updated 2009

Fire Music: *The Wire* 208 (June 2001)
Sun Ra: *The Wire* 163 (September 1997), revised and updated 2009

Modern Composition

John Cage: *The Wire* 161 (July 1997), revised and updated 2009
Morton Feldman: *The Wire* 210 (August 2001), revised and updated 2009
Musique Concrète & Early Electronic Music: *The Wire* 174 (August 1998), revised and updated 2009
Karlheinz Stockhausen: *The Wire* 163 (December 1996), revised and updated 2009
Iannis Xenakis: *The Wire* 259 (September 2005)

Avant Rock

Captain Beefheart

by Mike Barnes

Don van Vliet, aka Captain Beefheart, was born in Los Angeles in 1941. The double album *Trout Mask Replica* is still cited as an influence and inspiration by musicians of all persuasions, from Henry Kaiser to Mark E Smith. But ironically for someone so influential, his mark is usually only detectable in superficial traces in the music of his admirers. The paths he mapped towards a new musical language have rarely been explored and lie largely neglected.

Beefheart transcended his roots and influences in spectacular fashion. His most impressive music and lyrics sound like the outpourings of a creative wellspring with little predetermined structure or 'experimental' game plan to staunch the flow. He would undoubtedly have released more material had his career not been robbed of momentum by contractual and legal problems, and endless line-up changes for his group The Magic Band. But then again, as one ex-Magic Band member commented, maintaining a 16 year recording career on major labels with the sort of music Beefheart produced was a great achievement in itself. He was well aware of the worth of his output, suggesting in the 1970s that he needed a "new artform". Beefheart always felt that he should have been more commercially successful, and when he felt he had done what

he set out to achieve, he made a complete break from music in the early 1980s. He had always been a gifted visual artist, exhibiting since 1972, and during the 1990s, as plain Don van Vliet, he maintained a successful career as a painter. On the subject of his music, he prophesied in 1980: "Fifty years from now you'll wish you'd gone, 'Wow.'" A significant number of people have been exclaiming thus all along.

Safe As Milk
Buddah CD 1999, rec. 1967

Captain Beefheart and The Magic Band formed in the desert town of Lancaster, California in 1964. Initially influenced by the British Beat group invasion, they were a popular act who got their first break at the Hollywood Teenage Fair in 1965. The group's first commercially available recordings are collected on *The Legendary A&M Sessions* (Edsel), a sequence of singles originally released in 1966. The first Magic Band single, a cover of Bo Diddley's "Diddy Wah Diddy", is characterised by Beefheart's feral blues bellow and a monstrous fuzz bassline. The best and most significant track from this period went unreleased at the time (but appears on *Sessions*): Beefheart's own "Here I Am I Always Am". The song's rhythm 'n' blues structure relentlessly changes metre in a way that anticipates the developments on the debut album *Safe As Milk*. Beefheart's voice was already astonishingly well seasoned for someone in his mid-twenties, and it became more confident and potent on the *Safe As Milk* material. As well as French, Ry Cooder joined the group, fresh from playing guitar with Taj Mahal in The Rising Sons. *Safe As Milk* is a potent mixture of old and new: Delta blues, psychedelia, pop, rock 'n' roll and a shot of soul power. "Sure 'Nuff 'N Yes I Do" filches the riff of the blues standard "Rollin' and Tumblin", while the poppy "Yellow Brick Road" and the more radical "Zig Zag Wanderer" could have been written and performed by a number of contemporary groups.

"Electricity", on the other hand, exists in its own universe. Cooder recalls that Beefheart avoided standard 'four' beat because he thought it was "corny". In addition, immediately before recording the track, Beefheart decided to completely change the drum part into a shifting pattern of syncopations. Unfazed, French rose to the challenge of this 11th hour revision and the results are stunning. The song is loosely based around a square dance, and Cooder and rhythm guitarist Alex St Clair are magnificently incisive. Beefheart's singing peaks at the scalp-raising roar that blew out a microphone during the recording sessions – a feat he later repeated on TV.

Before The Magic Band, Beefheart – initially a reluctant singer – hung around with school friend Frank Zappa, adopting the Beefheart persona from a mooted film project, *Captain Beefheart Versus the Grunt People*, and recording some tracks with Zappa at the latter's Studio Z in Cucamonga, California under the name The Soots. In the 1970s Zappa announced that he was planning to issue a ten album set of Studio Z recordings, but so far only a few tracks have been officially released. The compilation *Frank Zappa: The Lost Episodes* (Rykodisc) contains half a dozen interesting Beefheart/Zappa collaborations, including the earliest Beefheart track in existence, the repulsive, scatological tour de force "Lost in a Whirlpool", recorded in Antelope Valley Junior College, Lancaster in 1958 or 1959. (In the song, Beefheart is flushed down the toilet by his girlfriend, and comes face to face with a big, brown, eyeless fish.) Other rare early material, including *Safe As Milk* outtakes, live recordings and more Soots material, can be heard on the bootleg CD *Captain Beefheart: The Early Years* (Beefmusic).

The Mirror Man Sessions
Buddah CD 1999, rec. 1967
(orig. Buddah LP 1971)
Strictly Personal
Liberty/EMI CD 1994
(orig. Blue Thumb LP 1968)

In November 1967 Beefheart and The Magic Band went into TTG's studio on Hollywood Boulevard to begin recording an album under the working title *It Comes To You In A Plain Brown Wrapper*. The initial sessions yielded four lengthy tracks that would eventually be released as *Mirror Man,* and around ten other pieces which were released separately in 1992. *The Mirror Man Sessions* CD finally put it all together for the first time, 32 years later.

Mirror Man is still erroneously dated as being recorded "one night in Los Angeles in 65". The "live in the studio" setting provides a close representation of The Magic Band in concert, where they would explore a few ideas at length. "Tarotplane" takes its title (but little else) from Robert Johnson's "Terraplane Blues", and during its 19 minutes includes references to Blind Willie Johnson's "You're Gonna Need Somebody On Your Bond" and Willie Dixon's "Wang Dang Doodle". This funky avant-Delta blues sounds like a jam session: the group are impressive, but don't seem to be heading anywhere in particular. Also featured are exploratory versions of "Kandy Korn" and "Mirror Man"; both would be re-edited and rerecorded a few months later for inclusion on *Strictly Personal*. There is an exquisite moment during "Tarotplane" when Beefheart first blows into the shenai – a North African horn reputedly given to him by Ornette Coleman – producing a garbled series of squawks in some distant key. This performance helps to explain John Peel's recollections of the effect Beefheart's shenai playing had on live audiences: "When he started playing that strange instrument, about half the audience would leave."

Strictly Personal was recorded six months after the above-mentioned sessions. Notoriously, it features phasing effects and backward tapes added surreptitiously by manager and Blue Thumb label boss Bob Krasnow, who released the album quickly in an attempt to cash in on the burgeoning acid rock market. Counter-rumours claim that Beefheart initially sanctioned the production, only disassociating himself from it when it was criticised by the US music press.

From the strange chorales of the lengthy "Trust Us" to the untrammelled bellowing of the rerecorded "Mirror Man" and the image-streams of "Beatle Bones 'n' Smokin' Stones", with the infamous "Strawberry Fields Forever" refrain which irked John Lennon, the *Strictly Personal* compositions exhibited the broadening of Beefheart's musical scope. Although Cooder had left the group, St Clair and incumbent guitarist Jeff Cotton were an impressive duo, grappling with increasingly serpentine lines, while John French's use of tabla rhythms carried the music beyond the four-square beat of blues, rhythm 'n' blues and rock 'n' roll. Beefheart demonstrated by "Ah Feel Like Ahcid", a fantastic mutation of a foot stompin' blues holler based loosely on Son House's "Death Letter" and Wille Dixon's "Spoonful". The phasing is occasionally intrusive, but overall it detracts little from the music, which, as Beefheart put it, shines through "like a diamond in the mud".

Trout Mask Replica
Straight/Reprise CD 1994, rec. 1969

Trout Mask Replica was released in summer 1969, but it still sounds like a signal retrieved from another time and dimension. Put more prosaically, it was a quantum leap from its predecessor in terms of structure and musical complexity. The difference is simply explained: Beefheart had recently had a piano installed in The Magic Band's communal rented house in San Fernando Valley, and began using it to generate new material. As he had no piano technique to speak of, the resulting 'compositions' were characterised by relatively short lines, inevitably in different metres. It fell to John French to capture the moment and transcribe these keyboard studies for the rest of the group to play. Building these heterogeneous layers into a structure and then coming up with drum parts to bind them together nearly drove him "nuts", French has admitted. The process wasn't any smoother thanks to Beefheart deciding on a whim that some parts should be played backwards.

The Magic Band now consisted of French and Cotton (renamed Drumbo and Antennae Jimmy Semens, respectively), plus two new recruits, teenagers Bill Harkleroad (aka Zoot Horn Rollo) on guitar and Mark Boston (Rockette Morton) on bass, who thought they were joining a psychedelic blues outfit. In the months leading up to the *Trout Mask* sessions, the group lived and rehearsed in conditions of grinding poverty, with French practising for up to 14 hours a day. The group members were definitely malnourished at times, though rumours (or allegations) circulated by the group that Boston lived on dog food and was too weak to leave his bed sound mischievous. Fistfights broke out and the atmosphere soured as Beefheart became increasingly tyrannical. "A comic book Mansonish gestalt therapy kinda thing" is how Harkleroad remembers the time.

The first piano-written track was the astringent chamber piece "Dali's Car". Beefheart's initial ideas would often run out of steam, and the group had to make imaginative leaps to complete the journey from A to B. "You guys know what to do," was his prosaic response to queries about how to tie up a song's loose ends. Gary Lucas (Beefheart's manager and guitarist later in his career) likened his compositional process to throwing a pack of cards into the air, taking a snapshot as they fell, then getting the musicians to reproduce the frozen moment.

"I got musicians who had never played before," explained Beefheart. "To get them past the 'I' consciousness, you know? That endless 'me, me, me'. Or do-re-mi, whatever that stuff is." This claim is fanciful to say the least: French and Harkleroad could both read music, and all four Magic Band members had been playing for years. But it is true to say that they had never played music like that on *Trout Mask Replica*.

Although it travels a long way from its sources, *Trout Mask Replica* is still infused with the essence of the blues. In isolation, some of the guitar lines aren't so different from the stranger articulations of Robert Johnson or Hubert Sumlin, Howlin' Wolf's guitarist. In addition, Beefheart threaded the music's tangled structure with threads of rock 'n' roll, avant garde jazz and poetry that looked back at the American cultural mythos through a kaleidoscope. When questioned about the record in 1991, he said that he had been "trying to break up the mind in several different directions, causing them not to be able to fixate".

The majority of the 28 tracks were put down in about six hours at Whitney Studios in Glendale, Los Angeles, with Zappa producing. With time added on for the vocal tracks and mixing, the record was complete in just four days. That was going it some, but the bootleg *Trout Mask Replica Rehearsals*, which features tapes of The Magic Band playing (without Beefheart) at the Cunoga Park house, highlights what an awesome unit the group had become.

There is too much on *Trout Mask* to summarise here, but two particular highlights are "Neon Meate Dream Of A Octafish", a delirious stream of sensual/sexual imagery (including "Meate rose 'n' hairs") declaimed over a spectacularly convoluted backing, and the a cappella "Orange Claw Hammer", a beautifully wrought, sea shanty style yarn about an old sailor's reunion with his long lost daughter.

American critic John Ellis bemoaned the fact that this mighty record was often just used as a novelty 'pot party' record. The fact that it works on that level and also stands as one of the most staggering pieces of music produced in the last 30 years is some kind of achievement.

Lick My Decals Off, Baby
Bizarre/Straight/Rhino CD 1991, rec. 1970

Just to prove that *Trout Mask* wasn't a fluke, *Lick My Decals Off, Baby* – Beefheart's favourite of his own albums – arrived just over a year later. Ex-Zappa drummer Art Tripp (aka Ed Marimba) joined, locking into a spectacular twin drumkit combination with French. Jeff Cotton departed, resulting in a

Magic Band sound that was by turns more open – with Tripp's marimba leavening the sound – and at times even more extreme than *Trout Mask*. The album contains some of Beefheart's most original music. The 'piano transposed to guitar' template was expanded for the sublime bass and guitar piece "Peon" (composed, miraculously, in one take), and the flamenco-inflected guitar solo "One Red Rose That I Mean". "Doctor Dark" is barely fathomable at first. The musicians seem to inhabit free time before cohering and then shooting off on a number of tangents simultaneously, and finally regrouping again. As the track fades, Beefheart, in fine voice throughout, sounds uncannily like Van Morrison. Harkleroad's thorny guitar, pitched against double percussion and Boston's flat, hollow bass, produced a sound that pushed even further into new territory. "What the music is going at is complete absence," Beefheart explained. "That's the way I did it. You can't think about that music. That music is moving so fast that if you think about it it's like watching a train go by and counting the cars. It's better to hear it without the mind so active."

Lyrically, *Decals* moved on from the environmental warnings of *Trout Mask* into apocalyptic landscapes. In "Petrified Forest", dinosaurs take revenge on the human race for their desecration of the planet – but there is humour, too, and sex on the title track. Practising the saxophone was anathema to Beefheart, and here he blasts at cacophonous full throttle all over the instrumental "Japan In a Dishpan" and "Flash Gordon's Ape". "That's his ego," reckons guitarist Moris Tepper, who joined the group in 1975. "He wrote this music and then he hears the band do the track and the track sounds amazing and he doesn't feel he's part of it. I think he covered up a lot of great music, but at the same time, watching him take out his big firehose and spray was real boss!"

The Spotlight Kid/Clear Spot
Warner/Reprise CD 1990, rec. 1972/1973

"I hate that album, it sucks," said Bill Harkleroad of *The Spotlight Kid*. Beefheart claims to have written it *for* the group, meaning that it was far removed from the sound and fury of *Trout Mask* and *Decals*, more overtly blues-based and easier to play. Harkleroad recalls that when the group started rehearsing the material "tempos got down to this zombie state". This is rather overstating the case. True, the album has a lugubrious feel, especially on the bleak "There Ain't No Santa Claus On The Evenin' Stage", but there are plenty of highlights, such as the sexual jousting of the characters on "I'm Gonna Booglarise You Baby", which rides out on an irresistible hi-hat/snare groove with Boston, Harkleroad and new guitarist and ex-Mother Of Invention Elliot Ingber skidding around on top. Many of the songs would become live favourites, including the awesome "Click Clack", a take on the perennial "train kept rollin" theme set to a shuffle beat that really does sound like it's played backwards.

Beefheart had often slipped playful blues references into previous songs. But having retreated temporarily from the innovations of his previous records, he became increasingly defensive in interviews, describing attempts to link him to the Delta blues as "just ignorant thinking". "A lot of those English boys copy people," he commented later, referring to groups that came to prominence in the 1960s blues/R&B boom. "I don't. Never did."

In 1972 Beefheart told *Creem* magazine that the music for *Clear Spot* had been written during an eight hour journey from Boston to Yale. If asked, The Magic Band would no doubt have disputed the timescale and perhaps the mechanics of composition. They were becoming dissatisfied with the lack of financial (if not critical) recognition for their contributions. Without claiming authorship of the material, Harkleroad claims that, with less overt teaching by Beefheart, both he and Mark Boston helped to shape much of the *Clear Spot* material.

Producer Ted Templeman, who had worked with other Warner Brothers acts, including Little Feat and Van Morrison, was drafted in to oversee the sessions. He wasted no time in letting Beefheart know who was in charge. Fallouts ensued, and there were rumours that Beefheart was denied access to the studio at critical times. Recently, Art Tripp said of Templeman, "We had him come in there and make it more commercial." Tripp also suggested that half the tracks on the record were "just like that normal crap you hear every time you switch on the radio. Except we had kind of a unique sound."

On *Clear Spot* that unique sound is warm and spacious, a world away from the dry angularities of *Trout Mask* and *Decals*. The group is at its most muscular, pumping this funky hoodoo music. "Too Much Time", with The Blackberries on backing vocals, is pure Otis Redding; so much so that the track was a hit on a Boston soul station until they discovered Beefheart was white. "Lo Yo Yo Stuff" and the horn-powered "Long Neck Bottles" are both witty and lascivious. And the album contains Beefheart's best known (and best) song, "Big Eyed Beans From Venus".

On its own terms, the avant pop and rock of *Clear Spot* is a massive success. Then, in 1974, came two albums that really did sound like the normal crap you hear every time you turn on the radio: *Unconditionally Guaranteed* and *Bluejeans and Moonbeams* (both Virgin CDs). Beefheart put his career in the hands of MOR svengalis the di Martino brothers, and went round extolling the virtues of Rod Stewart and The Stylistics. A handful of decent tracks are spread across the two albums, but most second-guess what commercial music should be like and come out sounding unbelievably lame. Ironically, they both failed to chart as high as the previous four albums. There is little point in trying to construct a revisionist apologia for this music, as Beefheart later advised anyone who had bought the studio albums to try to get their money back.

The former Magic Band members became Mallard, recorded two albums and disappeared. Beefheart disappeared too, disillusioned and thinking seriously about giving up music. But his old friend/enemy Frank Zappa threw him a lifeline, and in 1975 Beefheart toured with The Mothers Of Invention, a meeting which is documented on the sporadically brilliant *Bongo Fury* (Rykodisc). As well as featuring on Zappa's material, Beefheart contributes two compositions, "Sam With The Showing Scalp Flat Top" and "The Man With The Woman Head". After his recent nadir, these image-rich recitations boded well.

Shiny Beast (Bat Chain Puller)

Virgin CD 2006, rec. 1978

Interviewed in 1976, Beefheart claimed to have recorded an album with "the greatest band in the world", a young Magic Band he had taught from scratch. The group's keyboard player John Thomas clarifies: "Don was very fond of saying that he taught each of the musicians to play their instrument. But he virtually had to teach them how to play the music the way he envisioned it because there was no precedent for it. You bowed your own will in order to serve his vision."

Bat Chain Puller was a convincing return; powerful with a full, multifaceted sound. The Magic Band now comprised Thomas, French on guitars and drums, and guitarists (Jeff) Moris Tepper and ex-Mother Denny Walley. The title track – its rhythm adapted from a cassette recording of a train passing Beefheart's car, which was parked with the windscreen wipers on – is colossal, and the tale of an old hobo set to stunning music on "Odd Jobs" was equal to anything he had recorded. The big problem is that the album still hasn't been released. Frank Zappa was the executive producer, but the recording coincided with his lawsuit with manager Herb Cohen. He owned the tape but couldn't put it out. Neither could Warners, nor Virgin. That didn't stop Virgin from circulating some promo tapes, which subsequently became the source for numerous bootleg versions of the album.

A rerecorded version of *Bat Chain Puller*, retitled *Shiny Beast (Bat Chain Puller)*, was released in early 1978. About half the material is reworked from the *Bat Chain Puller* tapes. There are a couple of brilliant new tracks: the Zappa-esque "Ice Rose" (initially composed in 1967) and "When I See Mommy I Feel Like A Mummy". The album features Art Tripp's marimba and Bruce Fowler's trombone in a beautifully orchestrated, gloriously colourful sound. Perhaps it lacked the bite of the original *Bat Chain Puller*, but the airy production (by Beefheart and Pete Johnson) allows this joyous music to dance.

Doc At The Radar Station

Virgin CD 2006, rec. 1980

One thing *Doc At The Radar Station* didn't lack was bite: it was Beefheart's most abrasive record since *Decals*. The basis of Beefheart's creativity was always his spontaneity; he had often likened the process to going to the bathroom or combing his hair, and he was keen to share this turbulent mental throughput with the world: "I hope it gets people up and makes them move like I have to. I do it out of irritation – that's my drive. I have to do it. It's like sandpaper on a shrimp," he said. Once again the album recycles and remodels ideas and material from earlier sessions, including *The Spotlight Kid*, and a rerecorded take on "Brickbats", a cut from the original *Bat Chain Puller*. The new material is even better. "Making Love To A Vampire With Monkey On My Knee" is a compelling monodrama set to a group backing which includes mellotron, an instrument that Beefheart had taken a liking to, played in the iciest, spikiest way.

With Beefheart back on sole production duties, the sound is flatter; he stated that old blues records had no added reverb, so why should his music be "drowned in heavy syrup"? In addition, he wanted the music to be two-dimensional, like a painting. But The Magic Band had been listening to groups they had supposedly influenced, such as The B-52s and Devo, and wanted some of their production values. Keyboard and bass player Eric Drew Feldman recalls that when Beefheart left the control room, "I had the audacity to ask the engineer, '*Could* you make it a little warmer?' and he did. Don came in five minutes later and immediately said, 'Sounds different. The bass sounds different', and smoke came out the ears a little bit." The whole of *Doc* has this kind of edge.

Ice Cream For Crow

Virgin CD 2006, rec. 1982

With the benefit of hindsight, *Ice Cream For Crow*, Beefheart's last album, sounds like the subconscious tying together of a bundle of loose ends. New tracks sit alongside old, reworked material, and the original plan, in order to keep the budget down, was to include some of the tracks from the *Bat Chain Puller* sessions. But Frank Zappa, who technically owned the *Bat Chain Puller* master tape, refused to let Beefheart use any of the material unless he bought the tape outright. Fuelled by anger from his confrontation with Zappa, Beefheart began composing that night, producing an abrasive piano piece, "Oat Hate", which later became "Skeleton Makes Good". Along with another 'filler', "Cardboard Cutout Sundown"; it's one of *Ice Cream*'s best tracks.

Ice Cream features some fine music. The title track was a minor hit, and "Evening Bell", a showcase for Gary Lucas, was Beefheart's most challenging guitar composition yet. The reason the album doesn't quite match up to *Doc* is exemplified by "Hey Garland, I Dig Your Tweed Coat". Whereas on *Trout Mask* Beefheart belted his vocal over The Magic Band's turbulent backing and achieved an intuitive sort of coherence, here he sounds hesitant and that vital union isn't quite achieved.

Virgin were still keen to take up their option on another album, but Beefheart had already tired of the recording/touring routine, and apparently didn't think the terms were good enough. They even tried to guide him into acting by provisionally landing him a part in the killer bear movie *Grizzly 2* – with guarantees that Magic Band material would feature in the soundtrack. Beefheart wasn't interested. It was just "too corny". He was more concerned with pursuing his art career, which took off in the mid-1980s. Before he gave up music completely, he made some unreleased, abandoned recordings with artist Julian Schnabel. In 1984 he also began planning an album with Gary Lucas, which would include new material and an old, unreleased gem, "Hoboism", but when Beefheart revisited Lucas's apartment to start working on ideas he seemed "unfocused", and nothing was realised beyond rough drafts. Typically, Beefheart's appraisal of his departure from music was quite different: "I retired. I had to," he said. "I got too good on the horn and I got to the point where I thought I was going to blow my head right off. So I started a second life."

The Fall

by Stewart Lee

The Fall made their first appearance on vinyl in October 1977, on a 10" EP of recordings from their local Manchester punk venue, entitled *Short Circuit: Live At The Electric Circus* (Virgin). The two spindly songs, "Stepping Out" and "Last Orders", gave no indication that, nearly three decades and 27 studio albums later, The Fall would turn out to be the only group to survive the punk era with critical status undiminished and critical faculties intact. Over the years, the group has mixed rockabilly rhythms, pounding riffs, experimental collages, misappropriated electronica, a subversive pop sensibility, and a dark and often deceptive sense of the absurd. Frontman Mark E Smith's immediately recognisable anti-vocals, stream of consciousness lyrics and left-field literary references create a body of work unequalled in scope and sheer size by any other rock outfit.

Smith, The Fall's single longterm constant, is publicly disdainful of the cult of short-term nostalgia. Fall sets rarely include any songs older than the last couple of albums, unless they are seasoned covers of 1960s garage punk classics and old rockabilly riffs ripe for reinterpretation. Smith refuses to become a keeper of sacred relics, the living interpreter of his own back catalogue. The very notion of a Primer on The Fall would no doubt irritate Smith a little, as if someone were preparing his obituary, and the nature of the group's output and the passion of its followers makes it impossible to agree on generally accepted highlights. The most recent Fall record is always the most important one.

Perhaps appropriately, The Fall's recorded output has been in comparative disarray for some years, with semi-legal CD reissues mastered from scratched, skipping vinyl, songs mislabelled, and vital singles and session tracks completely overlooked. Compilation albums have been assembled from unsourced outtakes that were allowed to fall, in lean times, into the hands of unscrupulous labels, as if in exchange for plastic bags full of used fivers. There are more Fall live albums than necessary, and most are of a sound quality best described as no-fi.

The Fall
Live At The Witch Trials
Castle/Sanctuary 2 x CD 2008
(orig. Step Forward LP 1979)

Dragnet
Castle/Sanctuary CD 2008
(orig. Step Forward LP 1979)

Totale's Turns
Castle/Sanctuary CD 2008
(orig. Rough Trade LP 1980)

All the early Fall singles are collected as extra tracks on the satisfyingly thorough Castle reissues of their first and second albums *Live At The Witch Trials* and *Dragnet*. From the opening notes of August 1978's "Bingo Master's Breakout" 7", The Fall were sheltering from the spit-storm behind the convenient punk umbrella, while in fact defining themselves in opposition to any prevailing orthodoxies. As youngsters, Smith and his cohorts were nourished by the 1970s countercultural drip-feed of Krautrock, Iggy Pop, Captain Beefheart and weird Prog, and it could be argued The Fall became Peel favourites in the 1980s precisely because they reflected a decade of digesting the DJ's more extreme musical choices. The Sex Pistols may have inspired Smith to form a group, but there any comparison between the two ended. *Live At The Witch Trials* is characterised by Yvonne Pawlett's cheap and nasty keyboard sound, suggesting a toddler channelling Van Der Graaf Generator. Producer Bob Sargeant attempted to counterbalance the group's inherent griminess with a clean and shiny production job, resulting in a kind of grey, industrial psychedelia. *Witch Trials* suggests magic mushroom tea drunk from a dirty pub ashtray, an Ambrosian dishwater. It doesn't taste very nice, but it's probably good for you.

Although guitarist Martin Bramah and drummer Karl Burns were to be on-off members of The Fall for the next two decades, neither was present on *Dragnet*, which saw the arrival of three new members: future Radio 1 DJ Marc 'Lard' Riley and Craig Scanlon on guitars, and bassist Steve Hanley. Scanlon, a gifted interpreter of Smith's often incomprehensible instructions, spent the next 15 years reining in his improvisatory tendencies to define The Fall's majestically monolithic sound, alongside the similarly longserving Hanley's overhead powercable bass boom. Both *Witch Trials* and *Dragnet* contain the kind of paper-cut, spiky post-punk currently plagiarised by contemporary pop groups, but The Fall's vision remains too individual to assimilate easily.

Seven live albums of extremely variable quality document the group's 1977–80 incarnations. The best is Rough Trade's *Totale's Turns*, capturing The Fall infuriating various northern working men's club crowds as Smith audibly baits his colleagues into ever more intense performances. "Hey," he asks a heckler, "are you doing what you did two years ago? Yeah? Well, don't make a career out of it." This acidic put-down could be used to sum up The Fall's own ethos. The Castle reissue includes a Peel Session.

Grotesque (After The Gramme)
Castle/Sanctuary CD 2008
(orig. Rough Trade LP 1980)
Slates
Castle/Sanctuary CD 2008
(orig. Rough Trade LP 1981)
Live In London 1980
Castle/Sanctuary CD
(orig. Chaos Tapes MC 1980)
A Part Of America Therein, 1981
Castle/Sanctuary CD
(orig. Cottage LP 1981)

"C&N music is born," declared Smith's northern playboy alter ego R Totale on the sleeve of *Grotesque (After The Gramme)*. The cover, a Friday night out Giotto fresco in lurid felt tip by Smith's younger sister Suzanne, sums up *Grotesque's* tone perfectly. This record, and its attendant singles "Totally Wired" and "How I Wrote Elastic Man" – both collected on the Castle reissue – moved The Fall yet further from the prevailing punk template. As Echo and The Bunnymen and their indie rock contemporaries posited a vaguely mystical post-punk psychedelia, Smith turned The Fall into kitchen sink realists who found Lovecraftian horrors lurking down the U-bend. Collapsed Country & Western cliches and rickety rockabilly rhythms pinned and mounted various contemporary social archetypes – CB radio enthusiasts, long distance lorry drivers and ambitious émigrés – with an accuracy that escaped other lyricists of the era. While Paul Weller stuck "KICK ME" signs on the backs of be-suited businessmen and ran away, "English Scheme" explained the English disease in a hilarious stream of consciousness splurge of social theory, with exquisitely detailed supporting evidence: "*Your psychotic big brother who left home for jobs in Holland, Munich, Rome – he's thick, but he's struck it rich.*" "Impression Of J Temperance", "New Face In Hell" and "The NWRA" moved towards the expansive, narrative-driven epics that would characterise The Fall's best work in the near future.

The 10" mini album *Slates*, issued the following year (and augmented with a Peel Session and a single on the reissue), pursued the same themes in less forgiving terms, with song structures sacrificed to relentless repetition, as if Smith and his cohorts were furiously scratching the tracks into the vinyl themselves. *Slates* includes the incendiary "Leave The Capitol", a fevered vision of London at its most irritating, with buried lyrical nods to the forgotten mystic Arthur Machen, rendered over a pulverising descending guitar riff that never fails to excite. "*I laughed at the great God Pan!*"

Live In London 1980 is a sardine-tin recording of the group reaching towards ideas beyond their ability at the time, reissued with extra tracks. But *A Part Of America Therein – 1981*, though taped only a year later, reveals the group achieving its aims, with endless riffs approaching a trancelike effect. It includes a definitive, hallucinatory live reading of "An Older Lover", against which the *Slates* version sounds stunted. As usual, there are extra tracks on the CD.

Hex Enduction Hour
Castle/Sanctuary 2 x CD 2008
(orig. Kamera LP 1982)
Room To Live (Undilutable Slang Truth)
Castle/Sanctuary CD 2008
(orig. Kamera LP 1982)
Fall In A Hole
Castle/Sanctuary CD 2008
(orig. Flying Nun LP 1982)
Perverted By Language
Castle/Sanctuary 2 x CD 2008
(orig. Rough Trade LP 1983)

The Fall's recorded output from 1982 and 1983 is incomparable and indispensable. *Hex Enduction Hour* remains their greatest album, and the Peel Session that preceded *Perverted By Language* documented the group on the cusp of discovering a new and unique mode of expression that mixed rock's primitive structures with a transcendental, avant garde aesthetic. The *Hex* era is great art, made by people who did everything they could to avoid looking or sounding like great artists.

Hex Enduction Hour, issued in March 1982, is a masterpiece contained in a studiously non-designed sleeve, on which Smith has been let loose with green Letraset and a black marker pen. Like the music within, it is ugly, intriguing, confusing, profound and beautiful. Smith's lyrics balance recognisable fragments of narrative, and well chosen pop-cultural references with cryptically alluring phrases. "*You won't find anything more ridiculous than this new profile razor unit/Made with the highest British attention to the wrong detail/Become obsolete units surrounded by hail,*" he deadpans during "The Classical". The music sucks you in with overdriven steamroller riffs, but kicks you sideways with the percussive clatter of the double drumkit line-up, the stop-start rhythms and the uncharacteristic use of improvisation. The psycho-geographical incantation of "Iceland" was made up on the spot, "And This Day" was edited from a 25 minute jam and the aforementioned "The Classical" includes a bass solo. The single "Look Now", sung by Marc Riley, is omitted from the otherwise exemplary expanded Castle reissue, for indecipherable reasons.

Six months later, *Room To Live* – reissued with the rare live track "Words Of Expectation" – was considered a failure at the time, because of its refusal to follow the acclaimed *Hex* template. But its retreat into a loose-limbed, more fluid, fragmentary mode is typical of Smith's characteristic refusal to satisfy expectations.

By the release of *Perverted By Language*, Riley had been replaced by Smith's future wife Brix, whom he had met after a gig in Chicago, but the young American guitarist's eventually civilising influence was yet to be felt. Instead, the album finds The Fall at a peak of non-rock. The extended workouts of "Smile" and "Garden" achieve an impossible super-density. Smith, who'd been digesting Wyndham Lewis, is at his most elliptically intriguing. The *"Jew on a motorbike!"* refrain of "Garden" and his declaration in "Tempo House" that *"The Dutch are weeping in four languages at least"* are just two of many Fall lyrics that still seize fans at inopportune moments. On *Perverted* the group channelled the twang of Link Wray into a vortex of vast, surreal mantras and dadaist call and response chants. The reissue includes essential singles from the period, such as "The Man Whose Head Expanded" and the football-themed thrash "Kicker Conspiracy", live tracks and Peel Session album highlights that better the official versions.

Any live recording of this period is worth owning, including *Live To Air In Melbourne* and *Austurbaejarbio* (both Cog Sinister CDs) and the Bury 1982 set spread over the bonus discs issued with the inferior 1998 Cog Sinister reissues of *Room To Live* and the compilation *Palace Of Swords Reversed*. However, the superb New Zealand set, *Fall In A Hole*, finally reissued in a serviceable form, captures versions of the period's best material performed with an improvisatory fluidity Smith usually discouraged and disparaged.

The Wonderful And Frightening World Of The Fall
Beggars Banquet CD 1988, rec. 1984
This Nation's Saving Grace
Beggars Banquet CD 1997, rec. 1985
Bend Sinister
Beggars Banquet CD 1993, rec. 1986
458489 A Sides
Beggars Banquet CD 1990
458489 B Sides
Beggars Banquet CD 1990

After *Perverted By Language*, Smith seemed to have had enough of leading Britain's biggest unknown group and, emboldened by Brix's way with a winning hook and a clothes iron, The Fall entered a new phase by signing to Beggars Banquet, the batcave-like home of Gary Numan, Gene Loves Jezebel and The Cult. For the remainder of the 1980s, The Fall became a commercially successful alternative rock act, despite making no obvious concessions to public taste. They appeared on TV shows such as *The Tube* and *The Old Grey Whistle Test*. They did not look appalling. Smith wore long leather coats and eyeliner, as if attempting to beat the black clad hordes at their own game. On *Top of The Pops*, BBC cameramen tried to film up the skirts of Brix Smith and keyboard player Marcia Schofield. There were videos, 12" remixes, interviews in *Smash Hits*, collaborations with ballet dancers and middle billing at summer rock festivals. Indie guru producer John Leckie built an ongoing relationship with the group. Everything had changed.

Their Beggars debut, *The Wonderful And Frightening World Of The Fall*, marked a seismic shift of direction, with short, often poppy tunes and a minimal amount of the extraneous noise that had previously deterred listeners. Its attendant single "C.R.E.E.P." was shockingly radio friendly by Fall standards. My cousin, who had an inverted cross painted on her bedroom wall, bought the album and enjoyed the sinister pagan chanting, copped from TV's *Quatermass* series, that precedes its opening track, "Lay Of The Land". "Elves" stole its central riff from The Stooges' "I Wanna Be Your Dog" and sold it back to a new generation of fans who didn't recognise it. A previously undiscovered constituency was opening up, of disillusioned suburban teens, who a decade earlier would have been primed for punk but now wanted a new strain of outsider music.

This Nation's Saving Grace is a stand-out amongst their five Beggars albums, and drew in the merely curious with a clean production, catchy choruses, and something of the Gothic grandeur that passed for drama during those dreary days. "I Am Damo Suzuki", heavily indebted to Can's "Oh Yeah", flagged up The Fall's Krautrock influences back before anybody could buy CD reissues to follow them up, and the opening instrumental, "Mansion", fingered The Deviants' "Billy The Monster". The Fall were stealing from the greats. "LA" was a moody instrumental, in keeping with the nocturnal feel of the era, but the unerring repetition and impenetrable ranting of "What You Need" recalled *Perverted By Language*, albeit in shinier shoes. "Spoilt Victorian Child" and the contemporaneous, rockabilly-styled single "Couldn't Get Ahead"/ "Rollin' Dany" harked back to their thrash roots, and the moment in "Paintwork" where Smith accidentally erased a section of the tape confirms an ongoing faith in the artistic value of chance. *This Nation's Saving Grace* took the best of The Fall and force-fed it to fans beyond the reach of John Peel's end of year Festive Fifty countdown.

The following year's *Bend Sinister*, despite the fan-favourite cover of 1960s garage group The Other Side's "Mr Pharmacist", lost some of the ground *This Nation's Saving Grace* had gained in a quagmire of doomy songs, though "Dr Faustus", a kind of marching song for small mechanical goblins, was clearly indebted to Krautrock group Faust. *The Frenz Experiment* (Beggars Banquet CD 1988) included an unexpected pop hit, a cover of The Kinks' "Victoria". Indeed, the Beggars period, which ended in 1990, is best enjoyed via the two *458489* singles compilations of A sides and B sides, which document The Fall either creatively crowbarring their individual aesthetic into a borderline pop format, or else enjoying the artistic freedoms and experimental opportunities that B sides offered in the pre-download era.

I Am Kurious Oranj
Beggars Banquet CD 2000, rec. 1988
I Am Pure As Oranj
NMC CD 2000, rec. 1988

I Am Kurious, Oranj was the soundtrack to a collaboration with the progressive ballet dancer Michael Clark on a piece loosely based on the life of William of Orange, which eventually ran at the temple of culture that was London's Sadler's Wells. With the ballet *I Am Curious, Orange*, Clark and The Fall created a mild media panic. Today broadsheet newspapers are required to run reviews of the latest Pete Doherty biography, but in 1988 there was no context in highbrow circles for The Fall. The high culture/low culture barrier was breached, however briefly, as ballet dancers with bare backsides twirled to the title track's unusual fusion of offbeat reggae and seventeenth-century history. A spirited reading of William Blake's "Jerusalem", with its satirical sideswipes at compensation culture, reclaimed this righteous revolutionary anthem from rugby fans, public school assemblies and glib patriots. The stomping

rewrite of *Hex Eduction Hour*'s fragile "Hip Priest", entitled "Big New Prinz", survived in live sets until the early twenty-first century, where Smith's romanticised description of an undervalued artist became a self-fulfilling prophecy.

A belatedly issued live album, *I Am Pure As Oranj*, captures the strange, hostile ambience of the dance event itself. You can hear the audience stiffen as Smith's mumbled spoken word bit, "Dog Is Life", fills the expectant auditorium, punctuated by the inappropriate applause of excited fans. Other rock peasants have briefly dabbled in the realm of high art. Few have done it while simultaneously enjoying hit singles and backing giant dancing hamburgers.

Code: Selfish
Fontana CD/LP 1992

Brix left Smith and The Fall, and The Fall left Beggars for Fontana – a major label, where powerful cybernetic arms were grafted onto the body of an act that, on the evidence of their final Beggars release, *Seminal Live*, had perhaps shown signs of weakening. As his contemporaries descended upon seaside towns playing the hits, Smith poured scorn on the burgeoning punk nostalgia bandwagon, fashioning instead a Fall that sounded undeniably contemporary by bringing the group's sound into the digital age. A collaboration with dance producers Coldcut gave rise to the sublime stuttering beats of "Telephone Thing" on *Extricate* (Fontana CD/LP 1990), and by the following year's *Shift-Work* Dave Bush was on board, credited with "machines", augmenting a stripped-back quartet of longterm inmates Hanley and Scanlon on bass and guitar, with Simon Wolstencroft on drums. Live, The Fall began to sound like a computerised threshing machine, inexorably sucking everything before it into its gaping maw.

The standout album of this phase is *Code: Selfish*, with Smith's visions of a future Europe on "Free Range", and his comically acerbic deconstruction of thwarted provincial ambition on "The Birmingham School Of Business School", simmering with barely controlled contempt. "*The jumped-up prats/Laughing stock of Europe/Olympic bidding again and again/Exciting developments,*" he spat at the desperate

Brummies. Hanley's distinctive bass playing, usually delivered as a powerful throb amidst gnarly guitars, discovered a new precision amongst the computerised rhythm tracks, and Scanlon was free to play textures rather than riffs. "The Birmingham School" even included a guitar solo, albeit one that sounds contemptuous of the very idea of guitar solos.

The Infotainment Scan
Castle/Sanctuary 2 x CD 2008
(orig. Permanent CD/LP 1993)

Smith split from Fontana before he was pushed, signed to the independent label Permanent and released *The Infotainment Scan*, now reissued with an extra CD of supplementary material. The album, which peaked at number nine in the national charts, adapted Sister Sledge's "Lost In Music" to address the thorny issue of juvenile access to pubs and deconstruct the very notion of dance music. Smith found a sincere sentiment within Steve Bent's novelty record "I'm Going To Spain" that seemed to echo his own cultural displacement, despite being sourced from the Kenny Everett-compiled *World's Worst Record* album.

The Infotainment Scan has a strange and uncharacteristically wistful, melancholy quality to it. Lyrically, "It's A Curse" and "A Past Gone Mad" nailed the noxious modern phenomenon of media nostalgia years before Channel 4 began building entire TV schedules around remembering the 1970s and 1980s – but both betray a feeling of regret, of being a man out of time. Smith rails against the world whilst realising he is no longer the tastemaker's autodidact of choice. Even with a dance element to his music, he could pass for the titular subject of "Paranoia Man In Cheap Shit Room", a fearful figure *"in his early thirties/At the zenith of his powers"*.

The Twenty-Seven Points: Live 92–95
Castle/Sanctuary 2 x CD 2006

The Infotainment Scan aside, the mid-1990s remains The Fall's least interesting period; yet it's their most thoroughly documented, with six live albums – two of them doubles – covering the four studio albums released during the muddled years from 1993–96. These are supplemented by around four dozen outtakes spread thinly and repetitively over eight compilations on the ominously named Receiver label. As Britpop flourished, recycling retro-Mod aesthetics, there was little space for Smith's scorched earth attitude towards the past. Ironically, just as Pavement launched a career built on appropriating the sound of early 1980s Fall, the genuine article released a series of increasingly weak albums, vast portions of which sounded like a standard indie rock guitar outfit, albeit one fronted by a determinedly distinctive vocalist.

The 1994 *Middle Class Revolt* was the last record to feature the electronics of Dave Bush, and it was bulked out with high-fibre covers of The Groundhogs, The Monks and Henry Cow/Slapp Happy. Brix came back for the 1995 *Cerebral Caustic*, cowriting the album's standout track, "Bonkers In Phoenix", a satirical sound collage of summer festival experiences that basically graffitied over a sincere attempt at writing a genuine paisley-pop hit. She left for the final time during the tour for the 1996 *The Light User Syndrome*. The long-serving Craig Scanlon was sacked before the same album which, while offering some hope for the future, featured lacklustre guide vocal tracks over a sonic palette that's cluttered and unfocused. The lead-in single, the 17 minute, three part "Chiselers", described by Smith as "relevant to the recent experiences of Halifax Town football club", was notable for its length and audacity, but arrived on the album proper in a truncated form.

The period is perhaps best represented by the unfairly maligned, Smith-assembled live double album *The Twenty-Seven Points*. The album adds found snippets and spoken word sections into a sometimes unflatteringly honest, yet always entertaining, portrait of a group in creative crisis, yet nonetheless capable of genius. "Idiot Joy Showland" is abandoned after less than a minute. The otherwise unrecorded live track "Noel's Chemical Effluence" is a gradually uncoiling, lean and slinky slice of snake-charming music that ranks amongst the group's finest moments. But, on the whole, Smith was a man adrift. There seemed to be no obvious way forward for The Fall. Something was rotten in the state of dear Mark.

Levitate
Artful CD 1997

The Marshall Suite
Artful CD 1999

The Unutterable
Voiceprint 2 x CD 2008, rec. 2000

In April 1998 the last line-up of The Fall with any link – apart from Smith – back to its earliest officially recorded line-up fell apart acrimoniously in New York, though fans who have seen the video of the group's onstage collapse would be hard pressed to tell it apart from any number of similarly shambolic mid-1990s live fiascos. But Steve Hanley and Karl Burns were finally gone. This act of severance ultimately enabled the creation of a succession of completely new Fall line-ups. These gangs of anonymous young men, many only mewling infants when "Bingo Master's Breakout" hit the racks, were creatively unburdened by a shared history, or any sense of what The Fall were supposed to be. This, in turn, unburdened Smith himself, who increasingly resembled the last pink rabbit without any Duracell batteries.

The old gang's last gasp, the ungainly but effective *Levitate*, finds Smith sounding hoarse and thrillingly incoherent over clattering electronica that has none of the streamlined power of Dave Bush's contributions, and instead leaves the group in a heroic struggle with seemingly random hails of beats. In the midst of the chaos, courtesy of keyboard player Julia Nagle, comes the strange pastoral interlude in the middle of "Ten Houses Of Eve", and the piano instrumental "Jap Kid". *Levitate* works miracles with a Fall that had started to sound too much like itself, disguising them with multilayered vocals and noise for one last hurrah.

1998 saw Smith play gigs with hurriedly assembled three-piece line-ups, issuing the famous onstage disclaimer, "If it's me and your granny on bongos, it's The Fall." He released a spoken word album, *The Post Nearly Man* (Artful CD), but things became increasingly desperate. Then Smith returned with a new Fall that retained only Julia Nagle and *The Marshall Suite*, a record that ranks among the best of The Fall's career. Guitarist Neville Wilding helped assimilate Tommy Blake's

rock 'n' roll revenge number "F-oldin' Money" and The Saints' "This Perfect Day" into The Fall's oeuvre and "Shake-Off" and "(Jung Nev's) Antidotes" found new ways of meshing rock tropes, noise and Nagle's increasingly pervasive keyboards and electronica, without falling back into familiar patterns. "Touch Sensitive" – a chart hit that never was – later enlivened a Vauxhall car commercial, and was followed by a minor squabble over royalties.

The following year, *The Unutterable* was the last Fall album to feature Nagle. The high point amongst a playful and personable set was "Dr Buck's Letter", a menacing yet amusing reappropriation of the text of an interview with UK DJ Pete Tong. It's now available in a double CD 'Special Deluxe Edition'.

A World Bewitched: Best Of 1990–2000
Artful 2 x CD 2001

The Real New Fall LP – Formerly Country On The Click
Action CD 2007, rec. 2003

In 2001 the compilation *A World Bewitched* gathered together various rarities and collaborations in an alternative history of The Fall's 1990s output. It suggested a parallel career rather more daring than much of the decade's official releases indicated at the time. The same year saw yet another entirely new Fall line-up (featuring guitarist Ben Pritchard, soon to become a key player) release *Are You Are Missing Winner* (Castle/Sanctuary CD). The group knocked out an unapologetically simplistic set of high octane punk noise, free from feminine keyboard embellishments, as if to settle a score. In retrospect, *Missing Winner* is the sound of the new Fall clearing its throat before commencing the job of reclaiming the group's reputation, and releasing its best album for over a decade.

The 2003 *Country On The Click* was retitled *The Real New Fall LP* after bootlegged versions made it out in advance of the official release date. This record and its attendant singles meshed the pop sensibility of the Beggars Banquet years with the cohesion of the high points of the early 1990s. "Mod

Mock Goth" was an almost unbearably dense meditation on the Camber Sands All Tomorrow's Parties event, while the sinister football terrace stomp, "Theme From Sparta FC", could have been a number one single. The Fall were being extensively reviewed, rated and written about again.

50,000 Fall Fans Can't Be Wrong
Castle/Sanctuary 2 x CD 2004

Interim
Hip Priest CD 2004

Fall Heads Roll
Sanctuary CD/LP 2005

The Complete Peel Sessions 1978–2004
Castle/Sanctuary 6 x CD 2005

In 2004 *50,000 Fall Fans Can't Be Wrong* bucked a trend of unfocused Fall compilations to provide the first phase-by-phase overview of the group's history. Smith's fond imaginings that younger fans outnumbered the league of bald-headed men always present in his audience were becoming fact. And some spectacular live shows did nothing to disappoint. *Fall Heads Roll* consolidated The Fall's return to form, referencing the best of nearly three decades of different approaches. "Bo Demmick" and "Clasp Hands" rocked with the rockabilly rhythms of the Step Forward years. The monotonously mesmerising "Blindness", though far better in its Peel Session form, referenced the glory days of "Garden" or "And

This Day". Lyrically, Smith now deals in fragments and found phrases, sounding like no one but himself. Even if the complete narratives of *Grotesque* and the pin-sharp social satire of *The Infotainment Scan* appear lost forever, his voice is once again uncommonly clear – especially so on the vital late period masterpiece *Imperial Wax Solvent* (Castle/Sanctuary CD 2008), and even on the digital cut-up collaboration with German duo Mouse On Mars under the name Von Südenfed, *Tromatic Reflexxions* (Domino CD 2007).

Recent live recordings include the *2G+2* album (Action CD) and *Touch Sensitive Box* (Castle/Sanctuary 5 × CD), which document the same line-up playing largely similar material over six dates. *Interim* includes rare returns to the early 1980s songs "Mere Pseud Mag Ed" and "Spoilt Victorian Child", alongside spirited readings of new material in unusual settings. A fire alarm interrupts a rehearsal run-through of "Open The Box", but is assimilated despite its persistence. Finally, the six CD set of the group's 24 John Peel Sessions topped various polls at the end of 2005. Had it come out ten years before, it might have looked like a tombstone. Here lies The Fall and Mark E Smith. But luckily, Smith, though now in his fifties, is once again at the zenith of his powers and the *Sessions* collection is anything but a full stop. The Fall's Peel box, and by association their recorded output in general, reads as a secret history of the last three decades of popular music.

Noise

by Nick Cain

Reflecting in *Noise/Music: A History* (Continuum 2007) on the function of noise in twentieth century culture, Paul Hegarty wrote: "Noise is negative: it is unwanted, other, not something ordered. It is negatively defined – ie by what it is not (not acceptable sound, not music, not valid, not a message or a meaning), but it is also a negativity. In other words, it does not exist independently, as it exists only in relation to what it is not."

Early examples of what we now think of as Noise music were exercises in negative relation, attempts at cultural deprogramming conceived in opposition to then-dominant discourses. Throbbing Gristle's use of extreme subject matter in their late 1970s performances and recordings aimed to jam institutional information systems in order to liberate their audiences' thoughts and behavioural processes. Boyd Rice's *The Black Album* (1977) intended to purify its listeners' minds and allow them to experience primal states of awareness. The ramifications of these early developments played themselves out in 1980s Industrial music and power electronics, which explored linkages between Noise, transgressive behaviour and taboo imagery.

The story of Noise music since 1990 – the era this Primer focuses on – is the story of its progression from negative to positive connotation, of its gradual evolution as a musical language, a genre in and of itself, complete with codes, idioms and a historical narrative. Along the way it has shed many of its links to transgression and extremity, shifting its focus from the political to the musical – the sonic relationships Noise creates and allows, and the listener's interpretation and perception of them – and engaging less often and less directly with a broader cultural or societal context.

Since 1990, the two major developments in Noise music have been the primacy of Japanese Noise artists like Merzbow, Hijokaidan and Incapacitants in the 1990s; and, in the early twenty-first century, the hybridisation of Noise. In their search for new extremes of sound, contemporary Noise musicians have forced their music into direct cross-genre dialogues, in the process blurring or erasing altogether previously impermeable stylistic boundaries. Lasse Marhaug adding friction to Ken Vandermark's Territory Band, John Wiese improvising with Evan Parker, Dylan Nyoukis collaborating with Jaap Blonk – these are collaborations which would have been inconceivable only a decade before.

AMM's *The Crypt*, Evan Parker's solo soprano improvisations, the electronic soundworlds of David Tudor and Max Neuhaus, Gottfried Michael Koenig's computer compositions, the "sheets of sound" free jazz of Alan Silva's Celestrial Communications Orchestra, to name but a few examples: the avant garde has continually deployed Noise as a structural and textural device to expand or explode vocabularies of sound. In recent years, Noise music has reversed the process.

In addition to tracking the work of 1980s Noise progenitors like Merzbow and Hijokaidan and the musicians who have built on their innovations, this Primer documents the work of artists who don't regard their music as Noise, but who use Noise or elements of Noise as one part of a strategy, whether it be a performative or a sound art process, a means of reinvestigating a compositional process or the realisation of a philosophical framework. Their work has enriched the vocabulary of Noise, generating connections and frictions and suggesting different modes of sound organisation, and has played no small role in aiding the development of Noise into a legitimate, independent musical language.

Merzbow

Noisembryo
The Releasing Eskimo CD 1994

Venereology
Relapse CD 1994

Pulse Demon
Relapse CD 1996

Over the course of 30 years of activity, Merzbow (Masami Akita) has built up a discography numbering hundreds of albums, including the infamous 50 CD *Merzbox*, and attained a profile which no other Noise artist can match. Akita documented his 1980s output, which revolved around improvisations for electronics and acoustic instruments and objects, on dozens of cassettes and LPs on his own Lowest Music and ZSF Produkt labels. Merzbow's analogue era, which began roughly around the time of his first CD, 1990's *Cloud Cuck OO Grand*, is Akita's most sustained period of creativity, when he realised the latent potential of his 1980s work, accelerating it into a new variant of Noise.

Rainbow Electronics (1990), *Great American Nude/Crash For Hi-Fi* (1991) and the *Metalvelodrome* four CD set (1993) were dominated by wild, high speed oscillations of serrated electronics, which folded in and shredded piercing frequencies, spraying jagged shards of sound in all directions. The approach reached its apotheosis on *Noisembryo*, *Venereology* and *Pulse Demon*, all bona fide Noise classics which surge powerful pulses of momentum into viciously abrasive cut-ups. It began to level off after *Hybrid Noisebloom* (1997) and *1930* (1998).

In the past decade Akita has increased his rate of productivity exponentially, releasing in the region of 90 albums. A succession of albums themed around particular musical instruments and genres was followed by a series of animal-themed albums, emblazoned with endorsements of PETA and Greenpeace. Akita's shifting focus is certainly evidence of a restless creative spirit, though his digital era (from the year 2000 onwards) releases have been chequered at best.

Hijokaidan

Romance
Alchemy CD 1990

Windom
Alchemy CD 1991

Incapacitants

Fabrication
Alchemy CD 1992

Quietus
Alchemy CD 1993

After Akita, the two most important figures in Japanese Noise are Jojo Hiroshige and Toshiji Mikawa. Both are members of Hijokaidan, and Mikawa plays in Incapacitants with Fumio Kosakai, also a sometime Hijokaidan contributor. Though both groups had been operative in Japan since the early 1980s, they announced themselves globally with a concerted assault of releases on Hiroshige's Alchemy label from 1989 onwards. Albums like Hijokaidan's *Modern*, *Romance* and *Windom* and Incapacitants' *Fabrication*, *Quietus* and *Feedback Of NMS* established Alchemy as the premier Japanese Noise label, a status it retained for several years.

Where Merzbow associated Noise with fetishistic transgressions and automatistic artistic impulses, Hijokaidan and Incapacitants divested their Noise of any cultural meaning. Their overriding interest was in a sheer intensity of sound – *As Loud As Possible*, as one Incapacitants album put it. Analogue Merzbow's high-speed disintegrations span the dynamic range. By contrast, Hijokaidan and Incapacitants construct walls of Noise, the former's a monolithic high-end skree which subsumes instrumentation and vocals, the latter's comprised of multiple layers of endlessly fragmenting electronics.

In the past decade both groups have, like Merzbow, hit something of a plateau. Regardless, the cumulative impact of their breakthrough releases on 1990s Noise was little short of seismic. Their influence resonated profoundly with the second (Aube, CCCC, Masonna, Solmania) and third (K2, MSBR, Monde Bruits, Government Alpha, Pain Jerk) generations of Japanese Noise groups, and with legions of Noise artists scattered around the globe.

Whitehouse
Mummy And Daddy
Susan Lawly CD 1998
Cruise
Susan Lawly CD 2001
Bird Seed
Susan Lawly CD 2003

By the end of the 1990s, power electronics was in deep freeze. Fast forward a decade, and pioneering PE shock jocks Whitehouse – British duo William Bennett and Philip Best – were enjoying an unlikely vogue, universally hailed by Noise makers from Peter Rehberg to Wolf Eyes, their back catalogue the subject of an ongoing deluxe vinyl reissue programme, and their work unofficially inducted into the avant garde canon through a collaboration with the German New Music ensemble Zeitkratzer. The renaissance might well have begun with *Mummy And Daddy*, which embellishes the group's trademark scything tones with barrages of electronic loops and distorted percussion (replaced, peculiarly, by acoustic African-influenced rhythms on *Asceticists 2006* and *Racket* in 2007).

The vocals followed the instrumentation into bombast on *Cruise* and *Bird Seed*, with lyrics expanded into abusive screeds, delivered in sneering tirades. The invective's level of urgency was new, but Whitehouse's mission statement is as old as the hills: to present their listeners with extreme material as a means of forcing them to reassess their value systems and overcome their internal programming. Only then, runs the logic, will they be able to achieve the same level of perception and awareness as Whitehouse themselves. Three decades on, the concept of deprogramming doesn't seem like such a smart idea. "*Rise up! Rise up now!/Kill this fucking nightmare that is inside you*", spiels Bennett on *Racket*'s "Dumping More Fucking Rubbish". Delete the expletive, soften the tone slightly, and the rhetoric sounds not dissimilar to the manipulative pablum of fundamentalist preachers and self-help gurus.

Gate
Guitar
Majora LP 1992
Amerika
Majora LP 1993
A Handful Of Dust
Now Gods, Stand Up For Bastards/The Philosophick Mercury
No Fun Productions 2 x CD 2008
Birchville Cat Motel
We Count These Prayers
Corpus Hermeticum CD 2001

Occurring simultaneously with, but largely independently of, developments around the globe, Bruce Russell and Michael Morley's early 1990s Noise experiments were extrapolated from (and later fed back into) their work in pioneering form-destroying New Zealand Noise-rock group The Dead C. Morley's solo work as Gate slows The Dead C's downer dirges to a slothful instrumental crawl, flattening reverb-heavy guitar and synthesizer into a swampy, desolate churn, which *Amerika* elongates into opaque, reverb-swaddled drones and *Guitar* compresses into short, rough spurts of Noise.

Russell's collaboration with Alastair Galbraith as A Handful Of Dust is as airy as Gate is claustrophobic. *The Philosophick Mercury* (1994) and *Now Gods, Stand Up For Bastards* (1996) weave lines of wavering feedback tones and violin drones around each other, carving up space and meshing in gritty tangles of Noise. The albums were realisations of Russell's concept of 'free noise', a methodology of rock-based Noise improvisation, whose tenets he articulated in a manifesto. It postulated that all music is a subset of Noise and that free Noise is a mirror of reality, extolled the virtues of defective equipment and namechecked La Monte Young and the Theater Of Eternal Music.

Through his Corpus Hermeticum label, Russell promoted the work of a range of New Zealand Noise makers: Surface Of The Earth, Doramaar, Sandoz Lab Technicians, RST and Omit among them. He also championed the work of the key figure in the second, late 1990s wave of New Zealand Noise artists, Birchville Cat Motel (aka Campbell Kneale), whose Celebrate Psi Phenomenon imprint soon became a focal point for Noise artists and sound adventurers, Antipodean or otherwise.

Skullflower
Obsidian Shaking Codex
RRRecords CD 1993
Tribulation
Crucial Blast CD 2006
Hototogisu
Chimärendämmerung
De Stijl CD
Ascension
Broadcast
Shock 2 x CD 1996
Descension
Live March 1995
Shock CD 1995

List Matthew Bower's collaborators in chronological order and you'll have the beginnings of a timeline of the UK underground since the early 1980s: Stephen Thrower (Coil), Philip Best (Whitehouse), Gary Mundy (Ramleh), Stefan Jaworzyn, Neil Campbell, Richard Youngs and Simon Wickham-Smith, among others. From his early 1980s power electronics group Pure, through the long-running Noise-rock group Skullflower, and Total and Sunroof! to Hototogisu, Bower has repeatedly explored what he regards as the transcendent potential of Noise: its ability to induce temporary ecstatic states in both creator and listener, accessed through an intense physicality of sound experienced in the frenzied heat of the moment.

Early Skullflower albums served up sludgy psychedelic mantras, scouring grinding riffs with blasts of feedback and wah-wah. Experiments in free, droning sound, like *Obsidian Shaking Codex*'s 24 minute blackout "Smoke Jaguar", soon crept in. On hiatus for several years from the late 1990s, Skullflower resumed activity with the 2003 *Exquisite Fucking Boredom*, and since 2006 *Tribulation* have shed their rock moorings altogether in favour of excoriating Noise discourses, which recent releases have pushed further into distant reaches of rapturous bombast. Hototogisu's slew of albums more successfully articulate Bower's notion of the ferocious sublime. *Chimärendämmerung*'s streams of Noise-drone shear piercing feedback harmonics and starbursts of white-hot overtones, evoking void as much as bliss.

Stefan Jaworzyn played on Skullflower's first two albums and made a couple of appearances in Whitehouse. Ascension, his duo with percussionist Tony Irving, was a different proposition entirely. Like Masayuki Takayanagi and Rudolph Grey before them, Ascension exploded improvisation with Noise, combining the sophisticated interplay of Improv and free jazz with Noise's energy aggression of intent. Jaworzyn's barbed, piercing guitar lines were just as capable of generating dramatic tension and structural nuance, as *Broadcast*'s two richly architectural improvisations illustrate. Ascension expanded into Descension for a time with the addition of Simon Fell's bass and Charles Wharf's reeds, though scant regard is paid to the nuances of group interaction. The quartet's Noise onslaught achieves a density of sound comparable to Takayanagi's 1970s 'mass projections'.

Prick Decay
Guidelines For Basement Non-Fidel
Very Good LP 1995

Blood Stereo
The Magnetic Headache
Bottrop-Boy CD 2008

Dylan Nyoukis & Jaap Blonk
Dubbeltwee
Ecstatic Peace! LP 2008

Dylan Nyoukis
Inside Wino Lodge
No Fun Productions LP 2009

Dylan Nyoukis is as obdurate a presence in the UK underground as Matthew Bower, if a rather more enigmatic one. Since the mid-1990s his Chocolate Monk label has leaked out 170-odd cassettes and CD-Rs. His group Prick Decay essayed a Noise bricolage impishly bastardised from musique concrète, whose idioms it mangled into a 'dada junk spew'. Later known as Decaer Pinga, they're best heard on *Guidelines For Basement Non-Fidel*, which mashes tape-manipulated everyday sounds with primitive improvisations into murky collages and obtuse blasts. Tracks and albums are obscured with contorted titles, betraying Nyoukis's yen for scatology and his absurd, often infantile humour.

Nyoukis was one of the first Noise artists to incorporate sound poetry into his work – witness the vocal ululations of *The Magnetic Headache* by his post-Decaer Pinga group, Blood Stereo. The link is made explicit on *Dubbeltwee*, whose outlandish duo vocal improvisations Nyoukis crudely undercuts with electronic manipulations, generating juxtapositions so awkward they almost obscure his abilities as an improvisor. Similarly, *Inside Wino Lodge*, his most accomplished solo album, is lumbered with a self-defeating title and an icky full-frontal Xeroxed cover photo of a naked Nyoukis holding the hand of a naked toddler – gestures typical of this enduringly perverse figure.

Rudolf Eb.er
Psycho-Physical Tests And Trainings With Rudolf Eb.er And R&G/Schimpfluch Personnel
Selektion CD 1997

Runzelstirn & Gurgelstock
Asshole/Snail Dilemma
Tochnit Aleph CD 2000

Sudden Infant
Radiorgasm
Blossoming Noise CD 2006

Switzerland's Schimpfluch-Gruppe collective espouse a dissident variant of Noise firmly rooted in performance. Their work is a form of modern-day Actionism, reviving the 1960s strategies of Viennese artists like Otto Muehl and Günter Brus by transposing them into live performances – or "psycho-physical tests", as Runzelstirn & Gurgelstock's Rudolf Eb.er describes them – which confront their audiences with violent and/or humiliating scenarios. The first third of *Asshole/Snail Dilemma*, for example, documents a recording of a performance during which a trumpet is inserted into the anus of a female participant, her screams accompanied by dissonant string music.

The collective's music is fundamentally a live one, though their releases convey much of the performances' psychological impact through astute editing and reconstruction. Both *Asshole/Snail Dilemma* and *Psycho-Physical Tests* comprise material from several performances. Sustained passages of silence are interrupted by playful musical interludes, sudden bursts of noise and crescendoes of primal howling.

In addition to Eb.er, Schimpfluch's ranks number Dave Phillips, Daniel Löwenbrück of Raionbashi, G*Park's Marc Zeier and Joke Lanz of Sudden Infant. A form of regression therapy, Lanz's performances as Sudden Infant attempt to revert to or capture the essence of a purer, more childlike state of cognitive awareness, and to translate the subjective impulses of this mindset into sound. *Radiorgasm* (1991) enacts one such cathartic exercise, his agitated vocals abraded by passages of brittle Noise. Later releases display more finesse, but

Radiorgasm's raw power verbalises the primal tumult at the heart of Lanz's endeavour.

Lasse Marhaug
Tapes 1990–1999
Pica Disk 4 x CD

Jazkamer
Metal Music Machine
Smalltown Supernoise CD 2006

Fe-Mail
Skyklubb Fra Hælvete
Important CD 2004

Hild Sofie Tafjord
Kama
Pica Disk CD 2008

Even by Noise's hyper-prolific standards, Norway's Lasse Marhaug is an astonishingly productive artist. *Tapes 1990–1999*, a collection of material from the 70 or so cassettes he released in the 1990s, is a good entry point into his formidable discography. Compressing ten years into five hours, it runs the gamut from voice/electronic cut-ups to goofy collages, collaborations with Government Alpha and Macronympha, and wall-of-noise barrages revealing his debt to Japanese Noise.

Marhaug has since diversified further, testing out a bewildering range of styles in his solo work, collaborating with improvisors Paal Nilssen-Love and Frode Gjerstad, and injecting friction into Ken Vandermark's Territory Band. He was an early advocate of a cross-pollination of Noise and Metal, in his duo with Kevin Drumm, on stage with Sunn O))), and on Jazkamer's *Metal Music Machine*.

Lurking in Marhaug's lengthy list of collaborators are Fe-Mail, the duo of Maja Ratkje and Hild Sofie Trajord, welcome female presences in Noise's overwhelmingly male-dominated world. *Skyklubb Fra Hælvete* clears space in Noise's sound palettes for colourful melody and playful vocal interjections. Noise is just one of Ratkje's many ventures, along with composing for orchestras and improvising with Tafjord in Spunk. Marhaug's Pica Disk label released Tafjord's only solo release to date, an ever-evolving 41 minute torrent of sound conjured largely from a French horn.

Wolf Eyes
Burned Mind
Sub Pop CD 2004

Human Animal
Sub Pop CD 2006

Propelled by incessant touring and a flood of self-released cassettes and CD-Rs, Wolf Eyes emerged in the early noughties as figureheads of a groundswell of US Noise makers: Burning Star Core, Double Leopards, Prurient, Yellow Swans, Mouthus, The Skaters, Black Dice and so on. A geographically scattered and stylistically diverse alliance, they're united by a shared appetite for extremities of sound and a willingness to infect noise with methodologies gleaned from sources as varied as power electronics, sound poetry, minimalist drone and Improv.

Wolf Eyes themselves concoct an ungodly Noise hybrid which sucks fragments of US hardcore, Industrial, free jazz (they performed with Anthony Braxton in 2005), avant garde electronics and Death Metal into a sonic vortex. Cloaked in cartoonish horrorcore imagery, their music's obvious delight in its own intensity is as infectious as it is puerile. Their two Sub Pop albums mooted the possibility of a rapprochement with the indie mainstream, which unsurprisingly never transpired. *Burned Mind* and *Human Animal*, in fact, contain some of their most fierce and uncompromising material.

The momentum the releases generated has since dispersed somewhat, and Wolf Eyes appears to have been overtaken by its members' side projects. Like ex-member Aaron Dilloway, each works solo in any number of genre-blurring groups and collaborations, in addition to firing out scores of limited cassettes and CD-Rs on their labels, American Tapes, AA Records and Gods of Tundra.

Various
California
Ground Fault/Troniks/RRRecords 10 x LP 2006

John Wiese
Soft Punk
Troubleman Unlimited CD 2007
Circle Snare
No Fun Productions CD 2009
Joe Colley
Waste Of Songs
Oral CD 2006

California has a distinguished Noise tradition, beginning with the 1970s prankster antics of the Los Angeles Free Music Society (whose affiliate group Airway's 1978 *Live At LACE* album is an early genre touchstone), to GX Jupiter-Larsen of The Haters, Speculum Fight's Damien Romero and Joe Colley of Crawl Unit; younger musicians like John Wiese and RHY Yau; and newcomers Oscillating Innards, The Cherry Point and Sixes. Along with LAFMS alumni Solid Eye and several others, they're all represented on *California*, a compendious overview which showcases the state's diverse range of approaches to Noise making.

One of the most distinctive and articulate voices in contemporary noise, Wiese has consistently sought to develop his music by placing it in new contexts and absorbing the disparate ideas which result. *Soft Punk* folds the salvoes of tone-shredding harsh Noise of his early solo releases into elusive, shapeshifting cut-ups, articulating a variant of Noise which draws on musique concrète's spliced constructions. The approach is refined further on *Circle Snare*, where Wiese scrunches Noise currents into ungainly, looping structures which seethe with barely constrained energy – a reworking of digital Noise informed by vintage tape music. Wiese's collaboration with Evan Parker is foregrounded by his recent work in Sissy Spacek (a former grindcore outfit) and a duo with Burning Star Core's C Spencer Yeh, which undertake a serious engagement with Improv's idioms.

Joe Colley's *Waste Of Songs* elaborates on the work of the now defunct Crawl Unit. Like his 2005 album *Psychic Stress Soundtracks*, it exudes nervous tension. Colley, who frequently works in the field of sound art, develops sounds slowly and at length, disrupting linear progressions with curious, sudden transitions and cut-aways to volatile, abrasive electronics. Noise textures are deployed sparingly and structurally, inducing uncertainty and generating a palpable psychological unease.

Yasunao Tone
Solo For Wounded CD
Tzadik CD 1997
Yasunao Tone & Hecker
Palimpsest
Mego CD 2004
Hecker
Sun Pandämonium
Mego CD 2003
Russell Haswell
Second Live Salvage
Editions Mego 2 x LP 2008
R/S
One (Snow Mud Rain)
Erstwhile CD 2007

Yasunao Tone's *Solo For Wounded CD* is digital Noise, literally and conceptually – its sounds were created by covering a copy of his 1992 CD *Musica Iconologos* in Scotch tape and forcing a CD player to play it by pinpricking the tape to circumvent the machine's error-detecting system. The outlandish scrambles of glitches, clicks and jerks which result are the random end product of a sound-art process music. German computer musician Florian Hecker is as process-driven as Tone, but whereas Tone's work deconstructs modern technology to produce sound over which he has little control, Hecker's highly controlled compositions exploit the potential of decades-old algorithmic computer software. *Palimpsest* is a radically decentred Noise music, a sensorily overwhelming excess of sound events layered in multiple strata, reconfiguring themselves at sudden and unpredictable intervals.

Something of a landmark for digital Noise, Hecker's *Sun Pandämonium* carves swooping frequencies and oscillating tones into blaring sound arcs of near-psychedelic intensity. His 2009 release *Acid In The Style Of David Tudor* opts for a different model, sculpting tonal fragments into algorithmic swarms and obliquely angled, mutating waveforms. The jargon-riddled art theory essay clogging up its booklet signifies Hecker's move into the realms of sound art, prompted by his focus on the science of psychoacoustics, and an associated desire to explore the spatialisation of sound. His collaborator Russell Haswell's take on computer music is more immediate and intense – *Second Live Salvage* reconfigures retrieved recordings of live performances, sculpting them into immersively loud sound environments.

Cologne's Marcus Schmickler (aka Pluramon and Wabi Sabi) has also reinvestigated the lexicon of computer music, on his 2007 solo album *Altars Of Science*, in duos with Thomas Lehn and, on *One (Snow Mud Rain)*, Editions Mego's Peter Rehberg under the R/S alias. The pair's ferocious yet precise digital barrages ripple and crackle with electrical surges, firing out allusions to Noise, electroacoustic improvisation and live-processed digital audio. It's unlikely that any of these artists think of their music as Noise – Hecker, in fact, dismisses the term as linguistically invalid. But all of them use Noise, albeit as just one part of a complex vocabulary. Their work is another example of a historically rich tradition: of Noise engaging with experimental musics, cross-pollinating with them to take on modern, hybrid forms.

No Wave

by Alan Licht

No Wave was remarkably shortlived, yet its legacy is remarkably long lasting. The Contortions, DNA, Mars and Teenage Jesus and The Jerks – the four groups recorded by Brian Eno for the 1978 compilation that has become the era's definitive document, *No New York* – had all ceased to exist within a year or two. Yet these groups' impact was crucially felt in the New York rock and avant garde scenes for decades. John Zorn was a huge fan of DNA and has worked extensively with both Arto Lindsay and Ikue Mori. Sonic Youth aligned themselves with Lydia Lunch, Glenn Branca and many other No Wave veterans from the beginning of their career. In the 1980s Swans and Pussy Galore were indebted to the ultra-negativity the No Wave groups projected; in the 1990s Miami's Harry Pussy, Chicago's US Maple, The Flying Luttenbachers, Lake Of Dracula and The Scissor Girls all patterned themselves on the original sound.

In its purest phase, No Wave flirted with repulsion, poetry and antisocial attitudes, both lyrically and musically. Vocals were shouted or screamed. The playing was non-virtuosic – many players had only just picked up their instruments. The sounds were either clipped and sharp, or sprayed dissonance everywhere. Every song was a miniaturist sonic tantrum.

Unlike punk, No Wave denied rock's history and musical lineage; instead taking Johnny Rotten up on his suggestion that rock 'n' roll "has got to be cancelled". Later, its originators brought a variety of No Wave's subtextual influences to the fore, ranging from ethnic music to jazz and funk, to 1950s and 1960s rock and even modern composition. Eventually, New York's punk-funk, improvisation, dance, jazz and composition scenes would mingle with the remnants of No Wave, creating a kind of downtown pan-experimentalism that in some cases was more commercially minded too. Whatever it was, it was an outgrowth, but not necessarily a continuation, of a musical moment whose sonic severity obscured its broad horizons.

Other than the likes of The Velvet Underground, The Godz, Canada's Nihilist Spasm Band, John Lennon & Yoko Ono's *Plastic Ono Band* LP, and The Stooges, there were few antecedents to No Wave. As for their immediate contemporaries, Pere Ubu's 1975–76 Cleveland singles certainly pointed towards No Wave (and that group included future DNA bassist Tim Wright; other Cleveland No Wave émigrés included Adele Bertei of The Contortions and Bradley Field of Teenage Jesus). In New York Suicide had already been antagonising audiences with Martin Rev's numbing blocks of organ sound and Alan Vega's echoing shrieks; they also befriended Lydia Lunch and James Chance early on. Richard Hell and The Voidoids championed the new groups – Hell called Mars his favourite act long before the Eno compilation came out. Guitarist Robert Quine's berserk, trashy solos on *Blank Generation* must have prepared some punk listeners for No Wave, and Quine himself produced singles by Teenage Jesus and DNA, recorded a duo LP with The Contortions' Jody Harris, and much later a CD with Ikue Mori. The one other group of the era to approximate the No Wave sound was Half Japanese, who came from Washington DC via Detroit. Their earliest recordings of wildly detuned guitars and free-form drumming capture a decidedly more joyful noise; their post-Jonathan Richman lyrical outlook also separates them from the wracked poesy of the New York crowd.

Mars
Mars Live
Les Disques Du Soleil et De L'Acier CD 1994, rec. 1977–78

Mars were the first of the No Wave groups to form (as China) in late 1975. Mark Cunningham and Connie Burg (aka China Burg, Lucy Hamilton and Don Burg) had come to New York from Florida – along with classmates Gordon Stevenson, later of Teenage Jesus, and Arto Lindsay, later of DNA – to do experimental theatre, but wound up playing music instead. Lindsay was originally slated to be the drummer, but decided he would rather learn guitar. The pair met up with painters Sumner Crane (guitar and vocals) and Nancy Arlen (drums). The live tracks, here, from late 1977, show the group still sounding something like Television (especially on "Plane Separation" and "Compulsion") – Velvets-inspired two-chord songs with the occasional slide smear. By March 1978, songs like "Helen Fordsdale" and "Tunnel" had developed, with non-stop detuned guitar rants, stumbling drums and howled vocals. The complete Irving Plaza live set, included here from August 1978, raises the noise quotient even higher, as the climactic 13 minute version of "N-N-End" (with guest guitarist Rudolph Grey) sets up a forcefield of Silvertone blare

perhaps never equalled, even by Glenn Branca's later guitar armies. While "Outside Africa" has an almost Sunny Murray-style drum part, songs like "Fraction" and "Ich Bin Swat" have a more insistent, rumbling beat, and Crane's vocals on "Fraction" are truly alarming.

Glenn Branca
Songs 77–79
Atavistic CD 1996
Theoretical Girls
Theoretical Album
Acute CD 2002

Guitarist Glenn Branca also moved to New York City in the mid-1970s to pursue theatre, but was attracted by the CBGB's/Max's Kansas City punk scene. He joined forces with keyboardist/guitarist Jeffrey Lohn, forming Theoretical Girls in 1977 with future producer and Sonic Youth engineer Wharton Tiers on drums and Margaret Dewys on keyboards. They only released one single during their existence, "US Millie/You Got Me" (1978), but some of Branca's songs are collected on the *Songs 77–79* CD, while Lohn's were released as late as 2002 on *Theoretical Album*. The Lohn material is surprisingly straightforward, but powerful: "US Millie" is an anomaly, with its Terry Riley/Philip Glass-like keyboard part and drum corps snare; the bristling clusters of "Computer Dating" indicate the group's No Wave reputation more directly. Even Branca's 1977 "TV Song" is powerchord post-Ramones rock, but "You Got Me", "You" and "Glazened Idols", all recorded live in 1978, feature dissonant chord patterns, looping repetition, fractured time signatures and energetic bursts of clanging guitar. The group's Achilles' heel was vocals. Neither Lohn's nor Branca's are effective, and Branca's spoken word excursions are conspicuously arty. In 1978 Branca formed a trio, The Static, with Barbara Ess and Christine Hahn, to showcase more of his own songs. Their lone Theoretical single, "My Relationship/Don't Let Me Stop You", also appears on *Songs 77–79* and is a perfect distillation of loud, primitive rock overlaid with cruelly dissonant guitars.

Various
No New York
Lilith CD 2005
(orig. Antilles LP 1978)

In May 1978 the Artists Space hosted a four night festival including Theoretical Girls, DNA, The Contortions, Teenage Jesus, Mars and two groups featuring Rhys Chatham, The Gynecologists and Tone Death, among others. Brian Eno (himself a self-proclaimed 'anti-musician') had flown into New York that spring to master the second Talking Heads album, and attended the Artists Space performances. Eno loved what he saw, and approached the groups about making a record. They managed to persuade him to limit the participants to the four groups on what became *No New York*. Branca, for one, felt snubbed. "There was definitely some politicking that went down," according to Lindsay.

The recording was done in spring 1978 at Big Apple Studios, and the groups pair off by LP side quite nicely. The Contortions' "Dish It Out" could almost be a remake of Teenage Jesus' "Red Alert", but with vocals and a distinct James Brown influence. The Contortions sported the most conventional song structures and rhythmic feel – Don Christensen was the only accomplished drummer on the whole record – but Chance's sax bleats and abrasive shouts, Adele Bertei's elbows-only organ technique and Pat Place's whiplash slide playing kept them squarely in rock's vanguard. The Teenage Jesus tracks are their longest and most dolorous, with Lunch sounding wounded as she cries, "*The leaves are always dead/ The door is always closed/The garbage screams at my feet*" over her own open strings guitar and Field's lockstep drumming. Fittingly, her publishing company back then was called Infantunes; as there's a childlike, made-up feeling about her songs, although combined with a very adult sense of urban dread. Lunch's way of being progressive is to be regressive – taking rock instrumentality and songwriting to an almost prenatal stage as its next developmental step.

Mars and their number one fan, Arto Lindsay, take up side two. "Helen Fordsdale" and "Tunnel" are brought into sharper focus in the studio. "Helen" is the most exciting track

on the record, with drums and guitars flying over a bassline that could almost pass for Charlie Haden's "Song For Che", while Crane turns lines like, "*See who cares your hair in cars your arms detach your eyes fly by your torso in wax*" into long, guttural skids. "Hairwaves" is as ethereal as No Wave ever got, with Burg intoning cut-up lyrics while guitar lines crumble around her. DNA are the most disappointing group on the record. Robin Crutchfield's keyboard is simply annoying, while the group had yet to reach its full potential. But Lindsay's detuned Danelectro 12 string is used to stunning effect. Mori proves herself to be a natural percussionist, and indeed the most intriguing part of *No New York*'s DNA recordings (their first) is how much musicality these non-musicians have.

Teenage Jesus and The Jerks
Everything
Atavistic CD 1996, rec. 1978–79
Mars
Mars 78
Atavistic CD 1996, rec. 1978

Teenage Jesus's post-*No New York* output is far more bracing. The "Orphans/Less Of Me" single (Migraine 7" 1978) is fierce marching music, with Lunch barking out her lyrics over careening slide guitar. The instrumentals "Freud In Flop" and "Race Mixing" are even more frantic; "Baby Doll" reverts to a sludge tempo but the guitar and vocal achieve a full-tilt-screech. *Everything*, which collects this material, barely clocks in at 20 minutes – still twice the length of their average live set. Concurrently, Lunch formed Beirut Slump with Bobby and Liz Swope on vocals and bass, Sclavunos on drums and filmmaker Vivienne Dick on organ. They released one single and played live only three times, but the recordings released on Lunch's 1986 retrospective, *Hysterie* (Widowspeak), are startlingly accomplished. Swope is a terrifying vocalist (and lyricist), and the organ enhances the relentlessly creepy atmospheres. By the end of 1979 both groups had broken up.

Playing their final show in December 1978, Mars barely lived long enough to see the release of *No New York*. *Mars 78* reprises their *No New York* contributions, and some of the Irving Plaza live set, but also rescues tracks from the classic *Mars* EP, including the growly "Scorn" and the crackling "Immediate Stages Of The Erotic", whose cable buzz, feedback and punk-Schwitters epiglottal forays make it a jacked-up "White Cat Heat" for the late 1970s.

The Contortions
Buy
Ze CD 2004
(orig. Ze LP 1979)
James White & The Blacks
Off White
Ze CD 2004
(orig. Ze LP 1979)

The Ze label released these two Chance LPs simultaneously in 1979. *Buy*, including the token disco track "I Don't Want To Be Happy", finds The Contortions only slightly less urgent than on *No New York*, but the interplay between the instruments is even more intense, especially between Pat Place's slide and the underrated Jody Harris's feverish Jimmy Nolen perversions. Chance's vocals are still healthily aggressive, especially on a screaming take of "Contort Yourself". After one last "*hit me*" in "Bedroom Athlete", the group launch into a glorious din, led by George Scott III's overloaded bass, that stands as one of their finest moments on record.

Off White, recorded with the Contortions personnel, is more concept-bound, with plenty of race-baiting song titles ("Bleached Black", "White Savages", "White Devil", "Almost Black"). The album leads off with a tepid, August Darnell (aka Kid Creole)-produced version of "Contort Yourself", complete with handclaps and anonymous female backing vocals. From there things get worse, with an ill-conceived phone sex duet with Lydia Lunch called "Stained Sheets" and a ludicrous version of Irving Berlin's "(Tropical) Heat Wave". *Off White* picks up a little on the mostly instrumental second side; guitarist Robert Quine is thrown into the mix on "Off Black" and "Almost Black Pt II", which heats the otherwise listless funk vamps up to a burning No Wave blowing session.

These were the last recordings to feature the original Contortions line-up. ROIR's 1981 cassette *Live In New York*, reissued on CD as *White Cannibal*, finds Chance accompanied by various members of Defunkt. Though the music had settled into a more restrained jazz/soul/funk crossover, it occasionally veers off into harmolodic territory, briefly signalling No Wave's underexplored debt to the rhythms of Ornette Coleman's Prime Time and guitarist James 'Blood' Ulmer. Chance is still able to muster some punk energy on "Contort Yourself", but he's essentially redressed The Contortions as club entertainers.

Lydia Lunch
Queen Of Siam
Cherry Red CD 2009 CD
(orig. Ze LP 1980)
8 Eyed Spy
8 Eyed Spy
Atavistic CD 1997, rec. 1980

Lunch's first solo album is a triumph. Relying on piano and some horns for their ghostly settings, the 'infantunes' are now sung in a hushed, girlish voice. On the second side, she hired horn arranger Billy Ver Planck, of Flintstones fame, for a series of novelty numbers, including "Lady Scarface", "A Cruise To The Moon" and "Knives In The Drain"; they manage to swing pretty hard, bolstered by some of Robert Quine's most animated guitar solos. The record also achieves a film noirish effect that paralleled the tone of many of the underground films Lunch was appearing in at the time, working with directors like Scott & Beth B, Amos Poe, James Nares and Vivienne Dick. "Atomic Bongos" is a neo-surf number written by Pat Irwin, but beneath the surface it's really just "Baby Doll" bumped up a few dozen bpms. Lunch successfully retools her No Wave formula here to a variety of accessible forms without losing touch with her dark side. No mean feat.

Around the same time, Lunch formed her next group, 8 Eyed Spy, with Irwin on guitar and sax, Sclavunos on drums, The Contortions' George Scott on bass and Michael Paumgardhen on guitar. For her part, Lunch had stopped playing guitar and wouldn't pick it up again until her excellent instrumental collaboration with Connie Burg, *The Drowning Of Lucy Hamilton* (Widowspeak LP 1985). In 8 Eyed Spy she sang and wrote the lyrics, while the rest of the group came up with the music. The results are much closer to straight-up rock, rousing, sexy, swampy but still noirish, with Irwin's surf fixation becoming more prominent (he later formed The Ray-beats with ex-Contortions Harris and Christensen to follow the surf muse further). Scott devised some great cover versions, including a booming take of Bo Diddley's "Diddy Wah Diddy" and a down and dirty arrangement of Creedence Clearwater Revival's "Run Through The Jungle". It was quite an about-face from the year-zero stance of Teenage Jesus. Lunch's vocals are back to a piercing shout, and the lyrics concern various derangements of the heart ("*Love split with blood upon the floor/My wrists are ripped, my hem is torn*"). Though 8 Eyed Spy proved to be a popular outfit, Lunch quickly grew tired of playing 'rock mama' and left in the autumn of 1980. Scott died soon after. Several posthumous collections of their few studio and live recordings document the group. Although the recording quality varies widely, this Atavistic release is the most representative.

The Lounge Lizards
The Lounge Lizards
Editions EG CD 1990
(orig. Editions EG LP 1981)
DNA
On DNA
No More CD 2005, rec. 1981
Last Live At CBGBs
Avant CD 1993, rec. 1982

In 1979 Arto Lindsay began splitting his time between DNA and John Lurie's Lounge Lizards. Lurie had acted in films by Scott & Beth B and James Nares, alongside various members of Teenage Jesus and The Contortions, and he worked on the soundtrack to Scott & Beth B's *Vortex*. John recruited his brother Evan and longtime bassist Steven Piccolo for The Lizards, as well as Lindsay and drummer Anton Fier. Initially

labelled 'fake jazz', the group set out to do for Thelonious Monk what Chance and co had done for James Brown. Their early raucous work found a successful balance between No Wave and jazz, with Lindsay battling it out on the front lines with John Lurie's saxophone. By the time of their studio debut, recorded in 1980, the musicianship was considerably more polished. Lindsay is much lower in the mix, although up to his usual tricks (including a great solo on "Wangling"), and Evan takes several atonal organ solos – but most of the music is bop and film noir-style jazz, played for downtown tastes but still too trad to be considered No Wave.

Even so, The Lounge Lizards were integral to the cross-pollination within the New York scene, with Lindsay and Fier participating in Kip Hanrahan's enormous ensemble recording projects, *Coup De Tete* and *Desire Develops An Edge*, which recruited musicians from jazz, Latin, funk and rock. After they'd both left The Lounge Lizards in 1981, they worked together in Fier's avant/funk/pop supergroup The Golden Palominos, as well as in a trio with John Zorn in his DNA-inspired improvised song project *Locus Solus* (which also included Mori). To this day Lurie continues to lead The Lounge Lizards, which has become a veritable downtown Jazz Messengers/Bluesbreakers, spawning many of the mainstays of New York's current Improv scene. He also composed the soundtracks to Jim Jarmusch's *Stranger Than Paradise* and *Down By Law* (both of which Lindsay played on).

DNA didn't make another appearance on vinyl until 1981, by which time Crutchfield had left to form Dark Day and Tim Wright had joined on bass. This proved to be a decisive switch. The *A Taste Of DNA* EP (American Clavé 12" 1981), collected – along with almost everything the group ever recorded – on the No More Records disc, is a quantum leap forward, the music splintered and experimental. Wright is a formidable player with a commanding tone, Mori executes rapidfire rolls in the most unlikely places, while Lindsay's guitar sounds like breaking glass; his often unintelligible vocals dashed with high-pitched gasps. Most of the six songs barely last a minute, and the lyrics are correspondingly truncated and elliptical – the complete lyrics to "5:30" read: "*When bright blue eyes get* dark/I want another eye to look at/I want another mouth to water at/Thrown around in a room."

Documenting their final live show from June 1982, the longer duration of the Avant CD showcases this incarnation of the group at its best. Lindsay's Brazilian roots are beginning to show in the Portuguese he injects into "Brand New", "Action" and "New Low", as well as the bobbing, almost bossa feel of "New New". "Horse", an otherwise unreleased song that finds Wright slowly hammering one note into place as the others gradually join him for a series of crashing accelerations, is one of their most memorable performances.

Sumner Crane
John Gavanti
Atavistic CD 2005
(orig. Hyrax LP 1980)
Don King
Don King
Hyrax MC 1983

After the demise of Mars, Sumner Crane set about adapting Mozart's *Don Giovanni* for his own 'operetta'. For the resulting *John Gavanti* he enlisted Mark Cunningham on horns, Connie Burg on bass clarinet, Ikue Mori on strings and percussion, and Arto Lindsay and his brother Duncan (who contribute percussion on "The Samba" under the pseudonyms Arlindo and Dantas Lins). Released on Cunningham's Hyrax label in 1980, it remains the most daunting artefact of the period. Crane recites the lyrics in a mock bellow that sounds like a punchdrunk Blind Willie Johnson impersonating King Ubu, while the cacophonous music recalls Sun Ra's *Strange Strings*, Japanese gagaku and Korean pansori, without directly referencing any of them – or anything else.

Gavanti essentially laid the groundwork for the group Don King, originally a trio featuring Cunningham on trumpet and bass, Burg on bass clarinet and guitar, and Duncan Lindsay on drums. Named after the boxing impresario by Burg (who had wanted to call Mars 'Mick Jagger'), Don King's music on this cassette (reissued on CD by Cunningham in 2001) is skeletal and stark. The horns play off each other, while Lindsay thumps out vague, off-kilter rhythms that suggest jazz or Latin music.

Rhys Chatham
An Angel Moves Too Fast To See
Table Of The Elements 3 x CD 2002
Glenn Branca
The Ascension
Acute CD 2003
(orig. 99 Records LP 1981)

Rhys Chatham came of age in New York's minimalist scene, running The Kitchen and playing in a trio with avant garde composers Tony Conrad and Charlemagne Palestine. After a few compositional gear shifts he discovered The Ramones, began learning electric guitar and formed three groups, The Gynecologists, Tone Death and Arsenal. In 1977 he also developed his *Guitar Trio* for three electric guitars used as an overtone source played over a driving beat. By 1979, he was performing it in a group with Branca and Tiers from Theoretical Girls and Nina Canal from The Gynecologists. In 1980 he formed The Din and developed a piece for dance, *Drastic Classicism*, a 120-decibel roar of writhing, out-of-tune guitars and drums, making it the closest approximation of No Wave to be found in the annals of modern composition. Both pieces are included on Table Of The Elements' triple CD Chatham retrospective.

Branca had also developed the notion of taking downtown rock into the realm of composition. The Static started to develop longer pieces, and for Max's Kansas City Easter Festival in 1979 he wrote *Lesson No 1* (1980), an "instrumental for six guitars". Branca subsequently formed a six guitar group to record *The Ascension*; this "Lesson No 2" has the chugging tom-tom rhythm and sinister guitar sounds associated with the No Wave period, but longer tracks like *The Spectacular Commodity* and the title cut combine these with modern classical structures à la Penderecki or Ligeti. Branca soon took the next step into symphonic form, with unwieldy but often enthralling results.

Ut
Early Live Life
Blast First LP 1987
Y Pants
Y Pants
Periodic Document CD 1999

Women were notably involved in every No Wave group, and these two second-wave groups were all female. Ut formed in 1979 around Nina Canal. The three members would change instruments on stage after every song, and of all the post-*No New York* groups, they were the most committed to the No Wave aesthetic, a cross between DNA, Mars and The Raincoats. They retained the amateurish playing and angular, cheap guitar sound, but added drones to the mix; on songs like "Mouse Sleep" and "No Manifesto" they left drums off altogether. They relocated to London and lasted until 1989; as the 1985 "Fire In Philadelphia" on this live retrospective shows, they stayed true to No Wave right to the end.

Y Pants was Barbara Ess's post-Static trio. Using toy instruments, keyboards, ukulele, bass and drums, they were considerably more melodic and charming than their No Wave predecessors, singing lyrics like *"I washed my favourite sweater"*. If their vocals recall pioneering Swiss girlpunk group Kleenex and Britain's Slits, Y Pants also look back beyond their No Wave roots to 1960s girl groups for inspiration. Their haunting a cappella version of Lesley Gore's "That's The Way Boys Are" is an unheralded precursor to Riot Grrrl. This CD retrospective from Periodic Document collects the 1980 *Y Pants* EP Branca produced for 99 Records and the 1982 *Beat It Down* LP.

Various
Noisefest
ZG Music MC 1981

Three years after the Artists Space series, Thurston Moore curated the ten-day Noise Fest at another Soho gallery, White Columns. Branca, Lohn, Wharton Tiers's Glorious Strangers, Chatham, Lee Ranaldo & David Linton, Don King, The Blue Humans, Robin Crutchfield's Dark Day, Ut, Y Pants, Information and Mofungo all performed, as did Moore's trio with Kim Gordon and Anne de Marinis, who were making their debut under the name Sonic Youth. This UK-released cassette contains selections from the festival. Despite the name, much of the music is already heading in a new wave-ish direction – even Sonic Youth are a keyboard dominated entity at this point, except for a screeching slide solo by Moore. However, the spirit of 1978 still resonates.

Sonic Youth

by David Keenan

They came to raise rock, not to bury it. Building on groundwork laid by The Velvet Underground, The Stooges, The MC5 and Patti Smith, Sonic Youth manage to articulate the common aesthetic that links such outsider strains as free jazz, avant garde composition, No Wave and teenage rock 'n' roll. While helping to foster an international alternative rock community, from the bastard noise of post-hardcore groups like The Butthole Surfers, Pussy Galore and Big Black to stadium-hopping Lollapalooza punks, Kim Gordon, Thurston Moore, Lee Ranaldo and Steve Shelley continue to push their unique vision forwards, drawing sustenance and inspiration from countless diverse musics.

Sonic Youth have always been quick to refute any notion of being anything other than a contemporary rock outfit, aligning themselves early on with the burgeoning American hardcore movement more than the downtown art scene, despite their roots lying firmly in the latter via their links with No Wave, Glenn Branca's guitar ensembles and Gordon's experience contributing to *Artforum*. Yet their working strategies were largely intuitive. Their use of prepared guitars, alternative tunings and other 'non-musical' sound sources was born out of an intense, almost reverential approach to rock's freakout potential. The base elements of their music appear relatively simple: they build largely from straightforward rock rhythms, with Shelley's drums providing a solid anchor from which the guitars spin out into explosive peaks or clanging drones. All this underpins Gordon's, Moore's and Ranaldo's distinctive, untrained vocals, whispering/singing/screaming lyrics ranging from ironic commentaries on pop culture icons to hallucinatory images of totemic power. Sonic Youth's devotion to rock has spawned a phantasmagoric amplification of all they believed it stood for.

Contemporary music thrives on invigorating, unforeseeable paradigm leaps: it's as if a portal opens for a second and only those who are really listening see the opportunity to leap right through it. Sonic Youth's portal came both from No Wave's refusal and hardcore's burnout. Sonic Youth also give the lie to the old myth that record collectors never make good musicians. Sonic Youth's insatiable enthusiasm for contemporary manifestations of refusenik sound has meant that they have long enjoyed a symbiotic relationship with music's fringe zones. They've championed avant groups like New Zealand's The Dead C and New York's No-Neck Blues Band, while also enjoying a fruitful dialogue with the mainstream, signing to

Geffen in 1989 and bringing dissonance and freedom to stadiums around the world through their relationships with groups like REM and Nirvana. Indeed, their evangelical zeal spills over into the running of several of their own labels (Moore's Ecstatic Peace!, Shelley's Smells Like Records) dedicated to making available the kind of oddball beauty that would otherwise slip through the cracks.

Besides their label activities, all the members of Sonic Youth are involved in countless side projects and offshoots, duelling with first generation European improvisors, trading tapes with bedroom punk infidels and going head to head with the new generation of turntablists and laptop operators. Whatever they're tackling, they do it with a healthy irreverence, proving that rock made by intelligent, culturally literate musicians needn't be a terminally po-faced proposition.

Sonic Youth
Sonic Youth
Geffen CD 2006
(orig. Neutral LP 1982)
Sonic Death
Blast First CD 1993
(orig. Ecstatic Peace! MC 1984)

The folk-primitive sound of Thurston Moore's first group, The Coachmen, offers few clues to Sonic Youth's future. But through The Coachmen, Moore got to meet Kim Gordon, when she attended their penultimate gig. At the time she was playing guitar in CKM, a trio including Stanton Miranda, who was also involved with Rhys Chatham, an avant composer experimenting with massed guitar ensemble pieces, and Christine Hahn, who played with another future guitar orchestra composer, Glenn Branca, in The Static. Moore met guitarist Lee Ranaldo in the 16-piece guitar army Branca assembled to record *Symphony No 1 (Tonal Plexus)* in 1981.

As well as playing cupid to Moore and Ranaldo, Branca, in his role as Neutral label boss, midwifed Sonic Youth's first, self-produced record. At this stage they were a quartet with Moore and Ranaldo on guitar, Gordon on bass and drummer Richard T Edson. The guitars are naked, without the freeflowing fields of dissonance that would soon characterise their work. However, the Sonic Youth basics were already audible. "I Dreamed I Dream" is an embryonic version of the haunting monologues that Gordon would often front, only here Ranaldo doubles up with a beautifully sung counterpoint. "The Burning Spear" prefigures Moore's combinations of a gush of free associated images and coruscating, atonal guitar lines, often to extremely disturbing effect.

But the live *Sonic Death* is the most essential artefact of early Youth. Originally a cassette which launched Moore's Ecstatic Peace! label, its collage of live freakouts, scuzzy home tapes, audience abuse and inane conversations at once document and prophesy the excited, puzzled and sometimes hostile reception the group's raw tonalities met in their early years. Songs are announced and then abruptly faded or sped up on wonky tapes, while explosive riffs cut to arguments about hamburgers. Between the (wise)cracks there are moments where the group coalesce with torrential force, highlighted by a live version of "Early American", from 1983's *Kill Yr Idols* EP, where Gordon sounds lost and dazed, her voice carving icebergs from the static, while Moore and Ranaldo light up the night with atonal phosphorous sparks.

Confusion Is Sex
Blast First CD 2005
(orig. Neutral LP 1983)
Bad Moon Rising
Blast First CD 2003
(orig. Homestead LP 1985)

The contemporary Sonic Youth sound first flamed into being in *Confusion Is Sex*. Lyrically scarred with grotesque images of sadism, body horror and dystopian sci-fi, the album marked a descent into some dark places, from which they finally flew clear five years later with *Daydream Nation*. Their aesthetic was at its most punk here, with track lengths erring on the shorter side. But looking back, some of its most interesting moments are pieces considered minor at the time, even as they devastatingly illustrate the efficacy of their new alternate tunings. The primitively recorded album closer, "Lee Is Free", is a minimalist metallic symphony consisting of stretched steel strings played percussively to generate endlessly overlapping concentric patterns. Gordon's half-chanted, half-sung "Protect Me You" is an emotionally eviscerated proto-choral landscape. Reputedly recorded in the walk-in freezer of a deli near the studio, "Freezer Burn" is the sort of mile-high wall of muzzy feedback that would launch a thousand space rockers, despite the shock intrusion midway through, when it erupts into a lo-res live take of The Stooges' "I Wanna Be Your Dog". But rockers like "Inhuman", with its scything monomaniacal guitars, pack the biggest visceral punch. The album's uniquely murky sound was caused in part by a can of cola, which was accidentally spilled over the master tapes.

Sleeved in stunning American Gothic artwork that sets a flaming pumpkin head against a Manhattan skyline, *Bad Moon Rising* is where Sonic Youth really start to stretch out. It's very much a studio creation, with tracks segueing into each other on warped Möbius strips of guitar noise. *Bad Moon Rising* also marks the beginning of their interest in pop cultural autopsy with its inclusion of the "Death Valley 69" single, a demonic duet between Moore and Lydia Lunch that evokes the spiral of insanity that culminated in Charles Manson's apocalyptic murders in California. More significantly, the song allows the contours of their restrung guitars to shape the logic of the arrangement. From here on, the structure and mood of each track is determined by the physics and physicality of the guitar: how it's strung, string gauge, what tuning it holds the best and so on. Fortunately you don't have to conquer tonal string theory to dig the resulting compositions. Organic and amorphous, they forsake conventional verse/chorus forms in favour of a dialectic of expansion and contraction. Besides, *Bad Moon Rising* is where Sonic Youth started goofing off in earnest. Moore's stammered intro to "Justice Is Might" is an early incarnation of his Royal Tuff Titty persona; and Ranaldo's use of tapes is startlingly effective, especially when a snatch of The Stooges' über-teenage anthem, "Not Right", rips through his amp.

EVOL
Blast First CD 2003
(orig. SST/Blast First CD/LP 1986)

Sister
Blast First CD 2003
(orig. SST/Blast First CD/LP 1987)

By 1985, Sonic Youth's live sets routinely closed with the majestic "Expressway To Yr Skull". It is at once a rapturously beautiful song and declaration of musical freedom, where Moore's celebratory, quasi-cosmic sex imagery (*"We're gonna fire the exploding load/In the milkmaid maidenhead/We're gonna find the meaning of feeling good/And we're gonna stay there as long as we think we should"*) is offset by the howling air raid sirens ripped from Ranaldo's guitar, 'prepared' with drumsticks and screwdrivers wedged beneath the strings, before the track trails off into infinity on the back of tapped-out harmonics. Retitled "The Crucifixion Of Sean Penn" or "Madonna, Sean And Me", a studio version of "Expressway" closes the original vinyl version of their 1986 album *EVOL*. The album was trailed with the single "Starpower", the group's wicked first stab at bubblegum, but it's in no way indicative of the rest. *EVOL* turned phonetics and dynamics upside down with a series of psychotically forbidding song forms animated by the chillingly human howls drawn from Moore and Ranaldo's long-suffering guitars. *EVOL* was also Sonic Youth's first Stateside release on SST, the premier American hardcore label (Black Flag, Minutemen and so on), whose militant rock work ethic inspired Moore and co to get in the van. But, for all Moore's hardcore sympathies, Sonic Youth's music was already a world away from the muscular asceticism that characterised much of SST's output. Highlights include "Marilyn Moore", a purgatorial sludge that combines the clank of midnight trains with an eerily lonesome ambience; Gordon's somnambulant Hitchcock tribute "Shadow Of A Doubt"; and an early Kerouac-inspired road monologue from Ranaldo, "In The Kingdom #19", which Moore sabotages with a firework thrown at a clearly terrified Ranaldo in mid-song. *EVOL* also marked drummer Steve Shelley's replacement of Bob Bert in the drum seat. Tight and fairly controlled, Shelley wasn't an immediately obvious choice, at least not until you realise how well his percussion throbs serve as a homing beacon throughout the group's wildest extrapolations.

Reputedly intended as a concept album based on visionary sci-fi author Philip K Dick's writings, *Sister* is a much harder record. Sonic Youth jumpstart garage punk's caveman stance by crosswiring it with alternate tunings and bursts of atonal white noise. Mostly recorded live in an all-tube studio, *Sister* is the closest they've got to replicating the Sonic Youth live experience. Aggressively cranked guitar lends "(I Got A) Catholic Block" locomotive intensity; Gordon's hallucinogenic "Beauty Lies In The Eye" sounds like a dream beamed across centuries. But the rockers really define the set, especially the euphorically raging "White Kross" and the deranged cover of "Hot Wire My Heart", originally recorded by San Francisco murder punks Crime. *Sister* stands as the greatest rock 'n' roll record of the 1980s – if that isn't a contradiction in terms.

Jim Sauter/Don Dietrich/Thurston Moore
Barefoot In The Head
Forced Exposure CD/LP 1990

Lee Ranaldo
From Here To Infinity
SST/Blast First LP 1987

Harry Crews
Naked In Garden Hills
Widowspeak CD 1995
(orig. Big Cat/Blast First CD/LP 1989)

"We never considered ourselves as being 'out of tune'," Thurston Moore told an interviewer from the British TV arts programme *The South Bank Show* in 1989. "Out of standard tuning, maybe, but we think it's bolstering the tradition of rock to break out and freak with it." 'Freaking with it' brought the group to a creative juncture between free jazz, sound art and modern composition. Happily the Sonic Youth constitution encouraged group members to leave the confines of the group and explore new links. Moore's earliest and most

rewarding investigations of instant composition were undertaken with the horn players of Borbetomagus, New York's nastiest snuff jazz trio. The results are bellowing. Moore swings the great black weight of his mudcaked guitar as a deep, almost rhythmic backdrop for Jim Sauter and Don Dietrich's salivating foghorns. The sleevenotes by Thomas Pynchon succinctly sum it up: "Two free men met a slave. Everyone goes home barefoot. Right-fuckin'-on."

Ranaldo's vinyl sound art object *From Here To Infinity* features 13 minute-long, locked-groove tracks designed for maximal/minimal disorientation. Ranging from beautiful electronic whiteout through low level hums to punk turntablism that anticipates his collaborations with concept artist Christian Marclay, it almost outdoes Lou Reed's *Metal Machine Music* in terms of alienating thoroughness. If you can't find an original pressing, the Ranaldo compilation *East Jesus* (Atavistic CD) includes a couple of examples, along with early live material, singles and a bonus track taken from the same home-taping sessions that produced Confusion Is Sex's "Lee Is Free".

Kim Gordon, meanwhile, formed the shortlived trio Harry Crews with Lydia Lunch on guitar/vocals and professional wrestler Sadie Mae on drums. Their declared intention was to promote the work of author Harry Crews, a tough-assed chronicler of Southern life on the skids. Their crushing noise guitar and banshee vocals made them highly persuasive apostles of the Crews creed. Appropriately enough, Gordon aggressively projects her voice, stripping it of its narcotic quality, as she begins to mould the rocker persona soon to be unveiled on *Daydream Nation*.

Ciccone Youth
The Whitey Album
Blast First CD/LP 1988

Sonic Youth alter-ego Ciccone Youth's détournement of Madonna's "Into The Groove" paralleled similar dada-esque desecrations by the likes of Negativland and Culturcide. But with Sonic Youth it's always hard to tell whether their referential embrace is ironic pastiche or affectionate tribute. Their appetite for trashy pop culture in all its manifestations, which by this time had overtaken their interest in American Gothic, renders the dividing line between overground and underground null and void. Their obsession with Ms Ciccone dates back to EVOL (check "Madonna, Sean And Me"), but it was former Minuteman and Madonna fan Mike Watt who suggested forming a Madonna covers outfit. His contribution to The Whitey Album is a functional, straightforward take of "Burnin' Up", but the Youth single, "Into The Groovey", is a crude, fantastic karaoke job – a biro moustache on an Athena poster – with Moore singing along to the original Madonna cut through an overloaded mic while a crunching fuzz guitar doubles up on the changes.

The Whitey Album takes this cheap methodology even further, with Gordon's karaoke version of Robert Palmer's "Addicted To Love" (for which a video was shot in a booth in Macy's Department Store, New York). Sonic Youth's fannish enthusiasms have always taken them on some fruitful detours. As given away by the outsized sneaker footprint on the inside sleeve, The Whitey Album was seeded by their love of hiphop. Most tracks utilise simple, thudding drum machine patterns over which the guitarists layer waves of interference. It's as conceptually deranged as Faust's collage work, The Faust Tapes, and even includes a Krautrock tribute, "Two Cool Rock Chicks Listening To Neu!", which is exactly what it says. And Moore's Royal Tuff Titty persona supplies the funniest and lamest spontaneous freestyling this side of Ali G.

Sonic Youth
Daydream Nation
Geffen 2 x CD 2007
(orig. Blast First CD/2 x LP 1988)
Goo
Geffen 2 x CD 2005
(orig. Geffen CD/LP 1990)

With Daydream Nation, Sonic Youth made huge inroads into the popular consciousness, largely on the strength of its anthemic opening track "Teen Age Riot", which features a great riff and hilarious ultra-slack Thurston Moore lyrics: "It'd take a teenage riot to get me out of bed right now" (apparently inspired by the terminal apathy of Dinosaur Jr's J Mascis). Something about Daydream's production slightly blunts the guitars' chainsaw edges, but there are exceptions: the "Kissability" trilogy (every double album's got to have one), where Gordon's snotty, lung-straining vocal runs up against Moore and Ranaldo's big crunching downstrokes; and the great, wired "Silver Rocket" once again recalls Crime. More importantly, Daydream Nation – now available as a double CD 'Deluxe Edition' – establishes Ranaldo as Sonic Youth's most consistent songwriting voice, with tracks like "Rain King", which marries a psychedelic West Coast melody with explosive sonic breakdowns.

Caught up in the first stirrings of the Seattle rock explosion sweeping America, Sonic Youth took on Mudhoney as support act for their Daydream Nation tour, which paid off when Geffen signed them to an unusually artist-friendly deal that has left them free to work outside the label confines. Further, acting in an unofficial A&R capacity, the group recommended that Geffen sign Nirvana. They made a triumphant major label debut with Goo. Sharper sounding and more varied in attack, it works where Daydream Nation failed, with plenty of 'for the hell of it' guitar pyrotechnics and liberal doses of gonzo humour. Ranaldo's "Mote" is the album highlight, and that's not just because he forsakes his usual semi-spoken approach to really sing it. It's a dramatic psychodrama that accelerates into the kind of locked noise that permeated From Here To Infinity. The first single, "Kool Thing", features Public Enemy's bemused Chuck D, who manages a half-hearted "Tell it like it is!" in reply to Gordon's demands that he "liberate us girls from male, white corporate oppression". They go public with their Carpenters obsession on "Tunic (Song For Karen)", which makes great understated use of Ranaldo and Moore's increasingly melodious string work. They went on to cut a glitzy cover of "Superstar" for the Carpenters tribute album, If I Were A Carpenter (A&M), but on "Tunic" they channel messages from Karen in Heaven, where she's playing the drums again and hanging with Elvis and Janis Joplin.

William Hooker
Shamballa
Knitting Factory Works CD 1993
William Hooker/Christian Marclay/Lee Ranaldo
Bouquet
Knitting Factory Works CD 2000
Thurston Moore with Tom Surgal
Klangfarbenmelodie
Corpus Hermeticum CD 1995

One of the major catalysts in Thurston Moore's wholehearted conversion to New York avant garde and Improv was his encounter with William Hooker, a free drummer who first came to prominence during the New Thing's second wave in the 1970s. Hooker reappeared in the early 1990s, and his sextet album, *Subconscious*, released in 1993 on Moore's Ecstatic Peace! label, brought home the spiritual and emotional power of free jazz to a new generation. Mixing intense bursts of linear proto-rock propulsion with splurges of multi-directional temporal defiance, Hooker makes a well equipped sparring partner for Moore and Ranaldo. On *Shamballa*, a series of duets with Moore and avant guitarist Elliott Sharp, the startling vectors of Moore's freeform guitar recall the ululating, effervescent streams of John Coltrane's interstellar tenor sax. Hooker starts off holding down tight rhythmic shapes until Moore ditches the riffs for sound textures, freeing up Hooker to pilot them all the way out. Even as the context requires him to subtly reconfigure his vocabulary, Moore's distinctive guitar is instantly recognisable.

For his *Bouquet* date with Hooker and Christian Marclay, Ranaldo augments his arsenal with chains of bells and electronic devices, but again his guitar work is what really stands out, though the way he and Marclay relate sonically sometimes makes it difficult to work out who's doing what. Hooker, however, is in his element, and with no one willing to state the pulse, he gets plenty of opportunity to stretch his vertical logic to the max.

Tracking Ranaldo and Moore's extracurricular activities is a near impossible task, but it's exactly this kind of energy and openness to new situations that feeds back into Sonic Youth and keeps them sharp. Moore has kept himself loose by playing with saxophonist Evan Parker (*The Promise*, Materiali Sonori CD 1999); more than once with Loren Mazzacane Connors (try *MMRR*, also featuring Ranaldo and guitarist Jean-Marc Montera, Numero Zero Audio CD 1997); guitarist Nels Cline (*In-Store*, Father Yod CD 1996); and saxophonist Mats Gustafsson and multi-instrumentalist Jim O'Rourke in Diskaholics Anonymous Trio (*Weapons Of Ass Destruction*, Smalltown Supersound CD 2006). He has also cut some powerful sides with his regular sparring partners, the percussionists William Winant and Tom Surgal. *Klangfarbenmelodie*, his duo set with Surgal, is one of their best. Recorded live, there's a nice, slurred quality to the sound, with Moore alternating chugging clouds of sonic debris and screaming bursts of feedback, while the Shiva-like Surgal launches great divebombing runs on his kit.

Sonic Youth
Washing Machine
Geffen CD 1995
A Thousand Leaves
Geffen CD 1998
NYC Ghosts And Flowers
Geffen CD 2000

The 1992 *Dirty* album (Geffen) seemed a logical consolidation of Sonic Youth's increasingly structured approach to Noise. Caught up in a heavier touring schedule, it sounded like they were deliberately writing songs with stadium scale dynamics, operating under the illusion that a slightly airbrushed finish was all it took to smuggle their avant leanings past Pearl Jam fans and into the popular psyche. *Experimental, Jet Set, Trash And No Star* (Geffen CD 1994) was even more disappointing. Kurt Cobain's suicide had effectively ended the alternative rock honeymoon launched by the phenomenal success of Nirvana's "Smells Like Teen Spirit". Perhaps the dawning realisation that Sonic Youth had probably reached their maximum audience potential freed them up psychologically once more. Now unburdened by upwardly curving career concerns, they got back on course with *Washing*

Machine. The side-long jam "The Diamond Sea" recalls the great, blasted architecture of "Expressway To Yr Skull".

Another factor in their turnaround was Sonic Youth building their own Murray Street studio in Manhattan, and establishing their own label, SYR, as a repository for any material that was too extreme for Geffen to handle. Their SYR run of releases has also turned out to be an ingenious way of documenting work in progress. No longer having to watch the clock freed Kim Gordon up to return to guitar, and her playing on *A Thousand Leaves* (1998) revitalises Sonic Youth's six-string attack. She admits to not being as well versed in the language of improvisation as Moore and Ranaldo, and her playing feels all the freer for its lack of any conscious reference points. On the opening "Contre Le Sexisme", her lugubrious vocal harks back to the austere half-light of "Early American", as guitars shower the track with tentative sparks or cloak it in low level murmurs, while Steve Shelley sounds like he's sorting boxes at the bottom of a tunnel. The spindly intricacy of the guitars, and the group's attention to sonic minutiae, make parts of *A Thousand Leaves* sound most like Tom Verlaine's original Television blueprint: garage punks with an ornate take on Albert Ayler's *Spiritual Unity*.

Expanding the expressive possibilities of this new, spectrally detailed approach paid off in droves on *NYC Ghosts & Flowers* (2000). "Renegade Princess" is a great two-chord punk number that sounds like plugged-in Modern Lovers led by a teen-gang tough, before fading into forlorn ripples of damaged guitar. The album even has some discernible lead lines, most bewitchingly on Gordon's "Nevermind (What Was It Anyway)", with a snaking guitar sounding little nursery-rhyme note patterns throughout. The opening notes to the title track, lightly struck from a couple of open strings, sends shivers down your spine. Then Ranaldo narrates one of his most affecting monologues, while the group tentatively build chords into a miasmic throb that recalls the Kosmiche music of Manuel Göttsching's Ash Ra Tempel.

Goodbye 20th Century
SYR 2 x CD 1999

Kim Gordon/Ikue Mori/DJ Olive
SYR5
SYR CD 2000

Brought in as wild-card producer for *NYC Ghosts*, avant all-rounder Jim O'Rourke was later inducted as Sonic Youth's new bass player. Their relationship flowered during an earlier collaboration that became the third release. His bass role allowed Gordon's guitar playing to come to the fore in a move that made Sonic Youth's sound slightly less aggressive and more introverted. Recorded in 2000, Gordon's trio date with Ikue Mori (ex-drummer with No Wavers DNA, later with a string of excellent experimental drum machine releases on Tzadik) and DJ Olive is a series of meticulous electronic improvisations positioned somewhere between Los Angeles Free Music Society esoterica, straightfaced IRCAM squelch and the kind of early electronica experiments Rough Trade and Mute used to release. Gordon sings like a cut-up, obsessing over repetitious loops of almost infantile significance punctuated by little perfunctory guitar strums and juddering rhythmic burps. Mori's lush atmospherics create a sense of deep, silent space inside which every movement glows with obsessive detail.

Bidding farewell to the utopian experiments that motivated 100 years of avant garde composition, Sonic Youth's 'covers' album, *Goodbye 20th Century*, has a strangely nostalgic feel. Besides the O'Rourke-augmented line-up, the double set features contributions from New Music legends like Fluxus operative and Taj Mahal Traveller Takehisa Kosugi, composer and John Cage associate Christian Wolff, and William Winant, alongside Sonic Youth studio producer/engineer Wharton Tiers, Christian Marclay, and Gordon and Moore's daughter Coco (whose take on Yoko Ono's "Voice Piece For Soprano" is truly primal). Despite the forbidding nature of the terrain covered, which includes compositions by Steve Reich, John Cage and Cornelius Cardew, the results still sound very much like Sonic Youth. Inevitably the group work best on the pieces that encourage the greatest level of individual interpretation. Written especially for the group, Pauline Oliveros's "Six For New Time" is particularly effective.

Their interpretations offer invigorating proof of the way underground rock and conservatory avant garde have developed along parallel lines, even if few on either side of the tracks hitherto cared to admit the fact. Countless sound thinkers have interpreted the music; the point, as Sonic Youth have always maintained, is to change it.

Murray Street
Geffen CD/LP 2002

Sonic Nurse
Geffen CD/LP 2004

The annihilating wind, symbolically invoked by Sonic Youth's No Wave antecedents, arrived in the heart of downtown Manhattan on 11 September 2001. Sonic Youth's Echo Canyon Studio is located on Murray Street, a short distance from the World Trade Center; bassist Jim O'Rourke, who had been sleeping in the studio overnight after a late night mixing session on the new album, was awoken by the blasts and stumbled outside into the dusty aftermath of the attacks. *Murray Street* subtly reflects the shocked, nervous America of those days, from the sleeve photo of Moore and Gordon's daughter Coco picking strawberries beneath a protective net, and member photos snapped around Ground Zero, to the music's melancholy restraint. "The Empty Page" and "Disconnection Notice" are confrontations with the void: *"they seem to think I'm disconnected ... see how easily it all slips away"*, sings Moore, over forlorn chord progressions that, here and on the subsequent "Rain On Tin", are led for a walk rather than the forced marches of old. Even a quietly confident manifesto like "Radical Adults Lick Godhead Style" concealed a stillness at its core, as if trying to step back and glean strength and meaning from chaotic events. Overall there is a notably greater emphasis on composition and pacing, building to pressure points that subside into trickling rivulets of high-neck guitar tracery (suggesting a cross-generational marriage of The Grateful Dead and Television).

If *Murray Street* sounded like Sonic Youth's most 'mature' record to date, *Sonic Nurse* partially reinstated the rough edges and sparkling behind-the-bridge harmonics of *EVOL* and *Sister*, from two decades before. Gordon's vocals on "Pattern Recognition" and "Kim Gordon And The Arthur Doyle Hand Cream" still sound like a collapsed-lung purr, and there are equal measures of furnace-like noise guitars and clearcut lead lines. The closing "Peace Attack" was a devastating, impressionistic portrait of a nonchalant world leader in the run-up to launching a military strike (*"springtime is wartime"*); Moore inscribes the lyrics with a date (*"3 Feb 03"*) which contextualises the song in the midst of the build-up to George W Bush's invasion of Iraq. It's probably the closest Sonic Youth get to an expression of absolute clarity. (*Rob Young*)

Tropicália

by Ben Ratliff

Many still think of Tropicália as an existing stronghold of pop avant gardism, when in fact it was an art movement encompassing film, theatre, poetry and visual art as well as music, which emerged in direct response to the political oppression that took over in Brazil at the tail end of the 1960s. It lasted for just two years (1967–69), and produced only a handful of records.

In the hands of the best Brazilian songwriters, folklore and futurism, mass cult and high cult, keep colliding. In fact, you have to love collisions to get into Brazilian music; you can't cling to notions of purity, because its history has been defined by the fusion process. In the 1920s work of the early black samba composer Pixinguina, as documented on *Pixinguina 100 Años* (BMG Brazil CD), you can hear jazz and foxtrot-era horns on top of lurching Afro-Brazilian rhythms. In the 1930s the new white singers of samba-canção, a romanticised version of street samba designed for more middle-class audiences, produced a thoroughly successful fusion; where Anglos and Americans tend to deride white musicians for feeding on black music, Brazilians venerate them.

In the late 1950s bossa nova took the romanticism of samba-canção and turned it inward. João Gilberto and Antonio Carlos (Tom) Jobim were bossa's figureheads; the melodies came from Jobim, the rhythms and deportment from Gilberto. Almost immediately, both inside and outside Brazil, bossa nova was commercialised, made over as a lifestyle accessory. In the late 1950s and early 1960s, a time when America was wealthy, suburban and dreaming of tropical alternate realities, bossa nova was ripe for colonisation. On record, the results could be fascinating (Gilberto's and Jobim's famed collaborations with saxophonist Stan Getz), or kitsch (Astrud Gilberto and Walter Wanderley's *A Certain Smile A Certain Sadness*).

Back in Brazil, the years between 1964 and 1967 saw the emergence of several musicians who would become hugely influential; in particular, Chico Buarque, Caetano Veloso and Gilberto Gil. This was the post-bossa, pre-Tropicália period, the beginnings of what is called MPB (Musica Popular Brasileira). All three musicians were the beneficiaries of Brazil's post-war modernist resurgence. They had been in high school when Brasilia, the new capital, was constructed; when the 'concrete' poetry of Haroldo de Campos and Décio Pignatari emerged as Brazil's contribution to the literary avant garde; and when European high-modernist professors of music were imported into the colleges. They were in university when Cinema Novo, Brazil's version of the Nouvelle Vague, was born. And they had sufficient distance from the birth of bossa nova to do something with it: politicising it, filling it with fractious poetry.

The early music of all three is well worth hearing: the slowly building poems sympathising with the working-class Brazilians on *Chico Buarque De Hollanda Vol 1* (RGE CD); Caetano Veloso & Gal Costa's *Domingo* (Verve CD), a second-wave bossa nova record full of quiet, sweet, serious songs; and Gilberto Gil's more rhythmic and outgoing *Louvação* (PolyGram Brazil CD). Both *Domingo* and *Louvação* were produced and arranged by Dori Caymmi, who introduced subtle dissonances into his arrangements; his early work raised bossa nova to a new height.

By 1968, four years after the military had overthrown the progressive government of João Goulart, a pent-up frustration began to pour out of Brazilian songwriters, playwrights, filmmakers and artists. That year, Chico Buarque wrote a confrontational little play called *Roda Viva* about a pop star who is literally eaten alive by his public. Right-wing extremists in São Paulo, smelling political subversion, stormed the theatre where it was being staged and beat up some of the cast. The era of amiable, nationalistic protest-pop, as epitomised by singers such as Elis Regina and Edu Lobo, was giving way to a sharper form of cultural expression. "When the military came in," explains Christopher Dunn, author of *Brutality Garden: Tropicália and The Emergence of A Brazilian Counterculture* (University Of North Carolina Press 2001), "during the first two years there was a kind of redemptive protest culture, very invested in the idea that there was going to be a day of redemption coming soon, that the military regime was a passing aberration. By 1967 it was clear that that was false: the Left had seriously misread the situation, and that there was not going to be a return to civilian power."

Forged in the highly charged arenas of the competitive song festivals, the breeding ground for the generation of Brazilian musicians that emerged in the mid- to late 1960s, Tropicália was an attempt to express the great change a-coming.

On the back of the sleeve of *Domingo*, released in 1967, Caetano Veloso wrote: "My inspiration nowadays is tending towards very different directions to those followed until now."

Various
Tropicália: A Brasilian Revolution In Sound
Soul Jazz CD 2006

Tropicália was initially the name of a 1967 installation by the visual artist Hélio Oiticica; the film maker Luiz Carlos Barreto had seen it first and suggested the word to Caetano Veloso. Oiticica's piece was inspired by having lived in the slums of Rio, among what he termed the 'organic architecture' of poor Brazilians: half-finished structures, add-ons to cheap houses and so on. The piece comprised upright wooden posts draped with bright pieces of cloth (suggesting slum decoration), dirt paths and tropical plants. Inside one of the thrown-up structures was written, "Purity is a myth", a phrase that would seem to chime perfectly with the approach of the Tropicalistas.

Soul Jazz's compilation provides a decent 19 track overview of the genre's golden years. Musically, the musicians who would come to be associated with Tropicália were trading in their nationalism for a more inclusive aesthetic. "We had to demystify that fascistic insistence on cultural isolation," Gilberto Gil said later, referring to both the military government and the MPB nationalists, "and on the national meaning of Brazilian-ness." Besides their intense interest in bossa nova and the music of the northeastern Brazilian backlands, Veloso and Gil were fixated on The Beatles, and in particular *Sgt Pepper's Lonely Hearts Club Band.* This fixation was shared by Julio Medaglia (who produced Veloso's self-titled debut album in 1968) and Rogério Duprat, academic avant-gardists who had taken classes at Darmstadt in the early 1960s. In 1963 Medaglia and Duprat had co-authored the Musica Nova manifesto, the points of which included, according to Carlos Calado's book *Tropicália*, "the comprehension of artistic phenomena as part of industrial culture, the rereading of the past as an instrument to understand the future (instead of as the usual nostalgia), and the necessity of a participatory art".

When Gil met Duprat in 1967, the latter had quit his professorship at the University of Brasilia, convinced that serious music was dead. It was the invitation of the Tropicalistas to come and work with them that made him realise that the only sensible thing a classically trained composer could do in 1967 would be to move into pop music. Within little more than six months, Duprat produced five brilliant albums with Veloso, Gil, Gal Costa and, Os Mutantes, and the compilation *Tropicália, Ou Panis Et Circenses*, all of which were collected on the indispensable but now deleted five CD box set *Tropicalia 30 Años*. They are now available separately, as follows.

Various
Tropicália, Ou Panis Et Circenses
Universal CD 1995
(orig. Philips LP 1967)

The records produced by Duprat hinged on a knowledge and love of all Brazilian music, from bossa nova and samba-canção to lively northeastern folk forms such as forró and frevo, merging these homegrown elements with the new electric music emerging from the UK and America, and spicing it up with a dadaist love of outrage. *Tropicália* ... functioned as the movement's group statement; not just a sampler, it was a true collaborative work, with different singers on each track. One song, "Parque Industrial", was written by Tom Zé, who re-emerged in the 1990s after years of isolation to record two excellent post-Tropicália albums for David Byrne's Luaka Bop label: *The Return Of Tom Zé: The Hips Of Tradition* (1992) and *Fabrication Defect* (1998). According to Zé, the musicians gave the songs in voice and acoustic guitar form to Duprat, who then thoroughly transformed them.

Caetano Veloso
Caetano Veloso
Universal CD 2000
(orig. Philips LP 1967)

Caetano Veloso's self-titled album includes "Alegria, Alegria", whose filmic montage lyrics about modernity weren't so much overtly political as a statement of self-reliant happiness, a courageousness about life. The song's final refrain is "*Porque não?*" ("*Why not?*"), which could have been a challenge to restrictions imposed by the military government, or simply to the narrow, exclusive mindset of non-Tropicália musicians such as the MPB Nationalists and the Joven Guarda rockers. In any case, it has always been understood as protest, and acquired a new meaning in 1992 when Brazilians demanding the impeachment of President Fernando Collor sang it in the streets. The album also includes "Superbacana", one of a number of songs Caetano wrote at the time which both celebrated and lampooned materialist and technological culture. "The theatrical music could serve as a jingle or soundtrack for a publicity campaign," wrote Charles A Perrone in his essential book *Masters of Contemporary Brazilian Song* (University Of Texas Press). This is one of the things that must be grasped about the music of Tropicália: the simultaneous embrace of, and disgust with, modernity gives it its multidimensionality. If *The Who Sell Out*, a comparable work recorded the same year, was broadbrush satire by a bunch of musicians bursting with their own invincibility, Veloso's songs such as "Superbacana" and "Baby" were both audaciously poetic and vulnerably honest. "There's a great deal of melancholy in Tropicalismo," says Christopher Dunn. "As buoyant as some of those songs are, quite a lot of them are very sad; there are these allegories of the nation, about looking through the ruins of a history not to be." The best example of this is the song Veloso called "Tropicalia". The first verse, sung over dramatic, atonal strings, seems to be written out of a kind of astonishment at new machines, revelling in the glory of planes and trucks. The second establishes an image of "*The monument/In the central plateau/Of the country*". And then in the fifth verse reality sets in: "*The monument has no door/The entrance is an ancient street, narrow and crooked/And on the knee a smiling child, ugly and dead/Extends his hand.*" In a mid-1990s interview Veloso explained the song thus: "There is a reference to the creation of Brasilia, and the whole irony of building a monument when there was nothing to be commemorated: a poor country, under a military dictatorship, a dark, terrible monument."

Gilberto Gil
Gilberto Gil
Water CD 2007
(orig. Philips LP 1968)

Gilberto Gil's 1968 self-titled album, his second, is perhaps the most musically successful of all the Tropicália records. To beef up Gil's songs, Duprat used the snarling guitars of Os Mutantes in arrangements that also included twin wood flutes, bumptious brass sections, "Taxman" basslines and the sounds of passing cars. With "Pega A Voga, Cabeludo", Gil took an Amazonian folk song and with Duprat's help turned it into an improvised shout-along that sounded like a Swingle Singers session gone haywire, complete with smeared riffs of Lanny Gordin's guitar. Amid carnival rhythms and indigenous song forms, Gil's lyric themes reflect the anomie of modern middle-class striving. One song, "Ele Falava Nisso Todo Dia", explores the suicide of a 25 year old man from São Paulo who was more interested in his life insurance policy than his life. Gil got the idea for the song from a newspaper article. If that sounds familiar, a tropical echo of "A Day In The Life", it was one of many examples of the Tropicalistas chasing The Beatles.

Gal Costa
Gal Costa
Universal CD
(orig. Philips LP 1969)

Gal Costa's self-titled album opens with the strains of Caetano Veloso's "Não Identificado", but, more so than the albums by Veloso and Gil, the record is a bridge between Tropicália and the more straight-ahead Joven Guarda rock of musicians such as Roberto and Erasmo Carlos. While the other Tropicalistas rarely refer back to these early recordings, the album gave Costa hits that she still performs in concert, including "Não Identificado" and a version of "Baby".

Os Mutantes
Os Mutantes
Universal CD 2006
(orig. Polydor LP 1967)

Os Mutantes's debut album, again self-titled, contains the most studio processing of all the Duprat-produced records: spraycan tape hiss; backwards vocal tracks; amplified sewing machines. The group was a Zappa-esque avant pop troupe that hinged round the trio of guitarist Sergio Dias Baptiste, his bass and keyboard playing brother Arnaldo, and singer Rita Lee. Their choice of material was typically Tropicalist: a baião ("Adeus, Maria Fulo"), a samba (Jorge Ben's "A Minha Menina") and the John Phillips song "Once There Was A Time I Thought" ("Tempo No Tempo").

Edu Lobo
Cantiga De Longe
Elenco CD 1996
(orig./ Mercury Brazil LP 1970)

A second-wave bossa nova composer and singer who emerged in the mid-1960s, Edu Lobo, was part of the leftist, mostly government-tolerated MPB movement, along with Elis Regina and Geraldo Vandré. His early songs are full of the 'better times are coming' sentiment popular among the MPB musicians. He recorded for the Forma label, an important imprint of the new bossa nova founded by the producer Roberto Quartin (*Forma: A Grande Musica Brasileira* (Forma) is an excellent three CD compilation of tracks drawn from the label's catalogue).

After the military government passed the draconian, anti-intellectual statute known as Institutional Act Five in December 1968, Lobo moved to Los Angeles for a year. By this time, bossa nova was an aesthetic dead end. Ahead of Lobo's move to the USA, Tom Jobim, bossa's greatest songwriter, had recorded three albums of jazz-bossa fusions for the A&M and CTI labels. Later he would instigate two highly ambitious projects, the 1973 *Matita Peré* (Mercury Brazil) and 1971 *Urubu* (Warner Archives), which were partly conceived as homages to the 1920s Brazilian composer Heitor Villa-Lobos. Both records were dominated by billowing, expressionistic orchestral parts arranged by Claus Ogerman.

In a similar spirit of artistic renewal, Lobo made two records while in the USA: *Sergio Mendes Presents Edu Lobo*, a pop record for an American audience, and *Cantiga De Longe*, a far more sophisticated treatment of some of the same material recorded in 1970 with arrangements by Hermeto Pascoal and percussion by Airto Moreira, both of whom had played on the most memorable tracks on Miles Davis's *Live-Evil* that same year.

The album's title track is a delicious piece of cleanly written electric piano funk, while "Casa Forte" contains the layered vocal arrangements that would catch on like wildfire in American pop, used by everyone from The Mamas and The Papas to Mason Williams. But here they are in the service of a heavily rhythmic folk rock mysticism and a deliberately minimal approach to Brazilian song form such as the frevo.

Milton Nascimento
Milton
Verve CD 2000
(orig. EMI Brazil LP 1970)
Milton Nascimento/Lô Borges
Clube Da Esquina
EMI Hemisphere CD 1995
(orig. EMI Brazil LP 1972)

Milton Nascimento comes from the central state of Minas Gerais, not Bahia, and so was never part of the Tropicália movement. Nevertheless, he emerged in the middle of it as one of the most fascinating singers and songwriters of MPB, and has since become naturally associated with the likes of Veloso and Gil. His music has been both more country earthy and more orchestral than that of the Tropicalistas; it never had the sharp, urban frisson that characterised Veloso's recordings with Os Mutantes, for instance. And its visionary quality is an inward one, full of rich harmonies, whereas the Tropicalistas wrote critical, outward music. In interviews Nascimento has explained that anyone from Minas Gerais – where radio signals from Rio and São Paulo were blocked by the Serra de Mantiqueira mountain range – had to imagine half the songs they heard on the radio: one could copy the lyrics and melody, but harmonies had to be invented.

His first few records, made in the late 1960s and early 1970s, are gems: a beautiful blend of utterly original songwriting, the lyrics of Fernando Brant and the productions of Milton Miranda, who made the tracks massive with reverberation. Miranda came up with studio tricks that a musician such as Jim O'Rourke still echoes in his productions today: clean, direct-input guitars; an organ buried low in the mix; incidental scraping noises off in the distance. Listening to *Milton*, released in 1970, it's also easy to see what jazz saxophonist Wayne Shorter saw in Nascimento when he asked him to contribute to his 1975 album *Native Dancer*: vertiginous melodies, a layered approach to songwriting that packs several different songs into one before wrapping it up, and a rich vein of romantic fantasy. The album opens with a song called "For Lennon And McCartney", which lays down Nascimento's Brazilian identity at the feet of the First World musicians he loved so much: *"I am from South America/I know you won't know/But I'm a cowboy/I am gold, I am you/I am Mina Gerais"*.

The record which best summarises his approach is the 1972 double album *Clube Da Esquina* (*Corner Club*), which was jointly credited to the guitarist and singer-songwriter Lô Borges. The album was titled after the name given by the Brazilian press to the group of Mineiro musicians that congregated around Nascimento at the time. *Clube Da Esquina* is permeated with themes of travel, and it is one of those albums that are worlds unto themselves, unmistakably a collective effort, made by a group with unusual closeness of purpose. In fact, Nascimento and the members of the Corner Club lived together for six months in a beach house north of Rio before recording, and Wagner Tiso and Eumir Deodato acted as arrangers and orchestrators. With leisurely tempos, stacked harmonies, steeple bells and some wonderful chorded guitar solos by Toninho Horta, it echoes Chilean music as much as English pop; here, Brazilian popular music has thoroughly outgrown bossa nova.

Jorge Ben
África Brasil
Karonte CD 2002
(orig. Philips LP 1976)

Perhaps the least categorisable of all the Brazilian singer-songwriters who emerged during the 1960s is Jorge Ben. His initial second-wave bossa nova hits were recorded in 1963 (including the future standard "Mas, Que Nada"); by the end of the decade he was appearing on TV with all three factions of Brazilian pop: the Tropicalistas, the Joven Guarda and the post-bossa MPB protest singers, of whom Elis Regina was the queen. His songs weren't especially political: when the government cracked down on intellectuals with the passing of Institutional Act Five, which sent Caetano and Gil to prison and eventually to exile in London, Ben wasn't in danger. But he was a favourite of the Tropicalistas, and Veloso's memoir of the late 1960s, *Tropical Truth: A Story of Music and Revolution in Brazil* (Da Capo Press) includes a page on one of Ben's early songs, "Se Manda", in which the narrator sends a woman away without anger or anxiety. The song "summed up all our ambitions," writes Caetano; it was "a hybrid of *baião* and *marcha*-funk, sung and played with a healthy aggression and a naturally pop modernity that filled us with enthusiasm and envy."

From the beginning, that healthy aggression was primarily a product of rhythm, driven by Ben's slurring vocals and the hard attack of his guitar (he plays using just his thumb and forefinger). Instead of bossa nova's harmonic complexity, Ben's music was based on chants and repetition. One of his career highs is *África Brasil*, a record seriously influenced by the trance groove marathons of Fela Kuti and James Brown. It's impossible to underestimate the power of the 1970s black consciousness movement in Brazil, a nation where mixed-race citizens are the norm and miscegenation has been seen as a positive force at least since the 1930s. Black power has not only answered a deep need in Brazilian identity, but provided a way to challenge the government, who saw all social movements as possible communist plots. *África Brasil* is full of dense, body-moving music, with Ben's rough-hewn electric guitar leads and several percussionists building a tower of rhythm on "Xica Da Silva", recorded for the 1976 movie by Carlos Diegues, and the football chant "Umabaruma", which David Byrne included on his 1989 compilation *Beleza Tropical* (Luaka Bop), which is still one of the best one-stop introductions to Tropicália MPB and their offshoots.

Gilberto Gil
Refavela
Warners CD 2003
(orig. WEA Brazil LP 1977)

By the late 1970s, Gilberto Gil had already been working on large concepts: *Refazenda*, from 1974, attempted nothing less than a grand metaphor for regeneration, in music, art, history and personal life. In 1977 he played at the Second World Festival of Black Art and Culture in Lagos, and took a month to travel around Nigeria. Gil's ideas about an Afro-Brazilian consciousness crystallised, and soon after returning to Brazil he made *Refavela*, an album which melted together Nigerian highlife, reggae, rock, and themes dealing with Yoruba deities and the black power movement in Bahia. "Ilê Ayê" is still used as a theme song by the black-only carnival bloco of the same name in Salvador; while "Patuscuda De Gandhi" celebrates another black-associated group, Filhos De Gandhy.

In the early 1970s Gil had recorded a handful of live albums that showed how musically adept he was with his guitar alone (collected on the marvellous 12 CD box set *Ensaio Geral* on Universal). *Refavela* represents a major transition from that fast, highly improvised style to slower, deeper grooves. In addition, his lyrics began to address wider issues. For instance, "Era Nova" criticised the Western methodology of history in which eras were declared either beneficial or degenerate, suggesting a Taoist one instead, in which time was understood as cyclical.

Caetano Veloso
Araçá Azul
Abraxas CD 2007
(orig. Philips LP 1972)
Caetano Veloso
Nonesuch CD/LP 1986
Circuladô
Nonesuch CD/LP 1991

Taken together, these three records show the breadth of Caetano Veloso's temperament, and they make a case for the overrating of the Tropicália period.

The 1972 *Araçá Azul* was the result of self-enforced limitations: Veloso set out to spend no more than a week in the studio and come out with a record. All but one track is the result of this experiment, much of it solitary, and he didn't mind making music that might be ugly or repetitive. Both he and Gil were impressed by academic avant garde composer Walter Smetak (Veloso produced an album by Smetak for Philips in 1974), and the influence of Smetak and Rogério Duprat is heavily felt. "De Conversa" is made entirely with multitracked phonemes and mouth sounds. "Gilberto Misterioso" chew over the couplet *"Gil engenders/In Gil, a nightingale"* for over four minutes; and "Sugarcane Fields Forever" engineers segues between field recordings of samba-de-rodas (circle-dance sambas with handclapping and batucada drumming) and small, atonal segments like fever dreams. There's a suggestion of The Beatles' "Revolution No 9" here, but plugged into a particularly Brazilian mindset. Finally, "Epico", produced by Duprat, is Veloso's most dislocating piece of music, with sequences of atmospheric brass set against verses sung into a tape recorder on the street.

Veloso's first New York concert in 1982, at the age of 40, was his first time in the USA. Robert Hurwitz of Nonesuch Records heard him there and offered him a record contract on the spot. The first order of business in establishing him in America was to present him alone with his guitar, playing some of his better known songs from the 1960s to the 1980s. The resulting album wasn't released for another four years. It is a calm, centred collection of 13 songs, presenting Veloso as a master songwriter and a curious interpreter of American culture. It flirts with Americana, choosing Michael Jackson's "Billie Jean" as a medley outgrowth of Fernando Lobo's samba "Nega Maluca" (a typical Tropicalist gesture) and Cole Porter's "Get Out Of Town".

With *Circuladô*, we move forward to Veloso's 'middle age' period: the restless urge to shock is gone, but he is still striving as few singer-songwriters do. Among the tracks are a Noise guitar/free thought poem featuring Arto Lindsay; several beautiful ballads ("Itãpua" and "Boas Vindas"); a rant about (the first) President Bush's New World Order ("Fora Da Ordem"); while the title track is a poem by the concrete poet Haroldo de Campos set to music. Produced by Lindsay, the record uses a Brazilian group augmented by mercurial American sidemen including Marc Ribot, Melvin Gibbs and Butch Morris. It is sweet, polished and highly literate music.

Marisa Monte
A Great Noise
Metro Blue/Capitol CD 1996

An Arto Lindsay coproduction, *A Great Noise* sums up the work of the great female MPB figure of the 1990s. Recorded half live, half in the studio, it has modern Brazil's rich pop history all over it. The personnel also includes Carlinhos Brown, who sings and cowrites, and Moraes Moreira, guitarist in Os Novos Baianos, a 1970s carnival rock group that fused sambas with folk rock, salsa and hard-hitting, guitar led funk. Here, Monte does a version of the group's "A Menina Dance" from its great 1973 album *Acabou Chorare* (Som Livre), as well as covering two Tropicália standards: Veloso & Gil's "Panis Et Circenses", which Os Mutantes covered on their first album, and Gil's "Cérebro Eletrônico", the 1969 song questioning the end results of technology, which he wrote while kept under police surveillance within the Salvador city limits.

Arto Lindsay
Noon Chill
Rykodisc CD 1998
Vinicius Cantuária
Tucumã
Verve CD 1999

Linked by a similar production aesthetic, a similar lyric-writing style and the lead musicians' involvement in each other's work, these two albums lift up the entirety of post-bossa Brazilian pop and drop it in sonic modernity. (Both musicians also have connections with Caetano Veloso: Arto Lindsay has produced two of his albums since the late 1980s, while the singer and guitarist Vinicius Cantuária was a member of the group in the 1970s and 1980s.)

The records demonstrate the elasticity of the samba. Where bossa nova had obvious links with cool jazz in harmony and dynamics, it also has connections in rhythmic subtlety with downtempo club music, and tracks such as Lindsay's "Ridiculously Deep" and Cantuária's "Aracaju" show how useful and non-limiting Afro-Brazilian polyrhythms are to modern pop. The amazing thing about these records is that you can come away from them thinking that they are dyed in Brazilian colours, but they are not pure Brazilian artefacts; instead, they are wholly successful fusions.

Frank Zappa And The Mothers of Invention

by Edwin Pouncey

It was in the recording studio that Californian born guitarist and composer Frank Zappa (1940–93) felt most at home as an artist and musician. From his early apprenticeship days at Paul Buff's Pal Studio in Cucamonga to taking it over in 1963 and renaming it Studio Z, Zappa's personal interest in music – a diverse mix including R&B and doo-wop ballads, modern jazz and the orchestral music of such composers as Edgard Varèse, Igor Stravinsky and Anton Webern – remained important to him. Elements of all of these would find their way into his own rock and modern classical compositions.

The Mothers Of Invention (or The Mothers as they were originally called) were formed in Pomona, California during the early summer of 1965. The principal members of the group included Zappa on guitar, Ray Collins on vocals, Roy Estrada on bass guitar, Jimmy Carl Black on drums and, later, blues guitarist Henry Vestine, who left in 1966 to join Canned Heat because The Mothers were not interested in playing rural blues music (Vestine would go on to record with free jazz legend Albert Ayler). After securing a contract with Verve/MGM Records, the group entered the studio to record their debut *Freak Out!*, a revolutionary double album of rock and experimental music (heavily peppered with social satire) that would transport Zappa's musical ideas around the world.

As part of his definitive CD collection of live recordings *You Can't Do That On Stage Anymore* (released between 1988–92) Zappa included selected examples from the original Mothers Of Invention, which he had disbanded in 1969 in order to pursue a solo career. "While not exactly 'hi-fi'," he bemoans in the sleevenotes, "[these] have been included for the amusement of those fetishistic individuals who still believe the only 'good' material was performed by that particular group." Zappa was always irked by the fact that his fans actually preferred the music he made with The Mothers to that which he later produced as a solo artist, and with the various other groups of musicians he worked with afterwards that shared the name. He never quite understood that it was the group as an entity that people loved, and not just the leader of that group.

Frank Zappa And The Mothers of Invention
Joe's XMasage
Vaulternative CD 2005
Joe's Corsage
Vaulternative CD 2004

For those audiophiles interested in hearing Zappa at the controls (before his hair started getting good in the back) these two CD collections of Studio Z outtakes and other oddities are a must-hear. Joe's *XMasage* is a fascinating insight into his working methods, with dialogue between Zappa (aka Paul Jacket) and Ray Collins (aka Suckit Rockit) about "hope for all teenagers", alternate versions of two early songs ("Mr Clean" and "Why Don'tcha Do Me Right?"), a Varèsian electronic fragment called "The Moon Will Never Be The Same" and "GTR Trio", an acoustic guitar, bass and drums, bossa nova-style workout that proved to be the final tape recording before the studio was busted by the police the next night and closed down.

Joe's Corsage offers even more exciting archive material, with rare demo recordings that date from 1964 to 1965 when the original Mothers were formed. Here, songs that would later appear on the group's *Freak Out!*, *Absolutely Free* and *Cruising With Ruben & The Jets* albums are blasted out with all the raw power they can summon up.

Lead vocalist Ray Collins is particularly impressive, especially on the songs that would later appear on *Ruben & The Jets*. Collins's performance reflects a deep understanding of 1950s doo-wop and its effect on those who share his passion for the genre. Unfortunately his working relationship with Zappa was somewhat unpredictable. He left The Mothers in 1967, returned later that year and finally quit in the late summer of 1968.

Freak Out!
Rykodisc CD 2002
(orig. Verve/MGM 2xLP 1966)
The Making Of Freak Out Project/Object (fazedooh)
Zappa Records 2 x CD & 4 x CD 2006

Persuaded by MGM to change the name of his group from The Mothers (a name that the record company felt would be interpreted as a reference to 'motherfuckers') to the less controversial The Mothers Of Invention, Zappa entered TTG Studios in Hollywood with an (almost) unlimited budget to record rock's first double album, *Freak Out!*

Added to the original line-up of Collins, Black and Estrada, Elliot Ingber featured on alternate lead and rhythm guitar – he would later find fame as Winged Eel Fingerling in Captain Beefheart's Magic Band. Others involved included distinguished young black producer Tom Wilson (whose previous clients included Sun Ra, Cecil Taylor and Bob Dylan) and Zappa's 100-strong army of freaks, dancers and underground personalities known as the Mothers' Auxiliary. Those invited to take part included 60 year old dancer and sculptor Vito Paulekas (whose local 'Freak' commune was an important factor in the development of the early Mothers), future Monty Python animator and film director Terry Gilliam, and wild man of rock Kim Fowley, who was credited with playing the hypophone (Zappa's description for his big mouth).

The album containing some of Zappa's most valuable songwriting like "It Can't Happen Here", "Who Are The Brain Police" and "Trouble Every Day" (an impassioned journalistic account of the 1965 Watts Riots that could also be considered for nomination as the first rap song). The more experimental "Help, I'm A Rock", and especially "Return Of The Son Of Monster Magnet (Unfinished Ballet in Two Tableaux)" – described by Zappa as, "what freaks sound like when you turn them loose in a recording studio at one o'clock in the morning with $500 worth of rented percussion equipment" – owe more to performance art than 1960s rock indulgence, and have retained their power to shock and awe.

The full impact of Zappa's freaking-out philosophy and its place within his music overspills on to the two *MOFO (Making Of Freak Out) Project/Object* box sets of archive material that the Zappa Family Trust have recently made available. A plethora of basic tracks, remixes and onsite field recordings has been added to the original vinyl stereo mix, plus insights into the musical, social and cultural influences that were a part of its creation. The message transmitted is a call to arms to all who feel shunned by society. "We would like to encourage everyone who HEARS this music to join us," invited Zappa in his sleevenotes " … become a member of *The United Mutations … FREAK OUT*."

Absolutely Free
Rykodisc CD 2002
(orig. Verve LP 1967)

In November 1966 Zappa regrouped The Mothers (adding drummer Billy Mundi, keyboard player Don Preston and saxophonist Bunk Gardner to the core line-up of Collins, Black and Estrada) and entered TTG Studios in Hollywood to record their second album. The big budget that had been made available for *Freak Out!* was drastically cut, together with the amount of studio time. Undaunted by this setback, however, Zappa and The Mothers (with Tom Wilson again producing) emerged four days later holding a powerful riposte that tore into the plastic ideal of the American Dream and the political corruption that helped it thrive. Split into two sections, the first, "Absolutely Free", was a stinging rebuke against a 'plastic' society that was incapable of thinking for itself and could not communicate with anybody (or anything) that fell outside of its blinkered lifestyle. "Call Any Vegetable" jokingly urged the "Plastic People" to overcome their fear and try to make contact with these strange looking, lonely outsiders. *"Call and they'll come to you covered with dew,"* Zappa wrote. *"Vegetables dream of responding to you"*. Elsewhere, on the instrumental "Invocation And Ritual Dance Of The Young Pumpkin", Zappa includes the main theme to "Jupiter, Bringer Of Jollity" from Gustav Holst's *Planets Suite*, an indication that, despite the rock instrumentation and seemingly nonsensical vocal deliveries, this was serious music.

The second section, "The MOI American Pageant", ripped into consumerist society with shots to the head aimed at the war toy industry ("Uncle Bernie's Farm"), boozy businessmen ("America Drinks" and "America Drinks And Goes Home") and corruption and perversion at the White House ("Brown Shoes Don't Make It"). Compressed into a single seven and a half minute composition that was made up of 20 distinct lyrical and musical parts, the completed edit of "Brown Shoes Don't Make It" is Zappa at his creative and satirical zenith.

To promote the album, Zappa and The Mothers hired the Garrick Theatre in New York City for five months during the summer of 1967. At this venue they staged a constantly evolving performance piece called *Absolutely Free: Pigs And Repugnant* that echoed the work of such Happening artists as Jim Dine and Alan Kaprow.

We're Only In It For The Money
Rykodisc CD 1995
(orig. Verve/Bizarre LP 1968)

We're Only In It For The Money is one of Zappa's finest musical and social statements that justifiably satirised the 1960s flower power scene by exposing the corporate ugliness that was responsible for its creation. Central to the theme of the album is Mothers' house artist Cal Schenkel's cover, a perfectly aimed satirical swipe at Peter Blake's iconic cover design for The Beatles' contemporaneous *Sgt Pepper's Lonely Hearts Club Band*. Instead of silken Carnaby Street military uniforms, The Mothers were garbed in thriftstore drag, staring sullenly at the camera with the group's name picked out in rotting fruit and vegetables rather than sprays of flowers. Equally confrontational were the songs themselves. "Are You Hung Up?" and the caustic "Flower Punk" with its *"Well, I'm goin' to a love-in to sit and play my bongos in the dirt"* refrain mercilessly mocked the hippie hordes (who ironically were buying the album without realising that they were one of its main targets), while the almost journalistic "Concentration Moon" predicted the kind of governmental wrong thinking that resulted in Guantánamo Bay. "Mom & Dad" was a dig at parents who were too boozed up and hypnotised by TV to notice that their children were being slaughtered by the society they supported. All these were as politically and socially scathing as "Trouble Every Day" on *Freak Out!* or *Absolutely Free*'s "Brown Shoes Don't Make It". Sonic experiments like "Nasal Retentive Calliope Music" and "The Chrome Plated Megaphone Of Destiny" ventured into musique concrète territory, underlining Zappa's continuing interest in electronic music and modern composition.

When Zappa reissued *Money* in 1986, he chose to digitally rerecord the drum and bass parts, claiming that the original tapes had deteriorated by the time they were returned to him by the record company. Unfortunately, this tinkering ruined the feeling (and memory) of the original recording, a seemingly thoughtless act that caused many admirers of the original group to wonder whether one of the Mothers Of Invention's key albums had been desecrated not for the interests of quality control, but out of spite. (A 1995 edition of the CD restored the original version, with some audible tape deterioration.)

Lumpy Gravy

Rykodisc CD 1995
(orig. Verve/Bizarre LP 1968)

Civilization Phaze III

Barking Pumpkin 2 x CD 1994

The Lumpy Money Project/Object

Zappa Records 3 x CD 2009

Considered by many to be his best album, the recording of *Lumpy Gravy* gave Zappa his first opportunity to have his music played by a 50 piece studio orchestra (named by the composer The Abnuceals Emuukha Electric Symphony Orchestra & Chorus). Although he was still under contract with MGM, when Capitol Records commissioned him to write and record an orchestral piece for them in February 1967 Zappa leapt at the chance. Once recorded, however, the ensuing legal battle between the two record companies over ownership delayed *Gravy*'s release. This hiatus allowed Zappa to add vocal parts and radically alter the recording before it was finally released over a year later in May 1968.

For the vocal arrangements, a curtain-covered Steinway grand piano was fitted with two microphones, and a sandbag was placed on the sustain pedal. Visitors to the studio were then invited to squat inside the canopy of this Cagean prepared piano and improvise on suggested topics. Subject matter included pigs, ponies, grey smoke and other obscurities, all of which was recorded and edited by Zappa for inclusion into the final version of *Gravy*. When combined with the Varèse-style percussion interludes, slurred Stravinsky-esque orchestration and memorable pop and jazz anthems that formed the album, these strange, muffled discussions held under a piano give *Lumpy Gravy* an extra Fluxus feel.

Zappa revisited this experiment on *Civilization Phaze III*, his Synclavier (a digital synthesizer) 'masterwork', where the outtakes from the 1967 'people under the piano' sessions (together with newly recorded dialogue performed the same way) was incorporated into a selection of Zappa's Synclavier music, assisted by the large scale Ensemble Modern orchestra. The highlight here, however, is "N-Lite", a densely packed and meticulously arranged composition that had taken over a decade to perfect.

The complete *Lumpy Gravy* and *We're Only In It For The Money* recording sessions have now been released by the Zappa Family Trust as a noble triple CD set that includes the Capitol Records master of *Gravy* and a later remix, the original mono and later rerecorded mixes of *Money*, and an entire disc of unreleased material that reveals just how closely the two albums crossed over creatively. "I could take a razor blade and cut them apart and put it together again in a different order," Zappa said about his working methods, "it would still make one piece of music you can listen to. It's all one album."

Cruising With Ruben & The Jets

Rykodisc CD 2002
(orig. Verve/Bizarre LP 1968)

"Is this the Mothers Of Invention recording under a different name in a last ditch attempt to get their cruddy music on the radio?" queried Cal Schenkel's bulbous-nosed cartoon dog bandleader on the cover of The Mothers' fifth official album. Rather than being a device to display the group's possible commercial potential, however, *Ruben & The Jets* is Zappa's touching tribute to the rhythm 'n' blues and doo-wop music of his youth. Here, revised songs from *Freak Out!* like "How Could I Be Such A Fool", "You Didn't Try To Call Me", "I'm Not Satisfied" and "Any Way The Wind Blows" were supplemented with beautifully crafted doo-wop-style originals, several of which were cowritten by vocalist Ray Collins, who, like Zappa, was equally enchanted by the music of his teenage years. What seems like a cunningly crafted spoof on the surface turns out to be a genuine labour of love – so authentically presented that the record company felt the need to put a

Mothers Of Invention sticker on the cover in order to avoid confusion when the record was sent out to radio stations. The only indication that this was a Mothers album is Zappa's extended electric guitar solo on the end of "Stuff Up The Cracks" (a teenage suicide note in song form) that breaks free from the nostalgic feel of the rest of *Ruben* and trails towards psychedelia – thus linking the simplistic rock music of The Mothers' past with the more experimental and intellectually demanding music they were now playing at the behest of their equally demanding leader.

Alas, Zappa's meddlesome 1980s remastering job (with new string bass and drum tracks) intrudes on the replicated 1950s feel that nostalgically reverberated through the original recording, making the Rykodisc CD reissue virtually unlistenable. Until the original recording is properly restored, to hear *Ruben* at its best one must still diligently seek out the vinyl LP.

Uncle Meat
Rykodisc 2 x CD 2002
(orig. Bizarre/Reprise LP 1969)

Announced on the album cover as: "(Most of the music from The Mother's [sic] movie of the same name which we haven't got enough money to finish yet)", the soundtrack to *Uncle Meat* (a film project that began in New York City during the group's Garrick Theatre residency and took over two decades to complete) contains some of the greatest music the original group ever recorded together. Rather than the fragmented compilation of loose ends that the cover blurb implies, *Uncle Meat* is a fully realised Mothers album where every aspect of Zappa's musical interests are explored through the professional musicianship and bizarre humour of the various group members involved. The addition of drummer Arthur Dyer Tripp III (who had replaced Billy Mundi) and Buzz Gardner on trumpet was an extra bonus to the group's sound at this stage of their development. Alongside the strange guitar soloing of "Nine Types Of Industrial Pollution" (where Zappa's fretboard worrying resembles a Derek Bailey improvisation) and the operatic pachuco doo-wop of "Dog Breath, In The Year Of The Plague" are embedded such gems as the semi-

autobiographical "The Air" and "Cruising For Burgers", keyboards player Don (Dom de Wild) Preston's rendition of Richard Berry's "Louie Louie" on the Royal Albert Hall pipe organ, and the classically trained Ian Underwood's storming free jazz saxophone solo, whipped out live on stage in Copenhagen.

A large chunk of *Uncle Meat* is devoted to "King Kong", an extended instrumental in six sections with improvised solos by Preston, Underwood, Bunk Gardner and baritone saxophone player Euclid James 'Motorhead' Sherwood (who had joined The Mothers in 1967), which once again summons up comparisons with such 1960s free jazz sessions as Ornette Coleman's *Free Jazz* or John Coltrane's *Ascension*. On the original Bizarre Records double LP, "King Kong" was given an entire side, but for the double CD version it is stuck on the end of the second disc, almost as an afterthought, the rest being taken up with unfathomable dialogue from the problematic *Uncle Meat* movie that was finally released on video in 1988.

In October 1969 jazz violinist Jean-Luc Ponty recorded a version of "King Kong" for an album of Zappa instrumental covers, a further indication that this particular piece of music was leaning as much in the direction of jazz as it is that of rock. Ponty would later join Zappa as one of the players on his critically acclaimed jazz-rock solo debut *Hot Rats*.

Burnt Weeny Sandwich
Rykodisc CD 2002
(orig. Bizarre/Reprise LP 1970)
Weasels Ripped My Flesh
Rykodisc CD 2002
(orig. Bizarre/Reprise LP 1970)
Ahead Of Their Time
Barking Pumpkin CD 1993
You Can't Do That On Stage Anymore Vol 5
Rykodisc 2 x CD 1992

When Zappa disbanded The Mothers Of Invention in August 1969, he had already stashed away a considerable amount of recorded material by the group, which he would release later. The first of these was *Burnt Weeny Sandwich* (named after

Zappa's favourite late night snack), a selection of live recordings and studio pieces sandwiched between covers of two favourite doo-wop numbers – "W-P-L-J" by The Four Deuces and "Valerie" (mis-spelt "Valarie") by Jackie and The Starlites. The music of his youth collided head-on with his admiration for the works of Igor Stravinsky on "Igor's Boogie" and, especially on the beautiful "Little House I Used To Live In", Zappa shows how his own compositions were now comparable in quality to those by the twentieth-century composers he so admired.

Although the promised, ambitious 12 LP box set *The History And Improvisations Of The Mothers Of Invention* never materialised, scattered selections from this project would eventually surface on Zappa's Bizarre Records imprint. Complete with its gory, award-winning Neon Park cover of a man shaving himself with a flesh-shredding electric weasel, and a title that had been stolen from a cover story in a men's adventure magazine, *Weasels Ripped My Flesh* captured Zappa and The Mothers at the peak of their improvisational powers. Alongside an appreciative nod to avant garde jazz saxophonist/flautist Eric Dolphy (whose *Out To Lunch* was a personal favourite) on "The Eric Dolphy Memorial Barbecue", and the gung-ho rock guitar workout "My Guitar Wants To Kill Your Mama", Zappa added a stirring rendition of Little Richard's "Directly From My Heart To You", added Ray Collins's vocal to an instrumental section from *Lumpy Gravy* on "Oh No", and finished off with over two minutes of screeching feedback noise. Recorded at a UK concert in 1969, this was Noise music before the term had even been invented.

Ahead Of Their Time, an edited live recording of a Mothers performance at London's Royal Festival Hall in October 1968, was reluctantly released to appease those fans who still mourned the passing of the original group. The more substantial early Mothers archive haul, however, was reserved for the first disc of *You Can't Do That On Stage Anymore Vol 5* (part of Zappa's extensive 14 CD concert recording project) where every nuance of the group's on the road activities were painstakingly collected by their mischievous leader. These collected field recordings get to the very root of what The Mothers Of Invention were all about, as well as being an essential anthropological document on the history of the Los Angeles freak scene.

Mystery Disc
Rykodisc CD 1998
The Lost Episodes
Rykodisc CD 1996

These two important collections of archive material are an essential purchase for anybody remotely interested in the origin of Zappa's musical ideas and freak philosophy. *Mystery Disc* brings together on a single disc the two LPs that accompanied the first couple of volumes of his career-spanning *Old Masters* vinyl box sets – a perfectly pitched (albeit somewhat cynical) marketing lure to entice those fans who had already bought everything to buy it again. That said, there is much here to delight and excite the hardcore Zappa/Mothers devotee, with soundtrack music from Studio Z, historic recordings with Captain Beefheart, a previously unheard lecture segment from The Mothers' Festival Hall concert that was mysteriously omitted from *Ahead Of Their Time*, and much more besides. The original vinyl versions of *Mystery Disc* included the songs "Why Don'tcha Do Me Right?" and "Big Leg Emma", both sides of a lost 45 from 1967 that were then transferred to Rykodisc's CD version of *Absolutely Free* (for chronological reasons) and subsequently removed from the *Mystery Disc* CD.

The Lost Episodes expands on the *Mystery Disc* concept by unearthing recordings from the early period of Zappa's career, together with later material from the period after he had abandoned the original Mothers. Highlights include such 'anthropological relics' as a dialogue between members of Zappa's first group The Blackouts from the late 1950s and a field recording of The Mothers being visited at their New York loft studio by the NYPD (during their Garrick Theatre residency) for making excessive noise while rehearsing. Best of all, though, is a blistering 1963 version of "Fountain Of Love" (a song that would later appear on *Ruben & The Jets*) with Ray Collins vocalising over Zappa's fuzzed-out electric bass guitar. This superb, speaker-rattling rendition perversely transforms the crooning sentimentality of the original into a snarling garage rock beast, while ingeniously keeping the tenderness of Collins's heartfelt doo-wop harmonising intact.

It is a perfect example of Zappa's ability to take a recognisable musical form and creatively distort its sonic structure. By doing this, he opened up his audience to a wide range of unfamiliar, challenging music.

Funk, Hiphop & Beyond

James Brown

by Peter Shapiro

Call it the Muhammed Ali principle. If you talk up your own game as much as the Godfather of Soul, you've got to be one bad motherfucker. Listening to (and watching) James Brown walk it like he talks it with every glide, stride and shimmy is the main pleasure of his music. There's a vicarious thrill in watching Mr Dynamite camel-walk across a stage up to the mic to deliver one of his trademark grunts with precision timing. With James Brown, the tiniest gesture – a grunt, a shake of the head, an off the cuff vamp – meant everything. No one – not even Phil Spector or Trevor Horn – packed so much (timbres, forward motion, sparkle, intensity) into each bar. Even when Brown started to economise in the 1970s, he always understood what made pop music great in the first place: an immediacy and momentum that steamrollered all obstacles. Brown was at once the most superficial musician in history and the most profound: there was nothing below the surface of his performances, yet his links to an ancient tradition with roots in the community musics of West and Central Africa are glaringly obvious. Moreover, Brown was the most assertively black personality ever to be accorded mainstream acceptance in America. His esteem in both African American and white communities was enough to have him courted by politicians such as Vice President Hubert Humphrey for his "Don't Be A Drop-out" campaign. On the day Martin Luther King was assassinated, television stations in cities with large black populations aired a live James Brown concert in the hope that it would prevent rioting; it worked. As with Louis Armstrong and Jimmy Rodgers, it would be impossible to overstate his importance or overestimate his stature.

Moreover, unlike most legendary musical figures Brown's musical legacy has actually been treated with the respect it deserves. And it's a huge legacy. Not including side projects, he has at least 85 albums to his credit – not bad for a singles artist. For years Brown's best records languished in PolyGram's vaults, while disposable items such as *Sex Machine Today* (a 1975 attempt to recapture past glories) remained in circulation. Then the label placed Brown's catalogue in the hands of scholars and former associates like Cliff White, Harvey Weiner and Alan Leeds. They have subsequently produced a series of revelatory reissues that are landmarks of curatorial diligence and corporate largesse.

James Brown
Live At The Apollo
Polydor CD 1990

(orig. King LP 1963)

James Brown was born in a shack on the outskirts of Barnwell, South Carolina on 3 May 1933. Dancing for pennies as a sideline to picking cotton in his adopted hometown of Augusta, Georgia, he was arrested for breaking into a car to steal a coat when he was 15 years old. Paroled in 1952, he joined lifelong sidekick Bobby Byrd's Gospel Starlighters, who later changed their name to The Flames and stepped into Little Richard's shoes when he got too big to play local dates. Brown's irrepressible energy and acrobatics quickly garnered The Flames a following, and their first single, "Please Please Please" (1956), eventually sold over a million copies.

Before going on to rewrite the rules about the role of rhythm in Western music, Mr Please Please laid waste to the standard notion of a ballad singer. Like that other funky megalomaniac, George Clinton, Brown always wanted to be a crooner – in his fantasies he was a camel-walking cross between Louis Jordan and Billy Eckstine. Ray Charles may have brought the sound of gospel into R&B, but Brown brought into popular music the speaking-in-tongues possession exhibited by such shouters as The Five Blind Boys Of Mississippi's Archie Brownlee and The Swan Silvertones' Claude Jeter.

The greatest moment, both artistically and historically, of Brown's early career was Live At The Apollo. Convinced that his fans would want a document of his electric live show, Brown approached King Records supremo Syd Nathan to record some dates at Harlem's Apollo Theatre. Nathan refused, but Brown went ahead, even paying for the recording himself. Shelved until May 1963, Live At The Apollo eventually hit number two on the American album charts. It is undoubtedly one of the most brilliant performances of Brown's incandescent career. Live At The Apollo is pure physicality transposed to vinyl: flash, coruscating motion, bravado, urgency. Despite the crowd noise, Brown is so absorbed in the magnificence of his performance, hearing it now is like spying on someone

dancing in front of a bedroom mirror. The only problem with listening to Live At The Apollo, or any of his live albums, is how the crowd screaming alerts you to what you missed by not being there: Brown doing the mashed potato or good-footing it across the stage or throwing his cape off to come back to the mic one last time. Not only was Live At The Apollo a commercial and artistic triumph, but as a result of Brown's own financing and business acumen, the album, along with Ray Charles's growing independence, became a high profile symbol of the viability of African American self-sufficiency.

Foundations Of Funk – A Brand New Bag: 1964–1969
Polydor 2 x CD 1998

Beginning with Live At The Apollo, Brown embarked on an unparalleled period of world-changing activity that lasted until "Funky President (People It's Bad)" ended its R&B chart run at the end of 1974. During those 11 years, Brown singlehandedly (with some help from his group) orchestrated a tectonic shift in the foundation of music. Not unlike the compositional methods of Charles Mingus or Duke Ellington, Brown would sing and hum the song parts to bandleaders Nat Jones and Pee Wee Ellis, who would then transcribe them for the other musicians. Estranged from King over the Live At The Apollo affair, Brown adopted a holding pattern for the latter half of 1963 and the beginning of 1964, recording versions of "Caldonia" and "Things That I Used To Do" for Mercury subsidiary Smash. Then, in May, with newcomers such as saxophonists Maceo Parker and Nat Jones on board, Brown and his group recorded "Out Of Sight", which found a glorious middle ground between his screaming cover of The "5" Royales' "Think" and "Prisoner Of Love". With one ear tuned to the latest street slang and the other to Jesse Hill's 1960 proto-funk classic "Ooh Poo Pah Doo", Brown crafted a sinuous and sinewy groove that was as taut and lithe as his own dancing.

"Out Of Sight" was light years away from the mainstream of black American music as defined by Sam Cooke and Motown, but nothing could have prepared the world for "Papa's Got A Brand New Bag". Its bone-rattling effect was largely due to the fact that the master tape was speeded up during post-production to give the record a claustrophobic feel. As a consequence, the blaring horns, piercing guitar and ricocheting rhythm section sound that much more intense. Brown reduces the entire gospel vocal tradition to falsetto shrieks and guttural roars. But beyond the glare and flamboyance, "Papa" is also innovative: the 'chank' of the guitar part might well be the genesis of reggae. More significantly, the record upgraded the once anonymous instrumental bottom end to the be all and end all of music.

He followed "Papa's Got A Brand New Bag" with the equally marvellous "I Got You (I Feel Good)", "Money Won't Change You" and "Let Yourself Go". The call-and-response interplay between guitarists Jimmy Nolen and Alphonso 'Country' Kellum and the horn section on the 1967 "Let Yourself Go" marks the moment when the guitar began to supplant the horns as the main instrumental focus in Brown's music. Nolen and Kellum were brought even further up front on the two records that triggered the shift away from soul towards funk: "Cold Sweat" and "There Was A Time". With the exception of the incomparably *'nastay'* Dyke & The Blazers, nothing else at the time sounded quite like "Cold Sweat". On the record, Brown uses his voice as he uses his group – as a percussion instrument. The track features the catchiest horn hook ever; and during the *"give the drummer some"* interlude, you can hear drummer Clyde Stubblefield and bassist Bernard Odum inventing the next 30 years of music.

All of the above and a lot more are included on *Foundations Of Funk*. In addition to complete versions of "The Popcorn", "I Got The Feeling", "You Got To Have A Mother For Me" and "Brother Rapp", this double CD contains "Ain't It Funky Now", "Say It Loud – I'm Black And I'm Proud", "Funky Drummer" and a killer live version of "Out Of Sight/Bring It Up (Hipster's Avenue)" for which Brown summoned forth the greatest scream of his career. The highlight, however, is an unreleased take of "Cold Sweat", which gives a fascinating insight into his improvisational approach to composition.

Sex Machine
Polydor CD 1998
(orig. King 2 x LP 1970)

On the cusp of the 1970s, as if in anticipation of Prog rock's tyranny over complex time signatures and chord changes, Brown and his assorted barbarian pipers burst through the gates of dawn and instigated an uprising against the concept of 'progressive'. The 1969 "Give It Up Or Turn It Loose" and "Ain't It Funky" are nothing more than vamps on single-horn licks, with Brown grunting the respective title phrases a few times.

With the exception of Bobby Byrd and drummers Jabo Starks and Clyde Stubblefield, Brown's entire group walked out in March 1970 over a pay dispute. They were replaced by a band of Cincinnati teenagers called The Pacesetters who used to hang around the King studios. Renamed The JBs, the group's core members were two brothers, bassist William 'Bootsy' and guitarist Phelps 'Catfish' Collins. Quickly recognising the Collins brothers as gifted rhythm players, Brown forever banished the horns to the background of his music. The first record cut with the new group was "Get Up (I Feel Like Being A) Sex Machine", which ranks alongside "Papa's Got A Brand New Bag" and "Cold Sweat" as one of Brown's most influential releases. Only two things matter about the record: Bootsy's bass, which has more popping, slithering, sliding, strutting gangster lean than a hustlers' convention on Lennox Avenue, and Catfish's tersely angular chicken-scratch guitar. With Jabo Starks's minimal drum part for company, the tension built up by the liquid bass and rawboned guitar is staggering. After recording the nearly as good "Super Bad", The JBs rerecorded "Sex Machine" and simulated a medley of "Bewildered/I Got The Feelin'/Give It Up Or Turn It Loose" for a 'live' double album that was originally going to be titled *James Brown At Home With His Bad Self*. The album was eventually released with the title *Sex Machine*. Much of it was indeed legitimate live material recorded with Brown's 1969 group in Georgia, but it is The JBs' material, overdubbed with audience noise, that steals the show. The new version of "Sex Machine" is just as good as the single; "Bewildered" even surpasses the original version; and letting Bootsy loose on the "Give It Up Or Turn It Loose" groove is a bit like setting a fox in a chicken run.

Hot Pants
Polydor CD 1988
(orig. Polydor LP 1971)

Brown left King after *Sex Machine*. *Hot Pants* was his first album for Polydor, and if it is also his finest funk-era album, it is principally by default. For one thing, it is not a double and it has only four tracks. In addition, as the first album recorded after Bootsy and Catfish left to form their own group, *Hot Pants* is the greatest testament to James Brown's powers of regeneration through the vamp, which inaugurated his reign as "Minister of the new, new heavy funk". As minimal in their way as anything by Steve Reich, "Blues & Pants", "Can't Stand It", "Escape-ism" and "Hot Pants (She's Gotta Use What She's Got To Get Where She Wants)" relish the fact that they go nowhere fast – they hit their groove from the get-go and stay there for an average of seven and a half minutes. Without Bootsy's virtuosic if somewhat dominating basslines, the tracks on *Hot Pants* were anchored around Hearlon 'Cheese' Martin's droning yet fearsome guitar comps solo runs, and bassist Fred Thomas's rudimentary pulses. *Hot Pants* is groove as defined by the *Oxford English Dictionary* ("a monotonous routine, a rut"), almost completely stripped of its metaphorical connotations. An American Top 25 hit, "Escape-ism" is apparently the vamp the group played to kill time while they waited for Bobby Byrd to show up for the recording session of "I Know You Got Soul" (the CD reissue includes the complete 19 minute take with Soul Brother No 1 mumbling and stumbling his way through Little Willie John and Jimmy McGriff references). "Hot Pants" itself is basically Fela Kuti's career in nine minutes (minus the three conga players): mesmerising, hypnotic, interlocking polyrhythms; naive politics; and a less than salubrious view of women. Despite the notoriety and enormous commercial success of "Escape-ism" and "Hot Pants", "Can't Stand It" is the track that ushered in the era of 'the new, new heavy funk'. A remake of Brown's 1967 single "I Can't Stand Myself (When You Touch Me)", it marks the complete transition of the chicken-scratch guitar riff from an integral part of the rhythm section to the music's lead element. Catfish's guitar licks had a bell-like tone to them – they still sounded like they were played by an instrument capable of producing harmony and melody – but Cheese's runs are so intense that they sound as though they've got no tone at all, the strings reverberating without resonating.

This guitar sound survived as Brown's signature until the dawn of disco. Despite Jabo Starks's incomparable rhythm patterns and Fred Thomas's increasingly fluid basslines, singles such as the 1972 "There It Is" and The JBs' "Doing It To Death", and albums like the 1973 *The Payback* and 1974 *Hell*, hang almost entirely on the choked riffs of Cheese and Jimmy Nolen. *The Payback*, in particular, explores the deepest reaches of mantric wah-wah funk, with Tantric cuts that never resolve themselves.

Brown's last significant single of the funk era was the 1976 furious "Get Up Offa That Thing (Release The Pressure)", but by that point "The Original Disco Man" was eclipsed by a genre that took the concept of "Sex Machine" far more literally than the man who invented it.

The JBs
Food For Thought
P-Vine CD 1995
(orig. People LP 1972)

"Ladies and gentlemen, there are seven acknowledged wonders of the world," announced MC Danny Ray, introducing The JBs on stage. "You are about to witness the eighth." Brown was notorious for being a vicious taskmaster, but given the often ad hoc nature of his group, he had to be. With drummers subbing for sick bassists and trumpet players claiming to be sax players in order to land the gigs; with recording whenever and wherever it felt right, and with occasionally less than a week to rehearse a new group before hitting the road, the Godfather had to instil his troops with a sense of discipline and fear worthy of La Cosa Nostra.

With Brown laying down the law and trombonist Fred

Wesley arranging various riffs into vamps, *Food For Thought,* The JBs' first album under their own name, is easily as good as – if not better than – any of Brown's own funk-era albums. Comprised of three different line-ups (one including such fusion luminaries as Randy Brecker, Joe Farrell and Bob Cranshaw) recorded over six different sessions, *Food For Thought* makes it on pure kinetics alone. "The Grunt", recorded when the Collins brothers and drummer Frank Waddy were still in the fold, was probably the rawest track associated with Brown since "Cold Sweat". It features one of Bootsy's most swinging basslines alongside the greatest maracas-playing this side of Jerome Green; the boss's screams are replaced by a squealing sax that became the foundation of The Bomb Squad's productions for Public Enemy; the other horns are pure Afrobeat call and response; and it sounds like it was recorded in the studio bathroom. "My Brother" (probably devised as a novel way to get round payola) has a chicken-scratch riff outdone only by Nile Rodgers and Reggie Lucas, while "Pass The Peas", one of the three greatest songs ever written about food (the other two are Willie Bobo's "Fried Neckbones And Some Home Fries" and Irakere's "Bacalao Con Pan"), is introduced by Bobby Roach and Bobby Byrd waxing nostalgic about Southern treats like Hoppin' John and chitterlings.

Food For Thought was swiftly followed by *Doing It To Death* (1973). Nearly as good as The JBs' debut, it picked up where *Hot Pants* left off, with both the title track and "More Peas" (featuring Cheese and Nolen's most atonal guitars) clocking in at over 12 minutes. Brown's bizarre association with Richard Nixon reared its ugly head with the matter-of-fact priorities of "You Can Have Watergate, Just Gimme Some Bucks And I'll Be Straight"; but their next album, credited to Fred Wesley and The JBs, chose its political allies more carefully. Released in 1974, the theme of *Damn Right I Am Somebody* was inspired by one of Jesse Jackson's catchphrases, while the music was undoubtedly inspired by the success of Herbie Hancock's *Headhunters* album. Brown's first excursion into the realm of synthesizers produced the landmark tracks "Same Beat" and "Blow Your Head", with Soul Brother

No 1 himself playing the Moog riffs in a style that opened up street funk to the cosmic regions being explored by Hancock.

The JBs albums are only the most well known and successful of umpteen side projects, most of which appeared on Brown's own People label. When Brown's group walked out in 1970, they all, with the exception of Fred Wesley, recorded *Doing Their Own Thing* as Maceo & All The King's Men for the House Of The Fox label. When he returned to the fold, Maceo recorded *Us!* with The JBs as Maceo & The Macks in 1974. The ever-loyal Bobby Byrd was repaid with some of Brown's best grooves: "I Know You Got Soul" and "You've Got To Have A Job". Byrd's wife Vicki Anderson answered the Godfather's chauvinism with killer tracks like "Answer To Mother Popcorn (I Got A Mother For You)", "Super Good", "I'm Too Tough For Mr Big Stuff", and "Message From The Soul Sisters". Meanwhile, Marva Whitney's 1969 album *It's My Thing* came up with the perfect retort to The Isley Brothers' "It's Your Thing".

Rob Base & DJ E-Z Rock
'It Takes Two'
Profile 12" 1988
Public Enemy
'Rebel Without A Pause'
From *It Takes A Nation Of Millions To Hold Us Back*
Def Jam CD/MC/LP 1988

It is safe to say that hiphop would not exist without the Godfather. Brown more or less invented the breakbeat with "Cold Sweat", while "Give It Up Or Turn It Loose", "Get On The Good Foot" and "Funky Drummer" were all B-boy anthems. Hiphop pioneer Afrika Bambaataa paid tribute to "Brother Rapp"'s reconfiguration of rhythm by recording "Unity" with him in 1984. With a classic 1980s street-funk backing courtesy of The Sugarhill Gang's Keith LeBlanc, Doug Wimbish and Skip McDonald "Unity" was Brown's best record in ages, but his second coming would have to wait until Eric B & Rakim's 1986 single, "I Know You Got Soul".

Based on Bobby Byrd's Brown-produced track of the same

name, "I Know You Got Soul" helped usher in the era of sampling: as Stetsasonic put it, *"To tell the truth, James Brown was old/Until Eric and Rak came out with 'I Know You Got Soul'"*. "I Know You Got Soul" was so influential that a virtual James Brown appeared on hundreds of records in the late 1980s and early 1990s, and according to legend, Brown hired someone to check new releases for uncleared samples. "I Know You Got Soul" was rather literal in its Brown quotations, but in 1988 two records appeared that heard his disembodied shrieks and chopped-up beats as the main elements in a chaotic urban soundscape.

Cited as the greatest single of all time by *Spin* magazine in 1989, "It Takes Two" by Rob Base & DJ E-Z Rock ranks as one of the most breathtakingly immediate records ever made by someone who was not James Brown. Of course, the part that grabs you by the seat of your pants is a loop of James Brown's trademark yelp and grunt that electrified "It Takes Two" with Brownian motion. The loop (as well as the beat and the vocal hook) comes from Lyn Collins's 1972 single, "Think (About It)". Probably Brown's most important outside production, "Think" is his most sampled record after "Funky Drummer" and "Give It Up Or Turn It A Loose". *It Takes Two*, the duo's 1988 album containing the single, is still available on a BMG CD.

Where Rob Base and E-Z Rock had the technology to make Brown's energy positively bionic, Public Enemy and their producers, The Bomb Squad, turned Brown into white noise. Brown is all over Public Enemy's two classic albums, *It Takes A Nation Of Millions To Hold Us Back* and *Fear Of A Black Planet*, but he is torn to shreds, reversed, stunted and détourned. Aside from Chuck D's rap, Flavor Flav's interjections, a brief bridge and a synth bass, there is nothing on "Rebel Without A Pause" but a sample of "Funky Drummer" and a mindboggling sax loop from The JBs' "The Grunt". In the late 1960s and early 1970s Brown was the sound of Black Pride. In The Bomb Squad's hands, the sound of JBs' saxophonist Robert McCullough blowing his diaphragm out to produce an impossibly high-pitched squeal became emblematic of hiphop's menace and alienation. "The Grunt" also appears on "Night Of The Living Baseheads", which takes Brown's tantric funk to a new extreme. Built around a one-second trombone sample, "Night Of The Living Baseheads" doesn't even permit the tiny phrase to resolve itself, cutting it off before it finishes and repeating it throughout the entire track, creating more tension than Bootsy and Catfish managed on "Sex Machine".

James Brown
Star Time
Polydor 4 x CD 1991

Brown's new status as the detonator of the hiphop bomb was the impetus for PolyGram's ambitious 1990s reissue programme. No major figure has been treated better by back catalogue reconfiguration than Brown, and few box sets have been better received than *Star Time*. Almost universally hailed as the greatest album of all time upon its release, *Star Time* threatens a consensus as stultifying as that surrounding *Sgt Pepper*. Not only is it a near-perfect selection of the man's known music, it also features revelations like the original take of "Papa's Got A Brand New Bag", so you can hear how it sounded before the tape was sped up, and the first appearance of material scheduled for the aborted *Love, Power, Peace* live triple album. *Star Time* is that rare anthology: with only one dud track across four CDs, it makes an undeniable argument for the greatness of its subject. The one problem is that it underlines the absence of an equivalent iconic figure in contemporary music. Perhaps this is his ultimate legacy: by reducing popular music to its barest essentials and creating the source material for the first genre totally reliant on technology, James Brown killed the pop star.

Grime

by Simon Reynolds

Grime emerged from London's pirate radio underground. Its immediate precursor was two-step (aka UK Garage), which at the turn of the millennium was making a powerful break-through into the UK pop mainstream. Two-step had been shaped by the so-called 'feminine pressure' for singalong melodies and 'wind your waist' grooviness. Grime arose as a backlash against this crossover sound, a violent swing in the scene's inner gender-pendulum from yin to yang. Out went two-step's highpitched diva vocals, sensual swing and sexed-up amorousness; in came gruff rapping, stiff electro-influenced beats and raucous aggression.

MCs have been part of the pirate radio tradition for at least 15 years, going back through Garage and Jungle to the early days of Hardcore rave. By the end of the 1990s, however, the MCs were moving beyond their customary restricted role as party 'hosts' and sidekicks to the DJ. Instead of gimmicky vocal licks and 'praise the selector' exhortations, they began to rap actual verses – initially, extended takes on traditional boasts about their own mic skills, but soon getting into narra-tive, complicated metaphors and rhyme schemes, vicious dissing of rivals and even introspective soliloquies. The MC's rise swiftly eclipsed the DJ, hitherto the most prominent

figure on rave flyers or the main designated artist on record releases. The year 2001 was the turning point, when MCs shunted selectors out of the spotlight. So Solid Crew broke into the pop charts and the underground seethed with similar collectives modelled on the clan/dynasty structures that pre-vail in American hiphop and Jamaican dancehall.

Grime really defined itself as a distinct genre when the first tracks appeared that were designed purely as MC tools – riddims for rappers to ride. These Grimestrumentals were largely sourced in the electro diaspora – post-'Sleng Teng' ragga, Miami Bass, New Orleans bounce, Dirty South crunk and street rap producers like Swizz Beats. Like these genres, Grime doesn't go in much for sampling but prefers synths, typically with cheap 'n' nasty timbres that vaguely evoke the 1980s and often seem to be influenced by pulp movie video soundtracks, videogame muzik and even mobile phone ringtones. But in Grime's textured beats and complex pro-gramming you can also hear the imprint of the Jungle that most of these late teens/early twenties producers grew up on, alongside folk-memory traces of Gabba and Techno. Some-times you might imagine you can hear uncanny echoes of post-punk era electro-primitivists such as The Normal, DAF,

Cabaret Voltaire, or the calligraphic exquisiteness of Japan, Thomas Leer and The Residents.

Inherited from the period when two-step ruled the Top Ten, but also inspired by enviously watching the living-large of American rap superstars, Grime artists feel a powerful drive to invade the mainstream and get 'paid in full'. Pirate radio, a broadcast medium with a potentially vast audience, encourages this grandiosity. One peculiar byproduct of Grime's ambition is the scene's craze for DVD releases, combining documentary material with live footage. It's as if the scene is DIYing the sort of TV coverage it feels it deserves but isn't getting. Yet while some top MCs are being groomed for stardom by major-owned boutique labels, the day to day reality of Grime is grafting to get by in a narrowcast culture. Selling 500 copies of a track is considered a good result.

Unlike those globally dispersed microcultures such as Noise or extreme Metal, Grime is geographically concentrated. It is popular across London and has outposts in other UK cities, but its absolute heartland consists of a few square miles in that part of East London not served by the Tube. In truth, it's a parochial scene, obsessed with a sense of place, riven by internecine conflicts and territorial rivalries (the intense competitiveness being one reason Grime is so creative). Still, despite this insularity, Grime has never been easier for 'outsiders' to investigate, thanks to 1xtra (the BBC's digital radio station for UK 'urban' music; the trend for pirates like Rinse FM to go online as well as broadcast terrestrially; mail order; and the swarm of blogs covering the scene.

their frequent brushes with the law. In Grime terms, though, their single most influential track is this instrumental, which replaced two-step's sultry swing with an electro-derived coldness and rigour. This new starkness was a timely move given that two-step had reached the inevitable 'overripe' phase that afflicts all dance genres, its beats becoming cluttered and fussy. With its hard-angled drum machine snares and single-note sustained bassdrone veering upwards in pitch, "Dilemma" rediscovered the Kraftwerk principle: inflexibility can sometimes be funkier than suppleness. So solid, indeed: "Dilemma" is like a huge block of ice in the middle of the dancefloor, a real vibe-chiller.

So Solid affiliates DJ Oxide and MC Neutrino also scored a number one UK hit with "Bound 4 Da Reload". Initially a pirate radio anthem in 1999, "Reload" created a massive rift in the Garage scene. Older types loathed it, young 'uns loved it. Today's Grime heads would probably disown their teenage favourite as a mere novelty track. Which it certainly was, from the *Casualty* TV theme sample to the "can everyone stop getting shot?" soundbite from the UK gangster film *Lock, Stock and Two Smoking Barrels*. Gimmicks aside, Oxide's production is heavy, from the ice-stab pizzicato violins to the swathes of morgue-chilly echo (the track alludes to the rising blood-tide of violence on London's streets). Probably equally repellent to two-step fans was the nagging, nasal insistence of Neutrino's rapping, which is remorselessly unmelodic but horribly catchy. Instantly transforming two-step from 'the sound of now' to its current nostalgia-night status as Old Skool, "Reload" has strong claims to being the first Grime tune.

So Solid Crew
"Dilemma"
So Solid 12" 1999
Oxide & Neutrino
"Bound 4 Da Reload (Casualty)"
From *Execute*
East West CD 2001
(orig. East West 12" 2000)
So Solid are famous as the first MC crew to cross over big time (they hit number one with "21 Seconds"), and infamous for

Pay As U Go Kartel
"Know We"
From Various: *Smoove Presents Streetbeats*
Ministry Of Sound CD 2003
(orig. Solid City 12" 2001)
Wiley & Roll Deep
"Terrible"
Solid City 12" 2001

Circulating on dubplate as early as 1999, "Know We" was in constant pirate rotation by the time it was released, alongside "Terrible". Both are back to basics affairs: simple programmed beats, in each case adorned with the solitary hook of a violin flourish, functioning purely as a vehicle for the MCs. Another striking shared characteristic is the use of the first person plural. Each MC bigs up himself when it's his turn on the mic, but at the chorus individualism is subsumed in a collective thrust for prestige. "*Now we're going on terrible,*" promise/ threaten Roll Deep, and they don't mean they are about to give a weak performance – 'roll deep' itself meaning marauding around town as a mob. But there's a hint of precariousness to Pay As U Go's assertions of universal renown. The sense of grandeur is latent; they're not stars yet. What does come through loud and clear on both tracks is the hunger. "Terrible" starts with a Puff Daddy soundbite: "*Sometimes I don't think you motherfuckers understand where I'm coming from, where I'm trying to get to.*"

Genius Cru
"Course Bruv"
Kronik 12" 2001

Pay As U Go and Roll Deep pioneered Grime's criminal-minded lyrics. Taking them literally isn't always advisable, as the imagery of 'slewing' and 'merkery' is often purely meta-phorical, signifying the destruction of rival MCs in verbal combat, the maiming of egos rather than bodies. Still, the genre was not always so relentlessly hostile. Just before the Grimy era, Garage rap outfits like Heartless Crew and Genius Cru exuded playful bonhomie. The follow-up to their number 12 pop hit "Boom Selections", Genius' "Course Bruv" talks about spreading "*nuff love*" in the club and stresses that they "*still don't wanna hurt nobody*". The chorus even celebrates the rave-era ritual of sharing your soft drinks with complete strangers, the "*course bruv*" being Genius's gracious acquiescence to "*can I have a sip of that?*" Producer Capone weaves an effervescent merry-go-round groove of chiming bass melody and giddy looped strings, while the MCs hypnotise with the sheer bubbling fluidity of their chat. The verses are

deliberately preposterous playa wish-fulfillment: "*Number one breadwinner*" Keflon claims he's "*invested in many shares, many many stocks*" while Fizzy purports to date "*celeb chicks*", "*ballerinas*" and even have "*hot chicks as my household cleaners*".

Platinum 45 featuring More Fire
"Oi!"
From *More Fire Crew CV*
Go! Beat CD 2002
(orig. Go! Beat 12" 2002)

Pirate radio culture evolves in small increments, month by month. The onset of one genre or sub-flava overlaps with the twilight of its predecessor. There are rarely clean breaks. Still, every so often a track comes along that yells "IT'S THE NEW STYLE!" in your face. "Oi!" was one of them. Drawing on the most anti-pop, street vanguard elements in black music history – ragga's twitch 'n' lurch, electro's (f)rigidity, jump-up Jungle's bruising bass blows – producer Platinum 45 created a most unlikely number seven hit. Factor in the barely decipherable jabber of More Fire's Lethal B, Ozzie B and Neeko, and the result was one of the most abrasively alien *Top Of The Pops* appearances ever. The tune's pogo-like hard-bounce bass and uncouth Cockney-ragga chants mean that "Oi!" has more in common with Cockney Rejects-style punk than you'd imagine. "Oi!" was Grime's biggest hit to date, before the genre even had a name.

Musical Mob
"Pulse X (VIP Mix)"
Inspired Sounds 12" 2002

Widely regarded at the time as UK Garage's absolute nadir, "Pulse X" is actually a pivotal track: the scene's first purpose-built MC tool. Locating a new rhythm at the exact intersection of electro and Gabba, "Pulse" is virtually unlistenable on its own (those dead-eyed claps, those numbly concussive kicks). But in combination with a great MC, the skeletal riddim becomes an instant, massive intravenal jolt of pure adrenalin. It's not just the headbanging energy, though, it's the track's very structure that is radical. "Pulse X" was the first eight-bar tune, so called because the rhythm switches every eight bars, thereby enabling MCs to take turns to drop 16 bars of rhymes using both beat patterns. Far from being UK Garage's death rattle, "Pulse X" rescued the scene, rudderless and demoralised after two-step's pop bubble burst. The sheer phallomorphic rigour of "Pulse X" gave the scene a spine and a forward direction.

Dizzee Rascal
"I Luv U/Vexed"
From *Boy In Da Corner* ("I Luv You" only)
XL CD/LP 2003
(orig. XL 12" 2003)

Circulating as a white label from summer 2002 onwards, "I Luv U" turned London pirate culture around as much as "Pulse X". Legendarily creating the track in a single afternoon during a school music class, Dizzee took the same sort of sounds Musical Mob used – Gabba-like distorted kickdrums, shearing metal claps – and turned them into actual music. Add a teenage MC genius desperate to announce himself to the world and you have Grime's "Anarchy In The UK". The punk parallel applies because of the harsh Englishness of Dizzee's vocal timbre and the lovelessness of the lyric, which depicts the pitfalls of the 'dating game' from the POV of 'too much too young' 16 year olds whose hearts have been calloused into premature cynicism. Dizzee's snotty derision is almost eclipsed by the retort from female MC Jeannie Jacques, who throws *That girl's some bitch yunno* back in his face with the equally corrosive *That boy's some prick yunno*. The original white label featured the "Luv U" instrumental but tossed away on the XL rerelease's B side is the classic "Vexed". Dizzee's stressed delivery makes you picture steam coming out of his ears and the music – beats like ice floes cracking, shrill synth-tingles – renders obsolete the entire previous half-decade of retro-electro in one fell swoop.

Wiley
"Eskimo"
From Various: *Rinse 04: Mixed By Skepta*
Rinse CD 2008
(orig. Wiley Kat Recordings 12" 2002)
"Ice Rink"
Wiley Kat Recordings 12" 2003

Ex-Pay As U Go but at this point still Rolling Deep, Wiley invented an entire mini genre of low key, emaciated instrumentals: asymmetrically structured grooves based around sidewinder basslines that "Slinky downstairs" (as DJ Paul Kennedy put it) and glinting, fragmentary melodies. From his legion of imitators, these tended to be strictly MC-funktional beats; but in Wiley's case, more often than not the tracks are highly listenable standalone aesthetic objects even without rhyming. The first in an ongoing series of ice-themed tunes ("Igloo", "Frostbite", "Snowkat" and so on), "Eskimo" was the blueprint for this dinky yet creepy micro-genre (which Wiley dubbed 'Eskibeat'). "Ice Rink" took the concept of MC tool to the next level. Instead of just being sold as an instrumental for MCs to use, it was released in some eight versions featuring different MCs. Spread across two 12"s, "Ice Rink" constituted a de facto riddim album. Dizzee's turn is the standout, his scrawny voice oozing the impudence of someone at the top of his game, as he invites all haters to plant their lips upon his posterior: *Kiss from the left to the right/Kiss till my black bum-cheeks turn white.* Wiley's palsy of gated door-slam kicks and mercury-splash blips jostles with Dizzee for your attention.

Jammer
"Weed Man"
Hot Sound 12" 2003
Jammer featuring D Double E
"Birds In The Sky"
Hot Sound 12" 2003

2003 saw a slew of eight-bar instrumentals suffused with cod-oriental exoticism. As incongruous as a pagoda plopped smack dab in the centre of Bow, "Weed Man" is the supreme example of 'SinoGrime'. Produced by Nasty Crew's Jammer, the track is dedicated to *"all the marijuana smokers"* and appropriately the tempo is torpid to a triphop-like degree. The loping, sprained rhythm flashes back to David Sylvian & Ryuichi Sakamoto's "Bamboo Music", while the ceremonial bassline and breathy flute conjure mind's-eye imagery of Zen gardens and temples. But where Wiley's similar excursions Eastwards were fuelled by World Music record-buying trips, Jammer most likely derived his notion of oriental mystery from videogame muzik and martial arts movie soundtracks. "Birds In The Sky" has a similarly medieval atmosphere but, apart from the plucky twang of some kind of stringed Far Eastern instrument, is less obviously an ethnological forgery. The solo debut of one of Grime's greatest MCs, D Double E, "Birds" has a brooding, meditative aura. The lyric pivots around the bizarre trope of a verbal drive-by, the MC firing off word-bullets *"Like birds in the sky/Hit one of your bredrens in the eye."*

Riko & Target
"Chosen One"
From Various: *Run The Road Volume 1*
679 Records CD 2005
(orig. Aim High 12" 2004)
Ruff Sqwad
"Lethal Injection"
White label 12" 2004

Former Pay As U Go stalwart and man behind the ace *Aim High* compilations, Target here creates one of Grime's most stirringly cinematic epics, placing a heart-tugging orchestral refrain amid a strange decentred drum track whose flurries of claps and kicks seem to trip over themselves. This groove's sensation of impeded yet steadfast forward motion fits the lyric's theme of determination and destiny. In his smoky, patois-tinged baritone, Riko (another Pay As U Go alumnus) counsels calmness and composure to all those struggling, whether they're aspiring MCs striving to make it or regular folk trying to make it through everyday strife: *"Use your head to battle through/'Cause you are the chosen one."* The synth

swells favoured by Ruff Sqwad also have a cinematic grandeur, like a gangsta Vangelis. "Lethal Injection", though, is one of their more minimal efforts, consisting of a wibbly keyboard line, the boom of a heavily echoed kick drum and the Sqwad's rapidfire jabber, swathed in a susurrating shroud of reverb and background chat. Not a tearjerker like "Chosen One", but incredibly atmospheric.

Terror Danjah
Industry Standard EP
Aftershock 12" 2003
Various
Pay Back EP (The Remix)
Aftershock 12" 2003

You could justly describe Terror Danjah as one of the most accomplished electronic musicians imaginable. On tracks like "Juggling" and "Sneak Attack", the intricate syncopation, texturised beats, spatialised production and 'abstracty sounds' (Danjah's own phrase) make this a rare instance of 'headphone Grime'. Yet all this finesse is marshalled in service of a fanatically doomy and monolithic mood. The Gothic atmosphere of domineering darkness is distilled in Danjah's audio-logo, a demonic cackle that resembles some jeering, leering cyborg death-dwarf, which appears in all of his productions and remixes. "Creep Crawler", the first tune on *Industry Standard*, and its sister track "Frontline (Creepy Crawler Mix)" which kicks off *Pay Back*, are Danjah's sound at its most pungently oppressive. "Creep Crawler" begins with the producer smirking aloud (*"Heh heh, they're gonna hate me now"*), then a bonecrusher beat stomps everything in its path, while ominous horn blasts pummel in the lower midrange and synths wince like the onset of a migraine. From its opening 'something wicked this way comes' note sequence onwards, Big ED's original "Frontline" was hair-raising. Danjah's remix of his acolyte's monstertune essentially merges it with "Creep Crawler", deploying the same astringent synth dissonance and trademark bass-blare fanfares (filtered to create a weird sensation of suppressed bombast) but to even more intimidating and shudder- inducing effect.

Mark One versus Plasticman
"Hard Graft 1/Hard Graft 2"
Contagious 12" 2003
Loefah
"Bombay Squad"
From Various: *Grime 2*
Rephlex CD 2004

If you hadn't already guessed from the name, Grime inverts values. Dutty, stinkin', even disgustin': all are positive attributes in Grime parlance. So when I say "Hard Graft" is utterly dismal, you'll know this is the thumbs up. Grime often represents itself as gutter music. Mark One and Plasticman go further and deeper with this track, plunging into the sewage system. Full of clanking beats, septic gurglings, eerie echoes and scuttling percussion, "Hard Graft" makes you imagine pipes, storm drains, dank chambers. Mark One, Plasticman and their cohorts constitute not so much a subgenre of Grime as a side genre – soon to be definitively named dubstep – running adjacent to the scene proper. The sound is techy, MC-free and more danceable than Grime. Although a number of black producers are involved, you could fairly describe this style's sonic coding as whiter than Grime, and situate it on a Euro continuum running through Belgian Industrial Techno (Meng Syndicate, 80 Aum) through the cold Technoid end of rave (Nebula II) to No U-Turn's Techstep and Photek-style neurofunk (the beats on "Hard Graft" sometimes recall his "Ni Ten Ichi Ryu").

Plasticman's proximity to Richie Hawtin's Plastikman alias is telling. The black component to this side genre is dub. The clanking skank of Loefah (from leading dubstep crew Digital Mystikz) connects to a lineage of Industrial/rootical UK music: On-U, bleep 'n' bass, The Orb, Techno-Animal. A foundational track for the ponderous, slow-motion style known as half-step, "Bombay Squad" is built around what feels like a half-finished, or partially erased, groove: massive echo-laden snare cracks, a liquid pitter of tablas situated in a localised corner of the mix and … that's it, apart from the dark river of sub-bass that propels the track forward. The title's intertextual traces include Public Enemy's producers and 2 Bad Mice's rave anthem "Bombscare", but actually allude to the track's plaintive ululation by a Bollywood diva.

Wonder
"What"
From Various: *Smoove Presents Streetbeats*
Ministry Of Sound CD 2003
(orig. Dumpvalve 12" 2004)
SLK
"Hype! Hype!" (DJ Wonder Refix)
From Various: *Roll Deep Presents Grimey Volume 1*
DMC World CD 2006
(orig. Smoove/Ministry Of Sound 12" 2005)

Wonder works on the cusp between Grime proper and the Plasticman One/Loefah sound. "What" makes something compellingly atmospheric out of the most meagre components: a beat dragging like a wounded leg, sub-bass yawning ominously like a portal into the underworld, a dejected one-finger melody suggestive of an autistic desultorily toying with a xylophone, occasional dank blips of electronics. Overall, the audio mise en scène is something like 'twilight falls on the battle-scarred moon'. Also vaguely redolent of The Mover's gloomy brand of Ambient Gabba, Wonder's remix of "Hype! Hype!" replaces the perky original backing track (produced by the great Sticky) with a groan-drone of sick Technoise. This catastrophe in slo-mo makes a marvellously incongruous backdrop for the roaring vocal hook chanted by North West London crew SLK.

Jammer featuring Kano
"Boys Love Girls"
From Various: *Roll Deep Presents Grimey Volume 1*
DMC World CD 2006
(orig. Hot Sound 12" 2003)
Wonder featuring Kano
"What Have You Done"
From *Welcome To Wonderland*
Dumpvalve CD 2006
(orig. New Era 12" 2004)

Terror Danjah featuring Kano & Sadie
"So Sure"
Aftershock 12" 2004

The backing tracks are fabulous – Jammer's frenetic snare-roll clatter, Wonder's tonally harrowed synths, Danjah's aching ripples of idyllic electronics – but it's MC Kano who really shines. With some Grime rhymesters, the flow resembles an involuntary discharge (D Double E being the ultimate exponent of MCing as automatic poetry). But even at his most hectic, as on "Boys Love Girls", Kano always sounds in complete control. All poise and deliberation, he invariably sounds as though he's weighing up the angles, calculating his moves, calibrating which outcomes best serve his interests. That's blatant on "Boys" and "What Have You Done", both cold-hearted takes on modern romance that depict sex in transactional terms, a ledger of positives and minuses, credits and debits; a war of the genders in which keeping your feelings checked and maintaining distance is strategically crucial. But it comes through even in the gorgeous ballad "So Sure", on which Kano blurs the border between loverman and soldier drawing up plans for conquest: *"Ain't got time to be one of them guys just watching you and wasting time/Next time I'm clocking you I'm stopping you to make you mine"*. As much as the acutely observed lyrical details, it's the timbre of Kano's voice that's enthralling: slick yet grainy, like varnished wood, and knotty with halting cadences that convince you he's thinking these thoughts aloud for the very first time.

Davinche
Dirty Canvas EP
Paperchase Recordings 12" 2004
Essentials
"Headquarters"
White label 12" 2004

"So Sure" is an example of the burgeoning subgenre R&G, basically a transparent attempt to lure the ladies back onto the floor, after they'd been turned off by the testosterone-heavy vibe of tracks more suitable for moshing than sexy dancing. As the name R&G, short for 'rhythm and Grime' suggests, the mini genre replicates two-step's original move of copping American R&B's luxurious arrangements and diva-melisma. Alongside Terror Danjah, Davinche pioneered R&G with tunes like "Leave Me Alone". Too often these attempts at Brit-Beyoncé fall short owing to a lack of grounding in songcraft and the studio art of miking vocalists, and end up sounding slightly thin and shabby. So I prefer Davinche's instrumental efforts like the *Dirty Canvas EP* series. The quasi-soundtrack orchestration of "Stinger" – flurrying strings, decaying tones from a softly struck gong – are designed to swathe any MC who rhymes over it in an aura of slightly harried majesty. Built out of similar pizzicato elements meshed to a beat like a clockwork contraption gone haywire, "Madness", I'll wager, drew inspiration from the paranoia zone reached after one toke too many: racing thoughts, pounding heart, jangled nerves, the suspicion that you might just be losing your mind.

Grime is synonymous with East London, but other parts of the city are starting to get a look-in. Essentials, Davinche's crew, operate out of the South. This powerful sense of territoriality is integral to the concept of "Headquarters", which draws on the talents of a veritable battalion of MCs, some guests and some from Essentials' own barracks. At each chorus, a drill sergeant barks questions at the MC who's stepping up for his turn: *"State your name, soldier"*, *"State your location"* (usually 'East' or 'South', sometimes a specific postal district), *"Who you reppin'?"* (usually a crew, like Essentials, NASTY, Aftershock, but sometimes just *"myself"*). Then the sergeant orders each recruit to get down and *"give me 16"* – not press-ups, but 16 bars of rhymes. The amazing production seals the conceptual deal, the chorus being accompanied by cello-like instrumentation that's been digitally contorted into an unearthly wraith-like whinny, or a cyberwolf howling at the moon.

Lethal B featuring Fumin, D Double E, Nappa, Jamakabi, Neeko, Flow Dan, Ozzi B, Forcer, Demon & Hot Shot
"Pow (Forward)"
From Various: *Grime Wave Mixed By Semtex*
Antidote CD 2006
(orig. Relentless 12" 2004)

Following a failed mainstream-bid album, More Fire looked all washed up in 2003, but Lethal B rebuilt their street rep from the ground up. In 2004 his "Forward" riddim became the scene's biggest anthem. Renamed "Pow" on account of its main vocal hook, it ultimately barged its way to the outskirts of the Top Ten, achieving Grime's highest chart placing since ... well, "Oi!". The riddim is basic, verging on crude, a madly gyrating loop that resembles an out of control carousel. "Pow!", Lethal's chorus chant, evokes the fisticuffs of comic book superheroes. Matching the track's rowdy vibe (it was reputedly banned in some clubs for inciting mayhem on the floor), a squadron of top MCs lay on the ultraviolence, the cartoon flavour of which can be gleaned from Demon's immortal warning, *"You don't wanna bring some beef/Bring some beef you'll lose some teeth."*

Jammer featuring Wiley, D Double E, Kano & Durty Doogz
"Destruction Remix"
From Various: *Run The Road Volume 1*
679 Records CD 2005
(orig. White label 12" 2004)
D Double E & P-Jam
"Anger Management"
Dice Recordings 12" 2004

Like "Pow", "Destruction" is a rollercoaster of pugilistic noise and lyrical aggro, but Jammer's production is marginally more sophisticated, slicing 'n' dicing brassy fanfares (probably from blaxploitation movies) and filtering them to make a track simmering with pent-up rage. The four scene-leading MCs rise to the occasion, from Wiley's riffed variations on *"I know Trouble but Trouble says he don't know you"*, to Kano's quaintly Anglicised gangsta boast *"From lamp post to lamp post, we run the road"*. But the star performance comes from D Double. Sounding like he's battling multiple speech impediments, he expectorates glottal gouts of raw verbiage. "Spitting" is too decorous a word for his rhyme style: retching is closer. Witness Double's astonishing first six bars on "Destruction", a gargoyle gibber closer to hieroglyphics than language, seem-

ingly emanating from the same infrahuman zone Iggy Pop plumbed on "TV Eye". On Double's first solo single since "Birds In The Sky", rising producer P-Jam's snaking wooze of gaseous malevolence sparks one of the MC's most Tourettic performances. Barely tethered to the beat's bar scheme, Double seems to be wading waist deep through sonic sludge, *"sucking up MCs like a hoover"*.

Trim
"Boogieman"
From Various: *Roll Deep Presents Grimey Volume 1*
DMC World CD 2006
(orig. Aftershock 12" 2004)
Bruza
"Not Convinced"
Aftershock 12" 2005

Like most dance producers, Grime beatmakers typically invent a striking sound, then wear it out with endless market-milking iterations. Terror Danjah has often approached that danger-zone, but on "Boogieman" he shows how much scope for inventive arrangement remains in the "Creep Crawler" template. You can hear the cartoon-ghost 'wooh-wooh' touches best on the instrumental version, "Haunted" (on Aftershock's *Roadsweeper* EP). "Boogieman" itself is a showcase for rising star Trim, here honing his persona of scoffing imperturbability: *"I'm not scared of the boogieman/I scare the boogieman."*

On "Not Convinced" Danjah drafts a whole new template that reveals the producer's roots in drum 'n' bass. Again, though, the MC makes it hard to focus on the riddim. Bruza incorporates British intonation and idiom: the not-flow of stilted English cadences becomes a newflow. It sounds "brutal and British", as Bruza puts it. As his name suggests, the MC has also perfected a hardman persona that feels authentically English rather than a gangsta fantasy based on Compton or Kingston. He exudes a laconic, steely menace redolent of bouncers. "Not Convinced" extrapolates from this not-easily-impressed persona to create a typology of character in which the world is divided into the serious and the silly, the latter lacking the substance and conviction to give their words authority. Bruza addresses, and dresses down, a wannabe MC: "*I'm not convinced/Since you've been spitting/I haven't believed one word/Not one inch/Not even a millimetre/To me you sound like a silly speaker/Silly features in your style/You spit silly.*"

Kano featuring D Double E & Demon
Reload It
697 Records CD/LP 2005

"Reload It" celebrates the pirate radio and rave tradition of the DJ rewind, when the crowd holler their demand for the selector to "wheel and come again". Until Grime, the trigger for rewinds would be a killer sampled vocal lick, thrilling bass drop, or even just a mad breakbeat.

Nowadays, the MC being king, the crowd clamours to hear their favourite rhymes. "*This is what it means when DJs reload it/That 16 was mean and he knows it,*" explains Kano, before listing the other top dog MCs who get nuff rewinds

(two of them, Double and Demon, guest on the track). "*I get a reload purely for the flow,*" Kano preens, and you can see why as he glides with lethal panache between quicktime rapping and a leisurely, drawn-out gait that seems to drag on the beat to slow it down. The track itself, which is coproduced by Kano and Diplo, is all shimmery excitement, pivoting around a spangly filtered riff that ascends and descends the same four notes, driven by a funky rampage of live-sounding drums and punctuated by horn samples, Beni G's scratching and orgasmic girl-moans.

The Old Skool, breakbeat-like energy suggests an attempt to sell the notion of Grime as British hiphop, yet if transatlantic crossover is the intent, that's subverted by the localised, Grime-reflexive lyric. "Reload It" encapsulates the conflicted impulses that fuel this scene: underground insularity versus an extrovert hunger to engage with – and conquer – the whole wide world.

Dubstep

by Derek Walmsley

No matter which pieces of vinyl you buy, what equipment you play them on or how much you crank up the bass, the true low-end experience can never be appreciated except over a proper club sound system. It pulses through your body, prickles the skin, presses upon your face, confounds sensations of distance and depth. The feeling of bass is a crucial component of virtually all contemporary dance music. Dubstep is unique in the last 20 years, however, in taking the appreciation of bass to the level of obsession. This search for the killer bass vibration began at the end of the 1990s, at what seemed to be the end of the rave continuum that had run through London underground music from the late 1980s onwards. By this point drum 'n' bass had grown mechanistic and soulless; the effervescent sound of two-step Garage had been subsumed into the bland lifestyle branding of 'House and Garage'; and cocaine, a divisive vibe-killer compared with other club stimulants, was cheaper and more prevalent than ever. The vestiges of rave subculture – club nights, pirate radio stations, independent record shops – moved further towards the peripheries.

Dubstep and Grime developed in these margins – in opposite directions. Each took the smooth surfaces of Garage and inscribed upon it the harsh mark of urban life, but while Grime added a caustic layer of lyrical bravado, dubstep unravelled Garage into stark, brooding instrumentals. Grime pirate radio shows were about battle-ready MCs and splattering beats, a shout of self-assertion; dubstep became an echo of the bass vibrations that coursed through London music in the 1990s, a radar beacon for the post-rave diaspora.

There's also the question of location. Dubstep was nurtured in South London, whose languid suburban sprawl falls beyond the capital's underground train network, among the meandering overground routes and old industrial canal ways that have shaped a different pace of life compared to the rest of the city.

Dubstep began to emerge as a club phenomenon in 2005, triggered by tracks such as Skream's 'Midnight Request Line'. During the years in the wilderness, dubstep had infused London influences as various as digidub, Jungle and Techno. The obsessive bass fetishism of the early years now took on a more reverent and melodic quality, more akin to a love affair than an addiction. Dubstep started out in the early 2000s as a form of escape, but it soon took on a feeling of communion, completing a journey that explored the dark side before returning to the light. By relocating Garage around a central, omnipresent bass, dubstep had also performed a sonic inversion of the drum 'n' bass sound that had changed the course of 1990s dance music – percussion was now peripheral while the bass established the music's heartbeat.

Borrowing organically from all underground forms, dubstep pumps fresh blood through the ossifying structures of dance culture. Harking back to the golden years of rave, dubstep is imbued with nostalgia as much as futurism, and its search for lost utopias is timely in an era when technology is as much a threat to humankind as a comfort. Tracks by the likes of Burial and Shackleton are among the most elegiac and expressive electronic music has to offer.

Various
The Roots Of Dubstep
Tempa CD 2006
Horsepower Productions
In Fine Style
Tempa CD 2002

Dubstep may borrow reggae's bassline pressure and Jungle's low-end splatter, but you find its principal aesthetic in the London Garage scene of the late 1990s. The two-step Garage scene of the time condensed Jungle's breakbeat pressure to a ripe rhythmic bump. Simple enough for easy dancefloor pleasures, its lush layers of EQed detail were also compelling listening in their own right. Whereas Garage's vocal tracks celebrated romantic and/or sexual union, its dubbed-out B sides explored the genre's sensuous qualities in extended mixes that map terrain similar to that of Arthur Russell.

Producers such as Steve Gurley (Foul Play) and El-B (the latter a member of Garage crew Groove Chronicles) were initially better known for their remixes than their own tracks, but soon developed instantly identifiable styles, engulfing vocal tracks with diving basslines and explosive effects. Both feature on *The Roots Of Dubstep*, which compiles many of the elusive, vinyl-only releases that formed the foundation of contemporary dubstep. Gurley's 'Hotboys' dub employs only the most perfunctory melody, but its chopped and filtered percussion provide enough gratuitous hooks for a whole Timbaland

album. El-B's "Buck And Bury" is equally compelling in an altogether bleaker mode. While keyboard lines stutter to a halt as if they have stumbled up a dark alley, a ragga vocal bears witness to the weight of the bass: *"We're all inside, lock the studio, turn off the light … Come heavy, can't stop telling them me buck and bury."*

But Horsepower Productions, also featured on *The Roots Of Dubstep*, did most to map Garage's expressive outer limits. The prolific trio of Benny Ill, Nassis and Lev Jnr released a series of genre defining 12"s on Garage label Tempa and drum 'n' bass label No U-Turn's Garage offshoot, Turn U On Records. The interplay of the percussion alone can be spine-tingling – skittish snares and deft rimshots are mixed up with the punchbag thud of the kick drum. *In Fine Style* collects seven tracks from their back catalogue with six new productions. The percussion provides effortless perpetual motion while humming basslines, melodic droplets and noir dialogue slowly shift in parallax planes. In "Gorgon Sound" the rippling echoes begin to overlap and resonate, forming waves and crests that recall the aquatic House of Basic Channel.

DJ Hatcha
"Dub Express"
From Various: *Dubstep Allstars Volume 1 Mixed By DJ Hatcha*
Tempa CD 2003
(orig. Tempa 12" 2003)
Various
Tempa Allstars Volume 2
Tempa 2 x 12" 2004

In 2003 dubstep was simply 'the Croydon sound', and in this bleak wilderness of the post-two-step years, much of the residual activity in the nascent dubstep scene can be traced back to a single South London record shop and uptown club night. DJ Hatcha manned the counter at Croydon's premier Garage shop Big Apple Records, and here he met likeminded producers Skream and Digital Mystikz, cutting dubplates of their tracks for his sets at the intimate Garage night FWD>>. In these early years dubstep was a somewhat insular scene, with FWD>> frequently only half full, but Hatcha's determined promotion of early dubstep took the music from a cul de sac of adventurous Garage B sides towards a viable dance genre in its own right. Functional titles such as "Dub Express" and "Conga Therapy" provide a clue to the relentless physicality of early Hatcha DJ sets, with shuddering beats and skanking melodies barely able to settle into a single groove.

Hatcha and Big Apple were not the only players in the early years, however. Ammunition, the management behind FWD>>, also ran the influential Tempa label, whose first releases were almost entirely dedicated to the prolific Horsepower team. The first few *Tempa Allstars* EPs and *Dubstep Allstars* CDs are a snapshot of the raw energy driving this new sound, which FWD>> labelled 'dubstep'. The double 12" pack *Tempa Allstars Volume 2* is a vital snapshot of its early contrasting styles. The exotically titled "Amazon" and "Congo" from old heads El-B and Geeneus epitomise the rolling lushness of the earlier Garage sound, whereas tracks from newer producers such as Kode9, Digital Mystikz and Loefah explore bleaker, more forbidding spaces. The stark percussion of Digital Mystikz' "Give Jah Glory" juts up like mountain peaks at the edge of a rolling plain. D1's demented "Crack Bong" is the EP's boldest statement, with a bassline as thick and fat as a steel drum, and an appropriately manic snatch of dialogue from *2001: A Space Odyssey*: "*My mind is going ... there is no question about I ...*". The artists on *Tempa Allstars Volume 2* are still defining the rules of engagement with the music, exploring the perceived limitations of dubstep – its sparseness, synthetic qualities and primarily instrumental nature – and forging its most enduring qualities.

Various
Grime 2
Rephlex CD 2004

Despite their contrasting styles, there has always been a significant degree of cross-fertilisation between dubstep and Grime. Tracks such as Wonder's "What" and Plastician's "Cha" were popular with all DJs before either term had stuck as a label. So when Rephlex, assisted by the management behind Tempa and FWD>>, decided that their *Grime* compilations would comprise only instrumental music – rather than the MC-based tracks which truly constitute Grime – it was misleading, if understandable given the fluidity of the music. Even allowing for mislabelling, however, the first *Grime* compilation (from 2004) was something of a dud. A set of utilitarian underground bangers devoid of the MC chat that brought them to life on pirate radio, it was neither proper Grime nor exactly dubstep, owing more to the darker side of rave than to Garage.

But the second Grime compilation revealed a crucial change in emphasis. Indeed, it stands as a landmark in dubstep's development. By contemporary standards, the basslines are tame and the track structures extremely simple, but the detail is simply mesmerising. The murky, rave-tape ambience of the first compilation is superseded by a crisp, detailed sound palette. On Kode9's "Ping", sample libraries have been plundered for accordions, bells and musique concrète effects reminiscent of the BBC Radiophonic Workshop, and they are scattered in a beguilingly serene manner that recalls Wu-Tang productions. Digital Mystikz, the South London production team of Coki and Mala brought through by DJ Hatcha at Big Apple, provide the album's standout moments. On "Country Man" snares ping-pong around the echo chamber like bullets in a sealed room; "Cr7 Chamber" uses springy gamelan hits to provide it with extra bounce.

From the perspective of the actual MC-led Grime of the era, the repetitive nature of the material on *Grime 2* seemed somewhat basic. With hindsight, these tracks remain remarkably challenging; an electronic glide over alien terrain, seeking out new angles and contours.

Digital Mystikz
"Chainba"
DMZ 12" 2004

Coki
"Officer/Mood Dub"
DMZ 12" 2005

Mala

"Left Leg Out/Blue Notez"

From Various: *I Love Dubstep*

Rinse CD 2008

(orig. DMZ 12" 2006)

After gracing *Grime 2*, Digital Mystikz concentrated on their own DMZ label with fellow *Grime* alumnus Loefah. The early Digital Mystikz releases on DMZ extrapolated from their initial edgy brilliance. "Chainba" exudes a fractured, asymmetric energy, percussion hits skitting across a glacial surface of bleep and bass. If this debut was somewhat alien, by the time of the follow-up "Lost City" (DMZ 12" 2004), it was as if they had gone wholly native. A dub bassline is brutally filtered until it evokes an angry hornet, and percussion of every description is perversely mangled in the echo chamber.

2005 saw the launch of the DMZ club in Brixton, which was instrumental in teleporting dubstep out of the margins of dance culture and into the popular imagination. With the venue's hefty sound system came a renewed focus on pure, undivided heaviness, and the snatches of reggae that echoed around the early 12"s began to form the foundation of the Digital Mystikz sound. This is also evident on Coki's solo 12": "Officer" takes dubwise bass into cosmic regions, with a husky, tremulous bassline that sounds like it's carried on the wind, and wheezing trumpets reminiscent of The Specials' "Ghost Town".

But later tracks attempted to widen dubstep's horizons beyond the half-step dub trudge. When the duo channel their varied influences, which range from Techno to dancehall reggae, the results are highly innovative. Mala's "Left Leg Out" is a stark and compelling minimal roller in the vein of Lil' Louis's "French Kiss"; and his "Bury The Bwoy" (DMZ 12" 2006) is a menacing warrior charge that recalls the more primal reaches of On-U Sound's catalogue.

Benga & Skream

"The Judgement"

From Various: *The Roots Of Dubstep*

Tempa CD 2006

(orig. Big Apple 12" 2003)

Skream

Skreamizm 2

Tempa 2 x 12" 2006

"Midnight Request Line"

From *Skream!*

Tempa CD/2 x LP 2006

(orig. Tempa 12" 2006)

"Tapped"

From *Skream!*

Tempa CD/2 x LP 2006

(orig. Tempa 12" 2006)

Skreamizm 4

Tempa 2 x 12" 2007

Croydon's Ollie Jones (aka Skream) is dubstep's young prodigy, crafting hundreds of tracks on his PC before he was even old enough to drink in clubs. Like many prolific artists, his most enduring influence is his own previous work, and this fearless self-confidence is both his strength and an occasional weakness. His self-titled 2006 album was a prime example of stretching himself too far, incorporating smooth, jazzy beats and rash vocal collaborations. But throughout his career, his 12" releases have revealed a virtuoso's touch in radically adapting and reshaping his music.

Skream was working at Big Apple Records when he was barely a teenager. Honing his music skills at college, he began making beats on the downloadable Fruity Loops program with fellow Croydon resident Benga. Inspired by the bleak intensity of tracks such as El-B's "Buck And Bury", early Skream works such as his and Benga's "The Judgement" (with Benga) were volatile collisions of Acidic bass, trash movie samples and teeth-grinding textures akin to crushing metal. The positive vibes of the emerging DMZ sound turned his head around, however, and by 2005 he was using his music college experience to fashion a new melodic edge to his material. "Midnight Request Line", which circulated on dubplate for many months before its eventual release, was a breakthrough track not only for Skream himself but also for the scene in general, crossing over to Minimal Techno DJs like Ricardo Villalobos, and becoming a favourite for Grime MCs such as Roll Deep's

Skepta to rhyme over. Each of these audiences found something different to cherish in its dense composition. Most importantly, its central key change singlehandedly removed dubstep from the noir-ish cinematic shade of the post-Horsepower period and into a new era of melodic expressionism, which arguably found its key articulation in Burial's self-titled album.

Just as essential is Skream's series of *Skreamizm* EPs. The aquatic skank of the first was a key influence on dubstep's embrace of heavy, half-step beats, but in the second instalment the tempos are more fluid, the melodies more dramatic. The 'chorus' of "Welcome 2 The Future" triggers a succession of abrupt, double-time bass hits, as if the track's rhythmic gearbox had just smoothly clicked up a gear. The fourth instalment develops this Technoid side of his muse, with "Tek-A-Pill" as dexterously angular as anything dubstep has produced. The instrumental cut of "Tapped" (a ragged vocal version featuring Boy Better Know's JME features on Skream's later debut album) is equally good. Arpeggiated synths, modal chords and fat basslines are plaited together until it feels like all the available space (and oxygen) is running out; like a car flashing through an underpass at night, the sense of enclosure only heightens the impression of speed.

Loefah

"Horror Show"
DMZ 12" 2004
"Mud/Ruffage"
From Various: *Dubstep All Stars Volume 4 Mixed By Youngsta & Hatcha*
Tempa CD 2006
(orig. DMZ 12" 2006)

The Bug featuring Flowdan

"Jah War" (Loefah Remix)
From Various: *Warrior Dubs*
Planet Mu CD 2006
(orig. Ninja Tune 12" 2006)

As a rule of thumb, the most pedestrian dubstep is that which ignores the rich percussive pizzazz of the Garage years in favour of a heavy, half-step trudge. The exception to the rule, and the man whose work inspired numerous copycat beats, is Loefah, another member of the original Big Apple gang and partner in DMZ.

When it comes to basslines, Skream's may flash past your ears like a samurai sword, but no one cuts harder and deeper than Loefah. One of the original contributors to Rephlex's *Grime 2*, he became disenchanted with his tinny productions when DJ Hatcha gently mocked his use of hi-hats at the counter in Big Apple. "Fed up with bongos", he aimed for the loudest, cleanest mixdown possible, stripping out all extraneous elements and ramping up the bass. "Horror Show" pointed the way for his spare, architectural sound, with its kerb-crawling 70 bpm rhythm, echoed stabs like warning sirens in a spacecraft hangar, and an indefinable sense of unease emanating from garbled voices deep in the mix. A couple of years down the line, "Ruffage" brought his style to something approaching perfection. Interpolating influences from hiphop and electro, the kick drum and bass are as dense as a supernova, while echoes of sparse melody create an almost vertiginous feeling of space.

A supremely forceful presence in the sound systems of FWD>> and DMZ, where his DJing persona approaches that of a Japanese Yakuza, smoking slowly and impassively as panic ensues around him, Loefah's tracks feel implosive as much as explosive. His recent "Jah War" remix, with a vocal from Roll Deep's Flowdan, is another awe-inspiringly heavy workout; its elastic bassline like a bouncy asteroid of synthetic putty.

Kode9 & The Spaceape

"Sine Of The Dub"
Hyperdub 10" 2004
Memories Of The Future
Hyperdub CD 2006

Hyperdub, the label run by producer, writer, academic and Rinse FM DJ Kode9 (aka Steve Goodman), has been home to some of the most forward-looking music to emerge from dubstep. Kode9's own "Babylon (Dub)" from *Tempa Allstars Volume 2* (see above) takes a cross-section of Garage's rhythmic skip, using reverb and fuzz to tease apart the layers of hi-hat, clicks and snares. The first release on his own label, "Sine Of The Dub", took even more drastic measures. The warm bassline is replaced by an unrefined tone wave, and intermittent echoes are placed against a backdrop of airless, eerie silence. Spaceape's drawling vocal was chanced upon when he picked up the lyrics to Prince's "Sign 'O' The Times" in the studio and began adlibbing; his voice was then treated to resemble a man on his deathbed reciting his last will and testament. Such brutal reworking proves paradoxically close in spirit to that of Prince's apocalyptic original. The subsequent album, *Memories Of The Future*, explored equally perverse pleasures, the slow, ungainly funk of Kode9's beats and Spaceape's cavernous vocals evoking a future world of malfunctions and mutations.

Burial
South London Boroughs EP
Hyperdub 12" 2005
Burial
Hyperdub CD 2006

The most advanced dubstep to date has been the work of South London producer Burial, who purportedly chanced upon Hyperdub through the internet. While it is difficult to quantify exactly how much influence Burial has had on dubstep – certainly no one sounds exactly like him – one suspects that is primarily because other producers are still trying to grasp the impact of his work.

Inspired by the darkside drum 'n' bass of the Metalheadz label, Burial decided at the outset to avoid at all costs the rigid, mechanistic path that eventually brought drum 'n' bass to a standstill. To that end, his percussion patterns are intuitively arranged on the screen rather than rigidly quantized, creating minute hesitations and slippages in the rhythm. His snares and hi-hats are covered in fuzz and phaser, like cobwebs on forgotten instruments, and the mix is rough and ready rather than endlessly polished. Perhaps most importantly, his basslines sound like nothing else on Earth. Distorted and heavy, yet also warm and earthy, they resemble the balmy gust of air that precedes an underground train. Impersonal yet somehow familiar, the way Burial renders both intimacy and isolation via bass science is a key example of dubstep's capacity for emotional depth.

Burial's debut EP is a brooding journey through South London urban dread. The EP stands as dubstep's most abstract evocation of the modern cityscape; the title track features an arhythmic percussive skip, a bassline like a warm blast of city smog, and melodies that flicker into life like headlights on the ceiling of a darkened room. The *Burial* album mixes this brand of rolling, itinerant beats with disarmingly poignant Ambient interludes carrying titles such as "Gutted" and "Forgive". A melancholy tinge runs through the album, but the constant interplay of tension and calm, and of alienation and intimacy, offers the possibility of salvation around the next corner.

Benga & Hatcha
10 Tons Heavy EP
From Various: *10 Tons Heavy*
Planet Mu CD 2007
(orig. Planet Mu 12" 2006)
Benga
Diary Of An Afro Warrior
Tempa CD/LP 2008

In the early years, Benga's work was often overshadowed by that of his Croydon cohorts. But in 2006 he stepped up his game dramatically, churning out a series of crowd-slaying beats to satisfy all but the most hardcore DMZ raver. "10 Tons Heavy" and "Crunked Up" (the latter from *Diary Of An Afro Warrior*) are built solely for the purpose of providing a massive bass drop, where brutal electro stabs cut through the crowd. The splattering intensity of these tracks is echoed in the movie dialogue of "10 Tons Heavy" – *"He didn't just eat their bodies, he ate their souls . . . and I joined in."* "Night" – also on his debut album – was perhaps dubstep's biggest ever hit, a frisky Garage rhythm and naggingly catchy whistle riff that crossed over to House and jolted dubstep out of formulaic half-step beats in 2007. Beneath the playful funk, however, is the malevolence of old, with the fathomless cold spaces between the choruses bringing a new dimension to the notion of a bass drop.

Pinch
"Qawwali"
From Various: **10 Tons Heavy**
Planet Mu CD 2007
(orig. Planet Mu 12" 2006)

Peverelist
"Infinity Is Now"
From Various: **Dubstep Allstars Volume 6 Mixed By Appleblim**
Tempa CD 2008
(orig. Punch Drunk 12" 2007)

Although South London still exerts a strong grip on dubstep's collective imagination, Bristol has emerged as its second city, with the home of Massive Attack, Roni Size and DJ Krust now a base for the likes of Pinch, Peverelist, RSD and Skull Disco's Appleblim. Pinch's Subloaded club night and Tectonic label was a focus of the community in the early days, and his "Qawwali" was an idiosyncratic staple throughout 2006. Grafting tabla and harmonium samples and excerpts from Nusrat Fateh Ali Khan's *Musst Musst* album onto dubstep's rhythmic matrix, "Qawwali" is a simple but effortless translation from devotional bliss to dancefloor ecstasy. There is nothing that can straightforwardly be called a Bristol 'sound', and Peverelist's Bristol-only Punch Drunk label merely gives a sense of the breadth of the city's eclectic take on dubstep. His own productions exude their own, very distinct flavour – rolling, evolving bass-heavy rhythms that conjour a constant lurking pressure. The lush "Infinity Is Now" seems to constantly regenerate and reform before your ears.

Shackleton & Appleblim
Soundboy Punishments
Skull Disco 2 x CD 2007
Soundboy's Gravestone Gets Desecrated By Vandals
Skull Disco 2 x CD 2008

With their DIY-style covers, punk rock track titles and free party ethos, Skull Disco approach dubstep from an oblique angle. Yet the label, run by Londoner Shackleton and Bristol resident Appleblim, is home to some of the most forward-looking music in dubstep. Originally part of the select bunch of ravers at FWD>>, the pair's route into production began when a homemade Shackleton track found its way onto the free-spirited Mordant Music label, and the Skull Disco label followed soon after.

Rarely played by DJs, Skull Disco's stark deconstructions are virtual blueprints for the future possibilities of dubstep, with Shackleton's "Blood On My Hands", from the 2006 *Soundboy's Nuts Get Ground Up Proper* EP (collected on *Soundboy Punishments*) recently providing the raw materials for a minimal rework by Techno DJ Ricardo Villalobos. The original track eschews drum presets for dancing African percussion and is driven by an almost funereal sub-bass, creating a surreal union of Pole and The Mystic Revelation Of Rastafari.

On their split EP *Soundboy's Ashes Get Chopped Out And Snorted* (2007), which appears on the *Soundboy's Gravestone* double CD, Appleblim's "Vansan" is a superficially simple downtempo number, with a sober refrain and brushed steel textures, but an emotional charge is evident in the track's dreamy echo spaces. On the flipside, Shackleton's "You Bring Me Down" recalls nothing so much as Lee Perry's Black Ark years, with wonky percussion to the forefront and a lurking echo of a bassline, just out of the reach of the speakers. Paring down its core foundation, the bass, Shackleton excavates new, vacant spaces within the old structures of Garage. These elastic, pliable reformations of dubstep suggest that the genre has finally evolved beyond rigid formulas, reaching towards a new, organic maturity.

Fela Kuti

by Peter Shapiro

The one word that even the most pith-helmeted of World Music tourists – and perhaps even the man himself – has never tried to apply to Fela Kuti is 'charm'. Like most of music's greatest and biggest stars, Fela was an unrepentant swine; a towering presence, to be sure, but with a skyscraping ego to match. Music transformed the square, shy Fela Ransome-Kuti who was afraid of both women and drugs into a swaggering rockstar extraordinaire who made Jim Morrison and Mick Jagger look like cissies quivering in the corner of the classroom.

Fela's biography made for the kind of pitch that magazine editors salivate over: a guy with 27 wives who wears nothing but underpants and smokes joints the size of your forearm sets up his own commune-republic and does everything he can to antagonise the military government sitting on one of the world's largest oil reserves. The problem (at least for sceptics, scholars and critics) is that, like any performer – with the possible exception of Eminem – it is practically impossible to separate the man from the music and the myth. For fans, though, this is the very reason he is the thinking man's Bob Marley – Anansi (the trickster spider of Ashanti folklore), Superfly, Sun Ra, Kwame Nkrumah and Bruce Lee wrapped up in one vigorously unwholesome Third World hero package; a larger than life figure that could never be contained by one name, or even one life.

"I was born twice, man!" he told journalist Carlos Moore in 1982. "The first time I was born was in 193 ... [My] father asked this German missionary to ... name me ... You know what that motherfucker named me? Hildegart! ... I felt that name like a wound ... Bear the name of the conquerors? Or reject this first arrival in the world ... Two weeks after my first birth, my soul left my body for the world of spirits. What can I say? I wasn't Hildegart!"

The second coming arrived on 15 October 1938 in Abeokuta, Nigeria, a town set up in the nineteenth century as a home for freed slaves (and the home of author Wole Soyinka), when Olufela Oludotun Olusegun Ransome-Kuti was born to Reverend Canon Israel Oludotun and Funmilayo Ransome-Kuti. The young Fela was severely disciplined by his father, a minister and grammar school principal. Fela's nascent political consciousness was reinforced by his firebrand mother. Funmilayo founded the Nigerian Women's Union, perhaps the first feminist organisation in Africa, in the early 1940s, and was apparently the first woman to drive a car in Nigeria. Her campaigns for universal suffrage, Nigerian nationalism and socialist causes attracted such attention that she travelled to both the USSR and China, where she met Mao Zedong.

By the time he was a teenager, Fela's path was clear. His twin passions were rebellion and highlife, the music that emerged in coastal Ghana in the 1920s as a fusion of indigenous rhythms, palm wine guitar styles, Western military marches, church hymns and sea shanties. The urban elite in Ghana's coastal cities gave their patronage to brass bands, while in rural villages highlife was played by guitar-led groups. More important for the future direction of Fela's music, though, was EK Nyame, who was credited with popularising the guitar group strain of highlife and composing songs in Twi rather than the English of the elites. His type of highlife group became known as the 'concert party'. In the post-war years the concert parties effectively functioned as griots in a rapidly modernising Ghana by touring constantly, bringing music and news to isolated rural areas.

Perhaps more than anything else, it is this singular combination of political commitment and sense of theatre that gives Fela such iconic status. There are no less than three books on Fela in print. Masters At Work, Common, Mixmaster Mike, Sade and Nile Rodgers have all recorded tributes to Fela, while groups like Antibalas and The Daktaris have based their careers on his blueprint. Of course, when that blueprint is probably the most successful attempt to navigate the mind/body divide, to unite the power of the word with the power of the drum, to use the transformative power of music to uplift, you're bound to have followers.

Koola Lobitos/Fela Kuti & Nigeria 70
Koola Lobitos/The 69 LA Sessions
Wrasse CD 2001

In 1958 Fela persuaded his mother to send him to London, where he attended Trinity College of Music and studied the trumpet. Fela formed his first group, Koola Lobitos, with his friend Jimo Kombi Braimah, who had also travelled to London, and expatriate West Indians, mostly playing fairly

straightahead jazz. Upon returning to Nigeria, he formed a new Koola Lobitos in 1964. Later that year, Fela met Tony Allen, the drummer for The Western Toppers, and the following year asked him to drum for Koola Lobitos. Using Allen's prodigious skills at the kit (particularly the way he could blend, reinforce, echo and play off the conga and shekere percussion patterns), Koola Lobitos set out to create 'highlife-jazz', a deeper, more complex, more strident music than the lilting, calypso-oriented highlife of the time.

Koola Lobitos featured future Africa 70 regulars like Allen, trumpeter Tunde Williams, saxophonists Lekan Animashaun and Christopher Uwaifor. Of the group's singles collected on *Koola Lobitos/The 69 LA Sessions*, the roots of Fela's signature sound can be heard most clearly on "Ololufe Mi". Its bassline is much heavier than the easy, pan-diasporic swing that characterised the highlife around at the time, and the groove is forbiddingly deep and hypnotic. Fela's trumpet solo, though, has yet to throw off the shackles of jazz.

In 1969, at the height of the Biafran War (although he was a Yoruba, Fela sided with the Ibos who tried to set up the Biafran Republic in eastern Nigeria), Fela took his group to America. The 'tour' was a disaster, and the group ended up in Los Angeles with no money, no gigs and no visas. Eventually, Fela and his renamed Nigeria 70 scared up a couple of nightclub jobs, and he was introduced to Sarah Smith (later Isidore), an anthropology student and Black Panther. Smith turned Fela on to *The Autobiography Of Malcolm X* and Eldridge Cleaver, and Fela started to become more interested in his African roots, developing a pan-Africanism that could have only been born outside of Africa.

It was in LA that Fela wrote what he considered to be his 'first African song', "My Lady Frustration". He told Carlos Moore that the main rhythm was derived from something he remembered from London-based Ghanaian musician Ambrose Campbell, while others have claimed it was a rhythm from sakara, a heavily percussive genre that is almost exclusively made, and listened to, by Yoruba Muslims. While this may very well mark the birth of Afrobeat, the stamp of American funk was all over this record.

Despite its three minute duration, "Obe" might be a better starting point for Fela's re-Africanisation of funk. This was the first time his group achieved the near-impossible feat of creating music that is as dense, layered and chaotically packed as an overcrowded bush taxi, yet somehow simultaneously as wide and plush as the backseat of a stretch Lexus. "Wayo" is similarly deep, but with a more pronounced jazz leaning, and introduces what would become Fela's vocal trademark – his declamatory, drill sergeant singing style. "Ako" and "Witchcraft", though, still sound like Blue Note hard bop with Tony Allen and an octopus on congas sitting in for Art Blakey – not that that is a bad thing, of course.

Fela Kuti & Africa 70
Open & Close
Afrodisiac
Collected on Barclay/MCA CD 2001
(orig. EMI Nigeria LP 1971/EMI Nigeria LP 1973)

Sometime in 1970, Fela, back in Lagos now, renamed his group Africa 70 and started hosting Sunday afternoon concerts at his club, the Afro-Spot, where trays of dirt cheap Nigerian homegrown circulated among the audience. The Afro-Spot quickly became so popular that Bootsy Collins, Vicki Anderson, Jabo Starks and Bobby Byrd of The JBs visited the club during a 1970 tour of West Africa. Tony Allen claims that drummer Starks sat near him as he played, paper and pen in hand, attempting to chart his foot patterns.

The music that had The JBs trying to get on the good foot was probably something very similar to "Jeun Ko'Ku (Chop And Quench)" ('Eat And Die' or 'Glutton'), which became Fela's first hit in 1971 when it sold 200,000 copies. The re-recorded version that appeared on the 1973 *Afrodisiac* album reveals "Jeun Ko'Ku" as the first fully realised exploration of Fela's vision. While it is punchier than what would become the norm, "Jeun Ko'Ku" was a trance-funk epic built around a Tantric groove generated by Tony Allen that swirled so much, it resembled one of those hypnosis spiral effects from a 1950s B movie. While the music itself is as 'cosmic' as it gets, the scathing lyrics about a glutton sponging off everyone in sight

were as 'here and now' as you could possibly get: clearly directed at the regime of Lieutenant Colonel Yakubu Gowon, which saw the Biafran War as an excuse to further exert its power. On the same album, "Alujon-Jon-Ki-Jon" was based on a Yoruba folk tale explaining why the tortoise hides in its shell and was a more cryptic, and more musically sedate, attack on political patronage and cronyism. "Je'n Wi Temi (Don't Gag Me)", meanwhile, has the best percussion of any Fela record (and that's saying a lot for a group that distinguished between the lead and two 'rhythm' conga players) – icicles suddenly form in the rainforest at around the three and a half minute mark, sending a refreshing chill down the spine of the track. "Eko Ile", meanwhile, is Fela at his most strident, with a choppy rhythm and blasting horns that leap out of the speakers.

Like many of the albums discussed here, *Afrodisiac* has been reissued as part of Barclay/MCA/Wrasse/Universal's excellent reissue programme, which includes two six-LP box sets and a series of two-on-one CDs. On the CD reissue, *Afrodisiac* is teamed with Africa 70's third album (following *Fela's London Scene* and *Na Poi*), the 1971 *Open & Close*. The title track was ostensibly Fela's bid at a dance craze (Allen is an absolute maniac at the kit), but sounds more like the first flowering of his legendary lasciviousness. The rest of the album, "Swegbe And Pako" and "Gbagada Gbagada Gbogodo Gbogodo", combines the military horn fanfares from old school highlife with grooves so laid back and blunted they sound like James Brown coming down from a PCP high.

Roforofo Fight/The Fela Singles
Wrasse CD 2001
(orig. Jofabro LP 1972)
Shakara
MCA CD/LP 2000
(orig. EMI Nigeria LP 1972)

Along with his appearance on longtime ally Ginger Baker's 1972 *Stratavarious* album, *Roforofo Fight* and *Shakara* are the two albums responsible for bringing Fela to the attention of an international audience. They were both released in the

USA in 1974 on the legendary Editions Makossa label, and became major records at clubs like The Loft, Paradise Garage and the Roxy. The dark drum vortices and extreme pattern repetition of Fela's records made them perfect for disco's marathon trance sessions, and their ferocious rhythms interlocked with the heavily percussive nature of much early disco. (Africa 70 would address their relationship to disco on "Afro-Disco Beat" from Tony Allen's 1977 solo album, *Progress*.)

Despite its cover (an African version of *Electric Ladyland* with topless women forming the shape of Africa, a '7' and a '0', with Fela lying back in the centre of the '0', on his elbows, thrusting his groin in your face) and half the material which mirrors it, *Shakara* is perhaps the best, certainly most consistent album in Fela's prodigious catalogue of some 77 albums. The lyrics of "Lady" are Fela at his pig-headed worst – an attack on the 'hypocritical' brand of feminism practised by Westernised African women that mocks them for claiming to be as powerful as men while still wanting doors held open for them – but that groove, particularly the languorous main guitar riff, could redeem anything. "Shakara (Oloje)" is that strange combination of menacing, 'war drums along the Niger', slow grinding intensity and 'get up off your ass and jam' propulsion that only Africa 70 have ever mastered. Additionally on the MCA reissue is *London Scene*, a compilation of tracks from the Koola Lobitos era.

"Roforofo Fight" is Fela at his most engaging, scatting and mumbling and humming like Louis Armstrong possessed with the spirit of Clarence 'Frogman' Henry. Africa 70 sound like a mob watching the fight Fela is talking about: an intense groove of hissing shekeres, chattering congas and tightly coiled guitars. Then there's the definitive Fela keyboard solo and perhaps the best (certainly most in tune) horn playing on any of his records – the tenor solo, as on all the pre-1973 records, is by Igo Chico. With its nagging, dragging, endlessly repetitive beat, choked and constricted guitar riffs and honking horns, "Go Slow", about the horrendous traffic in Lagos, is more socialist realism. "Question Jam Answer" is pro forma James Brown funk trapped in a marijuana haze, but no worse for that, while "Trouble Sleep Yanga Wake Am" is essentially a

Fela ballad, a lugubrious half-stinker that threatens to ruin what is otherwise a true classic. The two singles added to the CD reissue are the 1972 'Shenshema', a dubby track featuring wild keyboards and what sounds like the Wivelsfield chapter of the Womens' Institute playing teacups in the background, and the 1973 "Ariya", a monstrous, lurching, 'boogaloo wading through quicksand' record that would be revisited numerous times by Fela and Tony Allen.

Fela Ransome-Kuti & Afrika 70
Gentleman
Fela Ransome-Kuti & Africa 70
Confusion
Collected on MCA CD 2000

(orig. EMI Nigeria LP 1973/EMI Nigeria LP 1975)

In many ways, *Gentleman* marks the turning point in Fela's career. By 1973 he had moved, with his entire entourage of around 100 people, into a two-floor house on Agege Motor Road in the Surulere district of Lagos. The entourage included the female singers and dancers featured on the cover of *Shakara*, who were also Fela's lovers. He called them his 'queens'. He also renamed the Afro-Spot, which would now be known as The Shrine, and started to smoke marijuana in quantities that would blind the entire population of a small island nation. "Igbe (Na Shit)" from *Gentleman* is an ode to the kind bud that fragments and twists and turns at all sorts of weird angles, but its sound suggests that Fela was on Mexican jumping beans rather than grass when he wrote it.

Gentleman, whose cover features a photograph of an ape wearing a three-piece suit, also marks the beginning of Fela's use of provocative sleeve art as an adjunct to his left-wing griot theatricality and to further bait the Nigerian authorities. For the next few years, many of his covers were designed by artist Ghariokwu Lemi, and depicted Fela's lyrics in a sardonic, satirical fashion somewhere between Pedro Bell's cartoons for the Parliafunkadelicment thang and the popular narrative paintings of African artists like Cheri Samba and Tshibumba Kanda-Matalu.

In early 1973 tenor player Igo Chico left Africa 70 and

Fela decided that he would learn how to play the instrument and replace him himself. For music fans, this was his most contentious move in a career of contentious moves. Fela's 'unique' sax style can be heard at the beginning of 'Gentleman' after the Stevie Wonder-ish keyboard intro, where his approach to harmony and syntax is like a feminist filmmaker bent on overturning narrative. Nevertheless, with churning funk and pidgin lyrics like *"I no be gentleman at all/Africa hot, like I am so/I know what to wear but my friend don't know/Him put him socks/Him put him shoes/Him put him pants/Him put him single … Him come cover all with him hat/Him be gentleman/Him go sweat all over/Him go faint right down/Him go smell like shit"*, "Gentleman" reinforced Fela's status as champion of the poor and as a political firebrand.

With his commune, unconventional cosmology and dedication to extended trance jams, Fela has been frequently likened to an African Sun Ra, and *Confusion*, a single track album from 1975, is where the analogy takes hold musically. The abstract and spacey opening five minutes and Franco Aboddy's Buster Williams-like bassline suggest many a night was spent at the commune with Fela's favoured Indian hemp, staring at the stars and listening to Herbie Hancock's *Sextant*. The bridge between the 'cosmic' beginning and the full-on Afrobeat section is pretty much the pinnacle of Afro-futurism, especially when Allen's drums really kick in around the 6'40' mark. Lyrically, too, "Confusion" is a masterpiece, with Fela using the Lagos traffic (and the three dialects he uses in the song) as a metaphor for the mess Nigeria was in.

Expensive Shit
Barclay CD 1999
(orig. Soundwork Shop LP 1975)

While many alternative communities have seen excess and debauchery as a way to challenge societal norms, Fela and his commune did more than just *épater les bourgeois*. He helped organise a pan-Africanist think tank with leading left-wing Nigerian intellectuals, formed a youth organisation called the Young African Pioneers, and bought a printing press in order to publish anti-dictatorship pamphlets. On 30 April 1974 the police raided the commune and arrested Fela for possession of marijuana. When he was released from prison two weeks later, Fela erected a barbed wire fence around the compound, declared it independent from Nigeria and named it the Kalakuta Republic ('kalakuta' means 'rascal' in Yoruba).

The police returned in the summer and attempted to plant evidence (more marijuana) on Fela. Fela asked to see the evidence and when the cops showed it to him, he ate it right in front of them. Remanded to prison again, the authorities demanded to see the evidence in his faeces, but his fellow inmates rallied round and Fela presented their untainted shit to the police for analysis. With no evidence, Fela was soon released and promptly recorded *Expensive Shit* to further lampoon the government.

The title track begins with an urgent rhythm guitar riff from Leke Benson and a very Bob Marley-like horn chorus, making this rebel music of the highest order. The song comically comments on his incarceration and has one of the great choruses of all time: *"Because why-o?/Because the shit dey smell."* Aside from this very personal indignity, excrement has an added resonance for Africans from former British colonies – the *oyinbo* (white man) used to punish Africans by forcing them to cart shit through the centres of towns (a theme Fela would return to in the 1979 "ITT"). "Expensive Shit" is also one of the definitive Fela club tracks, particularly because of his keyboard solo that begins around nine minutes in – as much a hallmark of House's two-fingered style as James Brown's solo on the 88s in "Sex Machine". The album's other track, "Water No Get Enemy", begins like the theme from *The Odd Couple*, and could very well be The Mike Post Orchestra except for James Abayomi's stick playing. Coupled on CD with *He Miss Road* (also 1975).

Kalakuta Show
MCA CD 2001
(orig. EMI Nigeria/Kalakuta LP 1975)
Zombie
Wrasse CD 2001
(orig. Coconut LP 1976)

On the morning of 23 November 1974 the police returned to Kalakuta, this time intent on busting skulls rather than making arrests or procuring evidence. Following the raid, Fela spent more than a week in hospital recovering. Undeterred, he returned to the studio in May 1975 to record *Kalakuta Show*, which would be the first release on his own Kalakuta label. Both the title track and Ghariokwu Lemi's extraordinary cover painting directly addressed the police raid, but without the comedy of "Expensive Shit" or "Alagbon Close", which recounted his first arrest. Reminiscent of the bloody vibe of Linton Kwesi Johnson's *Dread Beat An' Blood*, "Kalakuta Show" is all the more devastating for its matter-of-factness, for the way the downbeat but mesmerising and singleminded groove draws you in and then drops the bomb on you. The album's other track, "Don't Make Garan Garan", is largely Fela by numbers, but the keyboards make for a welcome respite from the carnage.

The raid on the compound only served to embolden Fela. His political attacks pulled no punches and he started to name names. Towards the end of 1975, he even changed his own name, ditching the 'Ransome', which he considered a slave name, in favour of 'Anikulapo' ('one who carries death in a pouch'). His full name now meant 'He who emanates greatness, who has control over death and who cannot be killed by man'. After recording "Zombie", Fela would have to call on the full force of his new name's occult powers.

"Zombie" is Fela's greatest record, a groove so intense, so vibrant, so militant that it could rouse a whole army of undead. Which is exactly what it did. Appended to Allen's funkiest drumming, stirring horn charts and percolating guitar riffs, the song's unrelenting mockery of the military regime and its foot soldiers bored deep into the Nigerian consciousness. Following its release, whenever Lagos's citizens saw a soldier on the street they would take on the mannerisms of a George Romero or Scooby Doo character – putting on a blank stare and marching with their arms outstretched in front of them. The message was reinforced by the more downtempo, more zombie-ish "Mr Follow Follow", but all the damage had already been done by the title track.

Needless to say, the Nigerian government didn't take kindly to the perverse 'dance craze' that Fela had started with "Zombie". On 18 February 1977, 1000 soldiers laid siege to Kalakuta with mortar fire. The soldiers beat, tortured or raped anyone and everyone that they could lay their hands on. Fela's 78 year old mother was thrown from a second floor window. Fela was again hospitalised (with fractures to his skull, arm and leg) and, inevitably, imprisoned.

Sorrow, Tears & Blood
Barclay CD 1999
(orig. Decca Afrodisia LP 1977)
Shuffering & Shmiling
Barclay CD 2005
(orig. Coconut LP 1977)
Coffin For Head Of State
MCA CD 2000
(orig. Kalakuta LP 1981)

As usual, Fela transmuted the government's brutality into devastating music. As with *Kalakuta Show*, *Sorrow, Tears & Blood*, the first record he made after the razing of Kalakuta, positively dripped with blood (the cover photo shows Fela on stage with his broken leg still in plaster). The title track is the diametric opposite of "Zombie", but just as effective, with Africa 70 evoking the black and white images of Civil Rights marchers in the American South striding grimly and determinedly onwards despite being pelted with rocks and garbage and set on by attack dogs.

Shuffering & Shmiling, meanwhile, was more of an exorcism. The intro to the title track is New York Garage five or six years early, while the lyrics were Fela's revenge on the 'turn the other cheek mentality' that the Christian missionaries had imposed on much of Africa: "*Suffer suffer for world/Enjoy for heaven.*" The original issue of *Shuffering & Shmiling* featured the stunning "Perambulator" on the flip which was later re-released, along with "Frustration", in 1983. The track sounds like the blueprint for Arthur Russell's "Go Bang #5", with Fela's psychedelic "Phantom of the Opera" organ slipping and sliding across hazy horns and an unforgiving percussion momentum. The lyrics, particularly the passage about haemorrhoids, urging doctors to use traditional African, instead of Western, medicine, only make it more bizarre.

On 13 April 1978 Fela's mother died from complications arising from the injuries she suffered during the army raid. The following year, as Olusegun Obasanjo was preparing to hand over his government to a civilian regime, Fela brought a replica of his mother's coffin to Obasanjo's house. The event was commemorated by *Coffin For Head Of State*, another extraordinary polyrhythmic dirge. Again, Fela took the opportunity to mock religion, throwing Islam along with Christianity into the bargain this time.

Fela Anikulapo-Kuti & The Egypt 80
Underground System
Kalakuta LP/Stern's CD 1992

After the death of Fela's mother, Tony Allen quit the group to pursue his own musical path. As Fela's wives (the 27 singers whom he married simultaneously at a ceremony during a concert in Benin City in 1978) started to abandon him too, Fela adopted an increasingly bizarre version of traditional spirituality. As he turned increasingly inwards, his music became more self-indulgent and fell out of favour with the Nigerian public, who preferred the more immediate thrills offered by juju and fuji. Under the influence of a spiritual vision, Fela renamed his group Egypt 80 for the excellent 1981 *Original Sufferhead*. Apart from both versions (Fela and Dennis Bovell's original and Bill Laswell's remix) of the 1985 *Army Arrangement*, most of The Egypt 80 albums are lethargic, jazzy affairs of exended length, the dragging feel compounded by Fela's more literal, wordier, less fabulistic lyrics.

Strangely, despite his deteriorating health due to AIDS, Fela's last album was perhaps the best of The Egypt 80 records – the torpor was gone. *Underground System* was characterised by a manic energy: blistering guitar riffs, overly excited horns and superfast vocal choruses on the title track; and dissonant 'Thelonious Monk on speed' piano lines, sibilant hi-hat and surging momentum on the great "Pansa Pansa". The political charge was still there as well, with Fela lamenting the state of Africa with one last desperate snarl at the former colonial powers and corrupt thieves now running the show.

It was a more fitting end than the Nigerian government would grant him. A few months before his death, he was arrested one final time, and paraded on TV in handcuffs, a frail, desperately ill man. Fela had refused all treatment for his illness except for traditional African medicine, and just before his death, he locked himself in his room and refused to eat. He died of heart failure on 2 August 1997.

Turntablism

by Peter Shapiro

I can't remember the last time I saw someone air-guitaring in public, but nearly every day I see some kid playing the great Technics in the ether as they groove to whatever Beastie Boys or DMX track is on the headphones. To say that hiphop has turned the tables (sorry) on rock hegemony might be overstating the case, but I'd wager more kids fantasise about being Mix Master Mike than Jimi Hendrix these days.

Of course, turntablism is about more than just dragging a record back and forth across a stylus, or segueing two tracks together nice and smooth. Considering the ubiquity of the vinyl record throughout most of this century, it's remarkable that so few musicians managed to make anything out of it as a tone and texture generator rather than as a playback device until the hiphop virus struck in the late 1970s. The first piece of music to envision the turntable as a musical instrument was John Cage's 1939 composition *Imaginary Landscape No 1* (see Cage Primer). While several composers took up Cage's challenge by scoring pieces for other items of electronic sound reproduction equipment such as the radio and microphone, the possibilities of the turntable as an instrument in its own right lay dormant until, in 1967, a Jamaican DJ called Kool Herc moved his sound system to New York, and helped set in motion a looping chain of events that would change the face of popular music for good.

Grandmaster Flash & The Furious Five
"The Adventures Of Grandmaster Flash On The Wheels Of Steel"
From *The Message*
Sanctuary CD 2008
(orig. Sugar Hill 12" 1981)

Afrika Bambaataa & Jazzy Jay
Death Mix
Traffic CD 2007, rec. late 1970s
(orig. Winley 12" 1983)

The story of what happened once Herc immigrated to the USA is now the stuff of hiphop legend. Settling in the Bronx in the late 1960s, he quickly set up his own sound system. When his reggae records failed to move crowds at the block parties where he played, he turned to funk, but the only part of the records he would play were the short sections where all the instrumentalists dropped out except for the percussionists. The 'break' was the part of the record that the dancers wanted to hear anyway, so Herc isolated it by playing two copies of the same record on two turntables: when the break on one turntable finished, he would repeat it on the other turntable in order to keep the *beat* going. At the same time, much further downtown in clubs such as The Sanctuary and The Tenth Floor, DJs like Francis Grasso and Larry Levan were developing the disco style of segueing records to keep the *groove* going.

Herc's breakbeat style laid the foundations for hiphop, but it was another DJ, Grandwizard Theodore, who at some point in 1977 or 1978 created its signature flourish. Theodore stumbled across scratching by accident, when he was practising in his bedroom and had his attention diverted. The sound of a record being rubbed across a stylus is hiphop's equivalent of the guitar solo, the climactic moment of intensity that everyone wants to emulate.

But the techniques developed by Grandmaster Flash became hiphop's riffs, the music's very foundation. Inspired by another hiphop pioneer, Pete DJ Jones, Flash brought DJing to a new level of sophistication by introducing the techniques of backspinning and cutting. Flash was the pioneer of the crossfader, cutting back and forth between records, slicing and dicing them and overloading the mixer's channels with brilliant, arrogant noise. With his phonographic flights of fancy, Flash made DJing into something more than just spinning records, creating audio montages that went way beyond the smart-ass shenanigans of the Dickie Goodmans and Bill Buchanans of this world.

The first hiphop singles were released in 1979 (ie The Fatback Band's "King Tim III" and The Sugar Hill Gang's "Rapper's Delight"), but Flash announced the music's true arrival with the 1981 "The Adventures Of Grandmaster Flash On The Wheels Of Steel". On one level, "Wheels Of Steel" was a collage of The Sugar Hill Gang's "8th Wonder", Queen's "Another One Bites The Dust", Blondie's "Rapture", Chic's "Good Times", The Sequence & Spoonie Gee's "Monster Jam", Grandmaster Flash & The Furious Five's "Birthday Party", The Incredible Bongo Band's "Apache", a *Flash*

Gordon record and a mock children's story lifted from an album called *Singers, Talkers, Players, Swingers & Doers* by The Hellers. In the studio, Flash recorded the track live on the decks; if he messed up, he erased everything and started again from scratch. He nailed it on the fourth or fifth take.

But "Wheels Of Steel" was more than just a collage; it was a cut-up that was *on beat* for the track's full seven minutes. Flash demonstrated that the turntable, despite its conventional usage, was a percussion instrument with a tonal range and expressive capability far beyond that of drums, woodblocks and marimbas. As audacious, assertive and aggressive as anything coming from New York's downtown art-punk fringe (check the vicious scratch that serves as the bridge from the children's story to "Birthday Party"), "Wheels Of Steel" remains hiphop's greatest feat of derring-do. Nobody since The Sex Pistols had so boldly and so authoritatively claimed new turf, and no one until NWA would mount such a vigorous challenge to the status quo.

Even more underground – in terms of its provenance and the number of people who actually heard it – was *Death Mix*, a bootleg of Afrika Bambaataa and Jazzy Jay playing a party at the James Monroe High School in the Bronx. Possibly taped sometime in the late 1970s (there is no official recording date), *Death Mix* was first released in 1983, two years after "Wheels Of Steel", on former doo-wop impresario Paul Winley's eponymous label. If it lacks the sense of danger and possibility in Flash's high-wire act, it sounds even more raw and, in its way, just as immediate. It has diabolical fidelity – the cuts and scratches sound terrible – but this only adds to the feeling that *Death Mix* is hiphop's equivalent of cave painting. In fact it sounds primordial, and since you can't hear the crowd, there's an eerie, palpable sense of ghostly absence in the record. Since *Death Mix* is more concerned with keeping the beat going, obliterating the kind of montage cuts and bold scratch-strokes employed by Flash, it is the only sonic evidence we have of the kind of sets that Kool Herc might have played in the mid-1970s.

Herbie Hancock
"Rockit"
From **Future Shock**
Columbia CD 1999
(orig. Columbia 7" 1983)

Flash and Bambaataa used the turntable to explore repetition, alter rhythm and create the instrumental stabs and punch-phasing that would come to characterise that sound of hiphop. Meanwhile, Grandmixer D.ST, a member of Bambaataa's Zulu Nation, was becoming the Dizzy Gillespie to Grand-wizard Theodore's Louis Armstrong. Having established his deck skills with his 1982 Celluloid single "Grandmixer Cuts It Up", D.ST's scratch solo on Herbie Hancock's 1983 single "Rockit" transformed the turntable into the hiphop equivalent of a lead guitar. (Today "Rockit" is best heard as part of the compilation *Street Jams: Electric Funk Part 1*, Skanless/Rhino CD, which also includes D.ST's "Megamix II: Why Is It Fresh?", a thunderous cut-up of tracks originally released on the Celluloid label.)

"Rockit" only reached number 71 on the *Billboard* charts, but its moderate crossover success (including regular airings on MTV) makes it one of the most influential hiphop tracks of them all. "Rockit" is cited by nearly every modern turntablist as the reason they started DJing, and even more than "Wheels Of Steel", the track established the DJ as the star of the record, even if he wasn't the frontman. A Material production, "Rockit" is a dense assemblage of Fairlight sequencers, Oberheim DMX drum machines and vocoders that moves with a dexterity belying its rump of steel skin. Despite the amount of detail packed into the track, everything is superfluous aside from D.ST's scratching – it's what you listen to and what you listen for. Epitomising the hiphop-jazz metaphor, D.ST approaches his solo as if he was playing at a cutting session at Minton's Playhouse in the 1940s. Nearly as in your face as "Wheels Of Steel", D.ST's scratching trashes Hancock and tells him to go back to the 1970s because *"this is our time now"*. (According to David Toop, D.ST scratched using a record of Balinese gamelan music.)

D.ST's technique cut 'real' musicians on their own turf;

but West Street Mob's "Break Dancin' – Electric Boogie" single, also released in 1983, and available on *Best Of Electro Vol 1* (Streetsounds CD/LP) was sheer punk negation. Based around a break lifted from The Incredible Bongo Band's "Apache" (1973), the track's cheesegrater scratching and note shredding was matched only by Philadelphia DJ Code Money's brutalist record mangling on Schooly D's early tracks. "Break Dancin'" moves with an irresistible sense of *flow*, but it also highlighted the limited tonal range of scratching, which was in danger of becoming a shortlived fad like the human beatbox. It would take the emergence of Code Money's hometown DJ brethren to push turntablism to the next level.

Gang Starr
"DJ Premier In Deep Conversation"
From **No More Mr Nice Guy**
Wild Pitch CD/LP 1989

Despite New York's continued pre-eminence in the hiphop world, scratch DJing was modernised 90 miles down the road in Philadelphia. While DJ Code Money was producing the most raw, vicious scratching ever recorded, other denizens of the City of Brotherly Love were creating the climate for the return of the DJ by inventing 'transformer' scratching. Developed by DJs Spinbad, Cash Money and DJ Jazzy Jeff, transforming basically involved clicking the fader on and off while moving a block of sound (a riff or a short verbal phrase) across the stylus. Expanding both the tonal and rhythmic possibilities of scratching, the transformer scratch epitomised the 'shopped-up' aesthetic of hiphop culture.

The only problem with the Philly DJs was their timing. In the mid-1980s hiphop was becoming big business, and the cult of the MC, the frontman, started to take over. As a consequence, the likes of Cash Money and DJ Jazzy Jeff were saddled with B-list rappers such as Marvelous and The Fresh Prince, and on albums they were usually accorded just one 'solo' track in which to get busy (check the bonus disc of scratch tracks from DJ Jazzy Jeff & The Fresh Prince's second album *He's The DJ, I'm The Rapper*). While DJs could shine at events such as the DMC World DJ

Championship, they were pushed to the sidelines when it mattered most.

Probably the most influential of all the Philadelphia DJ tracks was DJ Premier's "DJ Premier In Deep Conversation" from Gang Starr's 1989 debut album *No More Mr Nice Guy*. More than just a collection of Mach 1 scratches to display Premier's decks dexterity, "Deep Concentration" was an emotive sound assemblage that took in Kool & The Gang's "Summer Madness", Double Trouble's "Double Trouble", Billy Stewart's ululation from "Summertime", and the buzzing horn hook from Freda Payne's "Unhooked Generation". Of course the scratching was brilliant too, but what made the track the best turntable montage since "Wheels Of Steel" was its use of a piano loop from the introduction of "Summer Madness". At a stroke, Premier introduced an alien sense of ambivalence and melancholy to a genre normally associated with content-free thrills and spills, and paved the way for the emergence of such future turntable existentialists as DJ Shadow, DJ Krush and Peanut Butter Wolf.

Christian Marclay
Records 1981–1989
Atavistic CD 1997

While hiphop DJs were becoming more virtuosic on the turntables, the avant garde was becoming increasingly fascinated with mistakes. With a background that included studying at Massachusetts College of Art, Christian Marclay, unlike Flash or even D.ST, was almost certainly aware of the conceptual leaps made by Cage and the Fluxus artists. Inspired by Joseph Beuys's 'social sculptures', Marclay's brand of turntablism was an intervention into consumerism's cult of the object. Using mass-culture flotsam such as ancient Califone turntables hijacked from local high schools, and 50 cent records that he literally and figuratively cut up and rearranged, Marclay represented the self-consciously conceptual flipside of hiphop's 'necessity is the mother of invention' readymades.

Accenting the natural erosion of vinyl through use, Marclay constructed collages out of the skips, pops and background hiss of discarded secondhand records. By foregrounding surface noise, Marclay attempted to jolt the listener out of the reification created by the medium of recording. Marclay's most infamous 'releases' are the 1985 *Record Without A Cover*, an art object which was exactly what the title said it was; and *Footsteps*, the product of an installation piece in which 3,500 records lined a gallery floor for six weeks for people to trample on and were then packaged as regular albums. These projects – not dissimilar to the auto-destructive art of Gustav Metzger – drew attention to the sounds and noises of the record itself, rather than the music imprinted in its grooves, an idea that has subsequently entered the sonic lexicon of contemporary music, from the elegiac soundscapes of Philip Jeck (check *Surf* (1999) or *Stoke* (2002), both on Touch) to the creepily crackling soundtrack of David Lynch's film *Inland Empire*. It was taken to its logical conclusion by British art pranksters Project DARK, who constructed 7" singles made out of biscuits, wood, slabs of cheese and so on, and then played them back on battered turntables (hear their *Excited By Gramophones Vol 4*, Invisible CD 1998).

Marclay's art pranks were good, but his DJ sets are better. *Records* is a stunning collection of the collages he made during the 1980s, plus a recording of a short set he performed on Hal Willner's sorely missed TV show, *Night Music*. Marclay is just as much a performance artist as he is a sound manipulator, and the only problem with *Records* is that you can't see him callously throwing the objects that he has created out of abused records into the crowd or onto the floor at gigs, actions that are an integral part of his sets. Nonetheless, pieces such as "Brown Rain" (1982) and "Black Stucco" (1986) are wondrous collages of steel drums, ping-pong ball rhythms, string crescendos and rainforests of unidentifiable noise that are the sonic equivalents of a Henri Rousseau painting. An excerpt from a live performance, "His Master's Voice", is a more typical collage of a preacher railing against rock 'n' roll damnation with *"Push, push in the bush"* disco, Wagnerian chorales, Metal guitar spin-outs and Don Ho flitting in and out of the mix. Unlike many avantists, Marclay's conceptual pieces work just as well as his more 'conventional' compositions: check "Phonodrum", in which a guitar string attached to a stylus is dragged across records and wooden discs studded with nails to produce rhythms; or "One Thousand Cycles", which was realised by playing back the reconstituted discs Marclay had produced by literally cutting up records and gluing them back together.

The real masterpiece here, though, is the 1985 "Jukebox Capriccio", which is as whimsical as it is brilliant. Featuring squelching scratches, the synth hook from Soft Cell's "Tainted Love", kitschy xylophones, free jazz freakouts, ice-rink organs, cop show percussion and God knows what else, the piece imagines what Carl Stalling would have sounded like as a DJ. Surprisingly, it is one of the few turntablist pieces that takes advantage of the fact that the entire history of recorded sound is up for use.

Ground Zero
Ground Zero
Les Disques Du Soleil Et De L'Acier CD 1992

While scratching may be an aesthetic challenge to the concepts of ownership and copyright, the use of turntablism as an affront to the sanctity of the artwork has been embraced most dramatically by Japan's Otomo Yoshihide.

Hiphop might mutate and refocus the energies of old music in order to create something new, but with the possible exception of The Bomb Squad's productions for Public Enemy, there is a reverence for the notion of the Old School. Hiphop may rewrite tradition, but it never rejects it. For a different approach, listen to "WJAZ-1" on this debut album by Otomo's Improv group Ground Zero. Otomo uses the turntable as the foundation for a savage de(con)struction of the classic jazz mentality. While John Zorn drips sarcasm, imitating a boho jazz radio jock, Otomo subdues a Coltrane lick with shredding scratching before laying down a Jimmy McGriff Hammond organ groove for Zorn to blow ballistic sax over. "Massacring" is even more ferocious, with a sustained, barbaric bleat of guitar feedback extracted via the turntable from a pillar of classic rock and then spun back over itself until it grinds to a spluttering halt. Emerging contemporaneously with Rage Against The Machine, who do something very similar,

Otomo's scratch-imitating guitar patterns on "Sniper XR" are a potentially even more radical challenge to rock orthodoxy.

Unlike hiphop DJs, who operate largely within the framework established by Herc, Flash and Theodore, Otomo is a free jazz autodidact whose only reference points are ethnomusicology and an encyclopaedic knowledge of musique concrète. And, as is the case with other avant garde turntablists like Marclay or Philip Jeck, Otomo is even more concerned with sound for sound's sake than the hiphop DJs. Using the turntable to bolster the claustrophobia or mania generated by his group, the idea of the break is superfluous to Otomo. So, a snippet of Trouble Funk emerges from the din on "Chronicle-2"; music blurs into crossfaded static on "Silanganan Ingay"; and note-shredding axemen leap out of the stylus on "Euthanasia Drive" and "I X Love II BS M-Project 2". There's no need for a groove, or for anything to drop out, just as long as it's noise.

Martin Tétreault/Ikue Mori/Diane Labrosse
Île Bizarre
Ambiances Magnétiques CD 1998
Martin Tétreault & René Lussier
Dur Noyau Dur
Ambiances Magnétiques CD 1998

Although he doesn't dive headlong into the kind of backspinning information overload favoured by Otomo, Canadian turntablist Martin Tétreault uses a similar approach in which the stylus is the passageway to tundras of sound buffeted by gusts of howling static and populated with melting stalagmites and brittle icicles. On collaborative records such as Île Bizarre and Dur Noyau Dur Tétreault's primal scratching is performed with tiny gestures that evoke the invisible and inaudible microscopic worlds that exist in barnacled rock crevices, while his turntable tableaux are barren acid washes of denuded horns and strings.

DJ Q-Bert
Demolition Pumpkin Squeeze Musik
Dirtstyle CD 1994

In the early 1990s the appearance of US DJ crews such as Invisibl Skratch Piklz, The X-Men (later branded The X-ecutioners) and The Beat Junkies heralded the return of the hiphop DJ as a self-contained group. As Public Enemy put it on "Bring The Noise", "*A DJ could be band/Stand on its own feet/Get you out your seat.*"

This re-emergence of the DJ from the shadows of the stage dovetailed with a developing grass roots movement that set out to establish 'real' hiphop culture, one that would flourish in direct opposition to the materialism and violence that had come to characterise what groups such as Company Flow disparagingly referred to as mainstream 'rap'. While gangster-entrepreneurs such as Suge Knight, Dr Dre, Puff Daddy and others settled into a volatile collision with the established practices of the record industry, the new turntablists looked back to hiphop's origins as a street culture with its own language and codes of practice. As the intro to Z-Trip's "U Can Get With Discs Or U Can Get With DAT" (featured on *Return Of The DJ Volume 1*, see below) said, "*Ignoring the DJ in hiphop is like ignoring the guitar in rock 'n' roll.*"

Based in San Francisco's Bay Area, Invisibl Skratch Piklz (comprising Q-Bert, Mix Master Mike, DJ Disk, Shortkut and Apollo) were the most feted of the 1990s DJ groups, with turntable chops so awesome that they were banned from the very competitions that are the lifeblood of the turntablist scene. Emerging as a force in 1992 by taking the DMC World DJ Championship away from the odious DJ Dave from Germany (who actually air-scratched and did handstands on a moving turntable, as seen in John Carluccio's excellent DJ documentary *Battle Sounds*), The Skratch Piklz took turntablism back to the basics of scratching and cutting and away from grandstanding showmanship.

While turntablism was meant to be heard (and seen) live, it probably works best in the mixtape format, where the DJ's propensity for indulgent scientifical madness is reined in by the high 'thrills per minute' ratio that is crucial to the medium. Tracing its roots back to *Death Mix*, and popularised by New York radio DJ Kid Capri, the mixtape is emblematic of hiphop's basic guiding principle: flow and juxtaposition are

everything. If history is indeed over, then the aesthetic of the mixtape (along with the samplescape) has become post-history's overarching narrative, and turntablists are its epic poets.

The Odyssey of hiphop mixtapes, and very likely the greatest of them all, is Q-Bert's utterly devastating 1994 mix *Demolition Pumpkin Squeeze Musik*, which has been reissued on CD. With some help from fellow Skratch Piklz Shortkut and DJ Disk, Q-Bert unleashes his untouchable deck skills on a treasure trove of breaks that are so Old School that Q-Bert calls them 'pre-school'. Where Flash and Kool Herc created hiphop out of the syncretic readymade of the breakbeat, Q-Bert colonises and infests the break with his scratches and blocks of viral noise. With what would now be classed as rudimentary turntable skills, Flash's journey on the wheels of steel was more like a dip in the record crates. On *Demolition Pumpkin Squeeze Musik* the break is just the catalyst for Q-Bert's wildstyle jamming, which conjures a phonographic adventure through fantastic George Lucas-style mindscapes where the scratches sound like the shapeshifting video game characters of Q-Bert's imagination.

Demolition Pumpkin Squeeze Musik begins with Q-Bert 'duetting' with guitarist Alex Lifeson as he scratches over Rush's "Tom Sawyer" before quick-cutting to Eddie Bo's New Orleans funk classic "Hook & Sling". He proceeds to travel through "Tramp" (Lowell Fulson's version), Banbarra's "Shack Up" and Rhythm Heritage's "Theme From SWAT", transforming them all with the crossfader, and peppering them with dozens of snippets from *Style Wars* and *Wildstyle*. The mix's highpoint arrives when Q-Bert stretches Bootsy Collins's bassline on James Brown's "Give It Up Or Turn It Loose" and then breaks it down along with the guitar riff into The Blackbyrds' "Rock Creek Park".

Demolition Pumpkin Squeeze Musik inspired the approach taken by Japan's DJ Muro on his excellent *King Of Diggin'* mixtapes, and should be heard alongside other Skratch Piklz mixes such as Mix Master Mike's jawdropping 1996 12" "Musik's Worst Nightmare" (Down To Earth) and DJ Disk's *Ancient Termites* (Bomb Hip-Hop CD/LP 1998).

Various
Return Of The DJ Volume 1
Bomb Hip-Hop CD/2 x LP 1995
Return Of The DJ Volume 2
Bomb Hip-Hop CD/2 x LP 1997

Compiled by David Paul, editor of the West Coast *Bomb Hip-Hop* zine, *Return Of The DJ Volume 1* was the first album to be devoted exclusively to the hiphop DJ. Although it remained strictly underground, the second volume caught the leftfield zeitgeist and heralded the rise of turntablism (which was consolidated by the appearance of other relatively high profile DJ compilations such as Om Records' 1998 *Deep Concentration* and Axiom's *Altered Beats* from 1996).

While *Volume 2* contained brilliant tracks such as Radar & Z-Trip's manically tense "Private Parts", Kid Koala taking B-boys ballroom dancing on "Static's Waltz", and Z-Star's "Rockstar", a glorious condensation of the dope-addled experiences of the white American teenage male, *Volume 1* still sounds definitive. One highlight is X-Man Rob Swift's "Rob Gets Busy" routine. Picking up on an idea from Q-Bert (not to mention John Cage), who used to play tunes like "Mary Had A Little Lamb" on the turntable by manipulating a recording of a pure test tone with the pitch control lever, Swift uses the Technics's pitch control to mutate the Moog riff from The JBs' "Blow Your Head" before embarking on an exposition of the kind of beat-juggling techniques developed by fellow X-Man Steve D in 1990. Invisibl Skratch Piklz show off their battery of flare and crab scratches on "Invasion Of The Octopus People", while Mix Master Mike invoked the ghosts of Double Dee & Steinski with his "Terrorwrist" routine.

It wasn't all seat of the pants excitement, however. Peanut Butter Wolf's "The Chronicles" drew parallels with "DJ Premier In Deep Concentration" as well as DJ Shadow's influential Mo' Wax singles "In/flux" and "What Does Your Soul Look Like?" (both 1994), describing a melancholy journey through hiphop's short history that demonstrated both how much had been gained and how much had been lost.

Jazz & Improvisation

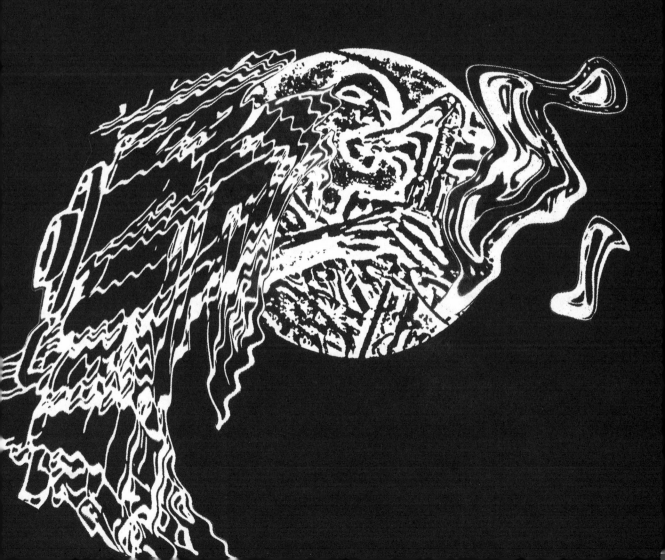

AMM

by Philip Clark

In 1966 a loose collective of London-based experimental non-conformists and inquisitive jazz musicians crystallised into the improvisation ensemble AMM. Guitarist Keith Rowe, tenor saxophonist Lou Gare and bassist Lawrence Sheaff had been members of composer Mike Westbrook's fledgling big band. Drummer Eddie Prévost (pronounced 'prevvo') had worked with Gare in a quintet that explored the hard bop of Max Roach and Sonny Rollins. They were soon joined by composers Cornelius Cardew and Christopher Hobbs, who threw an understanding of John Cage and Karlheinz Stockhausen into the already thriving mix.

Today AMM remain one of the iconic names in British Improv. The group are significant because they were the first to meaningfully employ a hybrid membership with backgrounds in jazz and post-serial, post-Darmstadt composition. Rather than improvisors arguing their point within an unfolding dialogue, AMM aimed at structures that enigmatically generated themselves during performance and that subsumed individual personalities into an ensemble ethos. Prévost has said that when on stage he "would not mind being invisible", and indeed early AMM gigs were often performed in the dark.

However, political infighting has been a key factor in AMM's evolution. Twice, warring ideologies have seen the group reduced to a duo. The Maoist politics of Cardew and Rowe provoked a faultline, and for a period gigs alternated between duos by Cardew & Rowe and Prévost & Gare. Then, in 1972, Rowe and Cardew left the group. Rowe returned in the mid-1970s and the personnel stabilised into a trio with pianist John Tilbury until 2004, when Rowe took exception to Prévost's critique of Rowe's current direction in his book *Minute Particulars*. As of 2009, AMM was a Tilbury/Prévost duo.

Despite the combative nature of AMM's internal politics, the group have always been open to sympathetic musicians. In 1968 New York School composer Christian Wolff played bass guitar with AMM while staying in the UK, and Cardew returned to the fold sporadically until his tragic death in 1981. Saxophonist Evan Parker, Arditti Quartet cellist Rohan de Saram and avant garde clarinettist Ian Mitchell have all had relationships to AMM rather like Neil Innes's to Monty Python – not quite card-holding members, but fellow travellers whose contributions are welcome.

Prévost has claimed that, of all these acolytes, it is Evan

Parker who has best internalised and understood AMM's aesthetic – begging the question: what *is* the AMM aesthetic? Frankly, that is impossible to answer fully. If one could provide a key to unlock the formula, then there would be little point in listening, although there are identifiable traits as true for their debut recording, *AMMMusic 1966*, as for *Trinity* (2008), their latest album at the time of writing (2008), AMM music – as it became christened – taps into a centring flow of sound, which the musicians, as responsive listeners, can either uphold or shift towards new ground. Each musician represents a separate layer of overlapping activity, and the music procreates an accumulative structure as these jagged layers dance in counterpoint to each other.

In Derek Bailey's *Improvisation: Its Nature And Practice In Music*, Prévost defines this musical responsibility as: "When the musical situation seems chaotic, when we are caught up in the maelstrom of sound, in which at times it is almost impossible to tell who or what is going on, that is the point when you have to 'distinguish' yourself, delineate your contribution, or else the enterprise is a meaningless cacophony." That 'maelstrom of sound', too, is something highly personal to AMM. Tilbury will often disguise his 'piano-ness' with a naturally soft touch and through understated preparations. Prévost's treatment of the drum kit with violin bows and other miscellaneous objects relocates it as an empiric sound source. Rowe's attitude to his electric guitar is arguably the most militant, as he lays it flat on a table, plucking strings with one hand and manipulating radio signals with the other, looking like he's forensically conducting an autopsy on the death of conventional technique.

Every fan would like to think AMM's covert acronym stands for something visionary and revolutionary, but it remains secret. Guesses range from the sympathetic Art, Madness and Music and Autonomous Modern Music to the less complimentary Association of Miserable Modernists, and a comment on the group's mainstream box office drawing power – Ain't Much Money. But perhaps it's fitting that the name lingers tantalisingly out of reach. Like the music itself. Prévost claims it should mean "whatever the experience of the music brings to the listener", and if anyone pinned a precise meaning down, it would be time to change the name.

AMM
AMMMusic 1966
Matchless/RéR CD
(orig. Elektra LP 1967)

AMM's debut originally appeared on rock label Elektra, a reminder that the group occasionally wound up on bills alongside Soft Machine, Pink Floyd, and even The Geno Washington Ram Jam Band. *AMMMusic 1966* was famously misfiled in the review section of old-timer bible *Jazz Journal* as being by The Cornelius Cardew Quintet. Already it's a distinctive AMM artefact, with Keith Rowe's Pop Art cover painting and Prévost's sage sleevenotes (footnotes and all) initiating a turbulent ensemble binge that's going in search of a music. Underneath, there were tensions in the ranks. Cardew rarely took part in weekly discussions aimed at defining what AMM should be and, apparently, had reservations about "the hurly-burly of collective activity".

The opening track, "Later During A Flaming Riviera Sunset", splutters into existence, with a drone in the bowels layered alongside embryonic AMM trademarks. Ebbing and flowing around the music is a disembodied voice kidnapped from a transistor radio. Slower moving piano figurations are contrasted against scurrying high register cello gyrations, while a fluctuating wash of colour from Prévost's cymbals gently ensures impetus; but so embedded is one sound in another that the ear is quickly diverted to the totality of the picture. Cardew's issues with the collective rise to the surface as he injects fractious piano gestures into the flow that have everything to do with Stockhausen's *Klavierstücke* or Boulez's *Structures*, but little to do with the here and now. Lou Gare's guttural tenor saxophone counters with an outburst that wouldn't be entirely out of place on a Coleman Hawkins record – a moment that encapsulates not only the inner conflicts of AMM, but of the UK experimental music scene in 1966 as a whole.

Keith Rowe's radio signals become symbolic of the outside world, and bring randomness into the equation. Slushy Mantovani strings are tuned in and suddenly dropped into the unfolding structure. Edward Heath – at the time the much ridiculed leader of the Conservative Party – also finds himself unwittingly incorporated, and these period details spar eloquently with the non-narrative time of the material surrounding them.

The Crypt: The Complete Session
Matchless 2 x CD 1992, rec. 1968
(orig. Matchless 2 x LP 1988)
Laminal
Matchless 3 x CD 1996, rec. 1969/1982/1994

Two years later, at AMM's seminal June 1968 session at The Crypt in West London, there had been a profound evolution. Out went Sheaff and in came Christopher Hobbs, and the music has appreciably matured. Individual parts are increasingly difficult to demarcate, and the interweaving between individuals operates at a level hitherto unattained. That said, the second track, "Coffin Nor Shelf", embraces a wide diversity of material. Gare's saxophone stubbornly tests the boundaries of how much jazz he can get away with, and the music bites back with sudden holes and vast electronic explosions that gash its surface. The end of the previous track, "Like A Cloud Hanging In The Sky?", has already challenged perceptions of scale by taking much longer than expected to wind down to a conclusion. Now the whole etiquette of 'endings' is overturned as an ambulance siren appears from somewhere. Is this sound from Rowe's radio or was it really passing outside? There is the muttered speech and a scream, then one person claps for a few seconds. But the atmospheric noise persists, and the audience don't know when – or if – the performance has ended. Footsteps stage right are presumably the musicians leaving the stage. Finally, it is over.

Laminal – so called because Evan Parker famously described AMM's music as 'laminar' – was issued to celebrate the group's 30th anniversary in 1996. If it's an overview you want, then this three CD retrospective could hardly be bettered and is a primer all by itself. Early AMM is represented with a stretching set, "The Aarhus Sequences", recorded in Denmark in December 1969. The classic trio incarnation follows with a 1982 set from Goldsmiths College in South London and AMM live in New York in 1994.

To Hear And Back Again
Matchless CD 1994, rec. 1973–75
(orig. Matchless LP 1978)
At The Roundhouse
Anomalous CD 2003, rec. 1972

The first ideological split within AMM saw Prévost accusing Cardew and Rowe of "cultural bullying" as they endeavoured to impose their Maoism. A duo incarnation resulted, which perceived wisdom tells us played generic free jazz, as Prévost and Gare dug back to their roots. Long passages on To Hear And Back Again substantiate this viewpoint, although other sections feel 'authentically' AMM. The album opens with Gare gnawing on something like a funk lick from Ornette On Tenor, supported by Prévost's relatively straightahead time. But on the second track, "To Hear" (track one on the original LP), the music evolves from Lester Young-like embellishment to mess with space and structural pacing. "To Hear" peters out midway, as Gare's exploration of tranquil sustained drones surrounds long stretches of silence. When it's time to go "Back Again", his ethereal melody lines hover against the spectral graduations of Prévost's cymbal work before probing the harmonic series.

To Hear And Back Again is a timely warning about forming judgements on the strength of one record. When, in 2004, Seattle's Anomalous label released Prévost and Gare's performance at London's Roundhouse as part of the 1972 International Carnival of Experimental Sound, a re-evaluation was urgently required. Gare begins by deploying all the energy and some of the gestures of free jazz, but the obvious idiomatic reference points on To Hear And Back Again aren't there. Instead they concentrate on the characteristic AMM obsession with vibration and a centring current of sound. Prévost defines ongoing time by creating elastic rippling on his cymbals, with his tightly strung snare drum pointing up passing landmarks.

The 46 minute track is titled "The Sound Of Indifference", an allusion to the free improvisor's lot in Britain. Both musicians cram more material than should ordinarily fit into the opening moments, and the performance imperceptibly unwinds to a complete stasis about 20 minutes later. This silence is busy and dangerous. A child's voice resonates in the distance and the audience evidently feels unnerved. But the duo know instinctively when to restart and metaphorically step back in time to an earlier energy level, which they pressure down to a deeper coma. The process recurs until clock time has dissipated into acute psychological disorientation.

AMM III

It Had Been An Ordinary Enough Day In Pueblo, Colorado
Japo/ECM CD 1991, rec. 1979
(orig. ECM LP 1980)

'AMM III', because this was effectively the group's third incarnation. Keith Rowe rejoined in 1976, signalling the end of the road for Lou Gare, who felt, "I could not go back after the freedom of the duo". Prévost and Rowe made a sparky and slightly belligerent pairing before John Tilbury came on the scene. In the meantime, It Had Been An Ordinary Enough Day In Pueblo, Colorado found itself on ECM. The oddly evocative title floats into earshot in the middle of the first track, "Radio Activity", gifted from the ether by Rowe's radio.

Rowe's guitar is unusually clear-cut and sounds more like a standard electric guitar than anything else in the AMM discography, although that doesn't stop him twisting its shapes into oblique contortions. Even Prévost's lively tom-tom work has an occasional rockist flavour, as though checking in with the zeitgeist of the era. This record may not find bits of your brain you didn't realise were there, as other AMM albums do, but it's a hugely entertaining stopover before the next 25 years nonetheless.

AMM

Combine/Laminates/Treatise 84
Matchless CD 1995, rec. 1984
(orig. Pogus Productions LP 1990)

Generative Themes
Matchless CD 1994, rec. 1982–83
(orig. Matchless LP 1983)

The Inexhaustible Document
Matchless CD 1994, rec. 1987
(orig. Matchless LP 1987)

Pianist John Tilbury's arrival in 1980 led to the stabilisation of AMM's line-up until 2004. Tilbury had deputised for Cardew on occasion and was fluid in AMM-speak, although his subliminally assertive musical personality changed the group fundamentally. Tilbury re-ignited AMM as a forum for improvisors and musicians interested in composition. Cardew's graphic score Treatise was the reason the composer initially approached AMM in 1965. On Combine + Laminates, three years after his death, AMM use pages from Treatise to "inspire and guide" an improvisation. Although, to quote Prévost, there's "no universal correlation between symbols on the page and the sounds musicians make", this exceptional performance doesn't sound much like AMM. The shapes and gestures created are unique to one night, captured in Chicago in May 1984.

Generative Themes is a rare studio recording, and the trio's ideas flow in abundance. The opening "Generative Theme" has a steely, suffocating sense of abstraction. The sonic palette is reduced to the near inert swaying of a few tautly handled brushstrokes. The second 'theme' loosens the lid, with recognisably pianistic tones steadily emerging from the ensemble whole, albeit given a surreal melt via Tilbury's sensitive preparations. Later the discourse focuses around an incessantly repeated high piano note that moves against radio signals like shortwave interference; Prévost too balances alienated sounds from his kit with hardy perennial drum tactics like rhythmic hi-hat rolls and steady triplets on his snare.

The next track is mainly quiet, apart from a solitary hammered low register piano cluster that adds lurching perspective to the ensemble continuum. Tilbury's background as a performer of composed music – with Morton Feldman a speciality – informs his unerring ear for how to avoid 'shock tactics' and mere 'effects'.

In *The Inexhaustible Document*, cellist Rohan de Saram adds his voice to this refreshed AMM, and holds a mirror up to new developments. Most of the album teeters on the brink of inaudibility, with the opening entrails of whispery instrumental 'shhh's and 'ohhh's underpinned by an irregular if insistent pulse. De Saram isn't in the improvisor's zone like the regular members, and perhaps he's wise not to try; instead he offers an outsider's running commentary on progress. Rowe's guitar work has Zen-like precision, and de Saram issues an arabesque of pizzicato notes in reply. Tilbury slips into a curiously distorted chorale and, at the end, de Saram sings a cello melody that would be conventionally sweet and singsong if only played two octaves lower. Now it suffers vertigo, and the key AMM aim of instrumental camouflage is accomplished.

Keith Rowe
A Dimension Of Perfectly Ordinary Reality
Matchless CD 1990
Keith Rowe & Toshimaru Nakamura
Weather Sky
Erstwhile CD 2001

When Keith Rowe showed up at a Mike Westbrook rehearsal with cereal boxes glued over his sheet music, it became clear that he was a soundscapist with little time for the lexicon of conventional music. *A Dimension Of Perfectly Ordinary Reality* is Rowe solo, although such is the repertoire of devices and radio voices that he's 'solo' only in the same way Harpo Marx is 'mute'. *Weather Sky*, recorded in France with Japanese no-input mixing board specialist Toshimaru Nakamura, is fantastic music but a significant marker of how far, by 2001, Rowe was already shifting from core AMM concerns. The music is a continuum that subsumes both protagonists in AMM fashion, but the wiry electronic drones and abrupt outbursts are confrontational in a way AMM never sought to be. The expanded ensemble MIMEO (Music In Movement Electronic Orchestra) was founded in 1997 and allowed Rowe to explore his growing interest in digital and laptop improvisation further with a younger generation of musicians like Kaffe Matthews and Phil Durrant. *The Hands Of Caravaggio* (Erstwhile 2002) paired MIMEO with John Tilbury in a concerto for piano, instruments and four laptops. For the best of Rowe alone, hear his *Harsh, Guitar Solo* (Grob 2000), an uncompromising set recorded live in Germany in 1999.

AMM
Newfoundland
Matchless CD 1992
Live In Allentown USA
Matchless CD 1994
Before Driving To The Chapel We Took Coffee With Rick And Jennifer Reed
Matchless CD 1996

AMM entered the 1990s an institution among its admirers but not sufficiently institutionalised to guarantee regular gigs or tours in the UK. Instead the group exploited their reputation in Central Europe and the USA, and issued regular tour updates on CD for listeners at home. *Newfoundland* – made where the title suggests – is one of AMM's finest recorded documents. It's another quiet one, with Tilbury's flawlessly honed mélange of Feldman-esque softs, Satie-style harmonic illusions and Cagean prepared piano rumbles. His lines have ornate internal complexity while never sounding cluttered, and wander in and out with supreme confidence. The music occasionally shows a playful side, as Prévost taps out jitterbugging wooden noises like Woody Woodpecker playing Dixieland traps; the dovetailing between three voices is both seamless and tersely ambiguous.

The CD sleeve of *Before Driving To The Chapel We Took Coffee With Rick And Jennifer Reed* splits its 65 minute duration into tracks, each labelled with a generic term from the Baroque suite: "Vivace", "Toccata", "Intermezzo" and so on. An "Aria" section zooms in on vocal-like sounds produced by Prévost bowing percussion instruments, while Rowe punches holes through a Billie Holiday record. This supple soundscape is quintessential AMM, but "Toccata" lunges at the listener with violent guitar noise and fidgety piano lines. Classical protocol demands that the piano is played smoothly, with dynamic levels held within strict parameters. Tilbury rebels – following these extreme louds, he tiptoes along the keyboard with ever increasing melodic circles that serenely loop the loop.

Live In Allentown USA is a monumental record that turns up the decibels. It's AMM's Industrial album, perhaps, with the brittle tone and clustery melodic intervals of Tilbury's clangorous piano introduction evoking Messiaen. But even here embedded subtleties are revealed, as chords are cunningly voiced to contrast conventional notes with others that have been prepared. Glissandi figures from Prévost and Rowe swell into electronic fanfares, and later cavernous chunks of metal march onwards with elemental force. But the ending is anti-rock 'n' roll – so quiet, your speakers struggle to keep up.

Eddie Prévost
Loci Of Change
Matchless CD 1996
Entelechy
Matchless CD 2005

Prévost was once branded the 'Art Blakey of Brixton', although these albums are testament to how inclusive his vision really is. *Loci Of Change* is in essence AMM rendered solo. Slowly evolving soundscapes move unhurriedly, their construction governed by Prévost's textural discoveries. Sustained wooden sounds chatter like crickets, while sliding pitches and percussive crackles have an autodidactic quality, in the manner of Harry Partch. "Bermondsey Breakdown" re-energises a more conventional kit set-up.

Entelechy generates 70 minutes of music from one tam-tam. Karlheinz Stockhausen did something comparable in *Mikrophonie I*, but Prévost goes deeper into tam-tam DNA. The final track rolls out over a half-hour duration and isolates overtones and timbral colour, allowing the instrument to punch above its conventional expressive weight.

John Tilbury & Evan Parker
Two Chapters And An Epilogue
Matchless CD 1998
John Tilbury & Keith Rowe
Duos For Doris
Erstwhile CD 2003

Tilbury's duo with free saxophonist Evan Parker became an instant classic among aficionados. If Rowe's *Dimension Of Perfectly Ordinary Reality* isolates his soundscaping contribution to AMM, then Tilbury's unerring 'rightness' – inventing structures on the hoof through sensitive note choices – is highlighted here. With accompaniment as sensitive as this, Parker seems liberated as rarely before. His lines coil through tonal centres to playfully caress melodic cells, revealing his formative devotion to jazz players like Lee Konitz and Paul Desmond.

Duos For Doris is benignly confrontational in comparison. Tilbury's stern entry on a low register note contradicts Rowe's airborne electronic hum, while rhetorical blood is spilt by Tilbury's full frontal clusters and Rowe's stubborn refusal to rise to the bait.

AMM
Tunes Without Measure Or End
Matchless CD 2000
Fine
Matchless CD 2001

The pace of AMM's structural revolutions may have slowed in the new millennium, but these records keep fresh sound sources in the ascendant. The beginning of *Tunes Without Measure Or End*, recorded at Evan Parker's free radiCCAls festival in Glasgow, puts Prévost centre stage, and his elegant choreography across the kit shows immense inner calm. Prévost turns his giant tam-tam into a one-man percussion ensemble, as resonant vibrations are tastefully captured and then looped via an electric motor taped to its side. Tilbury has an especially contrary moment near the conclusion, as his fingers alight on a standard chord sequence. It's effective because this is the one thing you *don't* expect to hear.

At the core of *Fine* is an intriguing paradox. The music was created with the dancer Fine Kwiatkowski for a festival in France, yet it is AMM's most static record since *The Inexhaustible Document*. Everything moves as though swimming through treacle, but the determination "to let the sounds be", as John Cage once expressed his own credo, is renewing to spirit and ears.

AMM & MEV
Apogee
Matchless 2 x CD 2004

AMM
Norwich
Matchless CD 2005

Apogee and *Norwich* are a summation, a parting of the ways and a new beginning. Perhaps it's unwise to view *Apogee* thus; the hindsight of knowing that Rowe and Prévost were at each other's throats might tempt listeners to put constructs on the music that aren't necessarily there. However, it unfolds with a palpable fin de siècle feel, a surprise considering the alluring possibilities of collaborating with members of another pioneering improvisation ensemble, Musica Elettronica Viva (MEV).

Frederic Rzewski, Alvin Curran and Richard Teitelbaum travelled to London in 2004 to record a collective studio session with AMM, and play separate sets at the Freedom of the City festival a few days later. Over the course of their joint Improv, AMM and MEV inhabit something of a life cycle. The music takes a long time to learn how to walk, has a productive and busy middle period and then experiences a slow but dignified death. It is instantly clear which strands are

AMM – hysteria from a bowed cymbal steps the music up a gear and is a Prévost fingerprint, while the outbursts of fragmented Shostakovich-like piano are obviously from Rzewski's keyboard. In fact, Tilbury struggles to assert himself in this sextet of possibilities, but he dominates the live set. His brutal opening chords and unrelenting attack threaten to shipwreck the rest of the ensemble, and a shellshocked solo coda that materialises as the permutation of notes he's been wrestling with is pursued to a natural endpoint. Rowe blasts detached and hostile DJ beats into the hall. Gone is the sensitive collective responsibility. It's clear that tectonic plates inside the music have shifted.

Rowe's work outside AMM and his increasing involvement with electronica and Noise practitioners lay at the centre of disputes with his former colleagues. However, Tilbury and Prévost carry on regardless, and the live set recorded at the University of East Anglia in Norwich reveals AMM music to be bigger than any single member. Coincidentally or not, previous performances have tended to hover around the 70 minute mark, but this new one is a lean 54 minutes. The music is spacious, and sounds disperse into silence, where Rowe's soundscaping once made the joins add up. Basic ingredients remain the same, but are cooked slightly differently. Prévost's unaccompanied entrance deals in jangling minutiae, which Tilbury's prepared piano neatly files into rhythmic configurations. There's a new meticulousness at play, both in this rhythmic clarity and in the harmonic implication of Tilbury's note-specific motifs, but also at the macro level. A curious percussive noise like a bronchitic rattlesnake recapitulates itself at key moments with the precision of a symphonist, and the ongoing structure keeps itself alive with possibilities.

Derek Bailey

by Philip Clark

"Strange stuff, music; a lot of it is highly suspect, I should say," Derek Bailey once mused in *The Wire*. Bailey often ruminated about music in the magazine, explaining his intricate, revolutionary worldview of improvised music with faultless comic timing and the wisdom of a sage.

When it came to wit, Bailey learnt from the best. In the early 1960s he was making his living as a session guitarist, and crossed paths with light entertainment royalty: Bailey played for Bob Monkhouse and Gracie Fields, accompanied Winifred Atwell (and her piano), and famously jolted Morecambe & Wise out of a meticulously rehearsed comedy routine by practising in the orchestra pit. Morecambe, the one *without* the short, fat hairy legs, shut Bailey up with a cutting ad lib that froze his fingers to the guitar. A proud moment indeed: Derek Bailey made Eric Morecambe improvise.

Meanwhile, on home turf in Sheffield, Bailey was discovering that his art lay far beyond showbiz – beyond, even, the advanced modal jazz of John Coltrane, Miles Davis and Bill Evans that he had been exploring with bassist Gavin Bryars and drummer Tony Oxley. The three men started playing together in 1963 under the moniker Joseph Holbrooke Trio (Holbrooke was a late nineteenth century British composer

who was famous for being hopeless, so a wickedly impertinent snook at composed music), and a 1965 rehearsal tape finds them transforming Coltrane's "Miles' Mode" into a point of departure for free improvisation.

A year later, when, aged 33, Bailey relocated to London, he was instinctively drawn towards drummer John Stevens and the scene surrounding his Spontaneous Music Ensemble at the Little Theatre Club in Covent Garden. The music played by Stevens's SME had evolved from a starting point in muscular free jazz, but was now also working towards a delicate 'hearing' music that stressed ensemble responsibility. But, unlike AMM, who submerged individual voices inside a collective group identity, Stevens wanted SME musicians to retain their signature sounds, working within the egalitarian ideal that each player was free to solo – but only if they were also opening up the space for other musicians.

Bailey made his recorded debut on the SME's landmark 1968 *Karyobin*, with Stevens, Kenny Wheeler (trumpet, flugelhorn), Evan Parker (soprano saxophone) and Dave Holland (bass), and in 1970 formed the Iskra 1903 trio with two Stevens acolytes, bassist Barry Guy and trombonist Paul Rutherford. Bailey's attitude towards improvised music was hardening. In the last interview he gave to *The Wire*, in September 2004, he acknowledged Iskra 1903 as "one of the best groups I've ever worked with", but explained that improvising groups tended to come with an inbuilt sell-by date: "After two or three years I'd had it … Everybody gets to know the music and as soon as that happens you stop improvising."

Years later, when Bailey was quizzed about the differences between how he improvised and, for instance, African drumming or South American music, he countered, "they are idiomatic and freely improvised music isn't". His chain of thought then probed the marrow of his aesthetic: "[Those musics] are the product of a locality and society … improvisation exists in order to serve this central identity. In freely improvised music, its roots are in occasion rather than place. Maybe improvisation takes the place of idiom."

Bailey's principles of what he would dub "non-idiomatic improvisation" led to pronouncements about music that could feel wilfully contrary when taken at face value. Despite improvising with saxophonists with real mettle, like Anthony Braxton, Steve Lacy and Tony Bevan, Bailey habitually complained about saxophone players whose muscular memories had jammed their fingers around jazz licks. Nothing needled him more than the mistaken assumption that what he played was an adjunct of jazz. "For me, jazz died in 1955," he notoriously asserted during that last *Wire* interview; but Bailey was not anti-jazz per se – what struck him as highly suspect was the notion of bebop, or any other branch of jazz, being played outside the social sphere that formed it.

The raison d'être behind Bailey's Company Weeks – a near-annual event staged between 1977 and 1994 – might also feel oxymoronic. Questioning the ideal that groups function best once the musicians involved have established an identity and repertoire of gestures, Company Weeks assembled musicians from disparate backgrounds within free improvisation and jazz, and dealt an occasional wildcard from rock (guitarist Buckethead in 1991) and modern composition (pianist Ursula Oppens in 1982). Over a week of performance, a hybrid language unique to those musicians, and specific to *that* moment, was allowed to generate. Once over, it was over: there was no suggestion that the assembled cast would reunite as a permanent group.

Bailey's biggest fear was that free improvisation itself had become a genre within an idiom within a genre, and in his last decade he sought out improbable company like Pat Metheny and onetime Miles Davis drummer Tony Williams, partly to blow apart expectations about the music he played. Bailey believed in live, alert, authentic playing. Music wasn't for academics, or to sustain corporate new release hype. Bailey reclaimed music for musicians, and for thinking listeners who wanted to marry music to life, rather than listen to it drone in the background with all the motivating clout of fridge hum.

Tony Oxley Quintet
The Baptised Traveller
Columbia CD 1999, rec. 1969
Tony Oxley
4 Compositions For Sextet
Columbia CD 1999, rec. 1970

These two records sounded the birth pangs of British free improvisation, and Bailey played on them both. Oxley was house drummer at Ronnie Scott's club during the period they were cut, and they document his journey from jazz to free playing. The earlier record is a self-conscious montage of stylised bop heads and Coltrane-like minor dirges that trigger pockets of free playing. Bailey's guitar clusters orbit a different planet from, for instance, Kenny Wheeler's clubbable lyricism, and are primed to act as whistleblower on the whole stylistic conceit. Despite its title, *4 Compositions* sounds like bona fide free improvisation, primarily because the jazz-centric archetype of front line and rhythm section has been dissolved into a unified, anti-hierarchical ensemble. Bailey's amplification and pedalling is not deployed to cultivate a rockist fingertip gloss, but splinters sound into a fragmenting slipstream that hijacks the grain. Bailey already sounds like Bailey, and also symbolic of the near future is his attitude: he is there as part provocateur, part enabler, demanding other musicians *play*.

Joseph Holbrooke '65
Rehearsal extract
Incus CD single 1999, rec. 1965

Derek Bailey
Pieces For Guitar
Tzadik CD 2002, rec. 1966–67

It would be a mistake to assume that Bailey arrived at Oxley's early sessions fully formed. When, in 1999, Incus released the "Miles' Mode" rehearsal tape, the surprise at Bailey's immaculate swing was nothing to the shock of hearing how violently Joseph Holbrooke trashed conventional jazz wisdom. The power of their intuition transforms Coltrane's notes into an impulsively concertinaed structure, just as the structure itself begins to crystallise. The music develops impetus of its own that challenges *them* to keep up with *it*. They sound like three men drowning in reverse.

Rehearsal Extract fills an essential piece of the jigsaw, and testifies to the early importance of 'occasion' over 'place' – Oxley played jazz drums, Bryars was also a composer and, as Bailey said, "the most successful way we could play together was free". And *Pieces For Guitar*, released in 2002 on John Zorn's Tzadik label, clarified another important aspect of Bailey's prehistory. In his sleevenote, Bailey explained that "my strongest influence at the time was Webern", and these formative tracks find him exploring how best to utilise the objectifying screen of serialism within improvisation – through composition.

Tzadik's cover art proclaimed that here within were Bailey's "own written compositions!!", a prospect so implausible they highlighted their tagline in incredulous bold type. Not that Bailey allowed himself to drown in 12 tone doctrine: the earliest piece, *G.E.B*, falls towards conventional harmonic progressions and bass patterns that serialism uproots. Other pieces morph the guitar into percussive rubble as far removed from George Benson as Cage's prepared piano is from Haydn. Composition, for Bailey, was merely a route to mould serial practice to the guitar, something that becomes apparent when he plays improvised rethinks of his written material at the end. When Bailey turns up on those early Oxley records, the impact Webern made on his ear and imagination is striking.

Evan Parker/Derek Bailey/Han Bennink
The Topography Of The Lungs
Psi CD 2006
(orig. Incus LP 1970)

The Topography of the Lungs places Bailey in the epicentre of a now established free improvisation 'scene'. The record enjoyed mythological status for decades because only a lucky few could actually hear it: any possibility of a reissue had been scuppered by the Byzantine arrangements made when Evan Parker angrily quit Incus Records in 1987. Bailey's death subsequently freed Parker to issue *Topography* on his own Psi label during 2006.

Parker has spoken about how the sessions were conducted in an atmosphere of indigence and frustration (Parker and Dutch percussionist Han Bennink were stuck in traffic and showed up late; Bailey was livid), and the record's brutal hysteria is no playact. In the midst of the opening track, Bennink reaches into the air like a Venus flytrap and snares the energies flying around his sticks with a reverberating clatter that jumps the music into shellshocked quiet. Bailey's monolithic, glutinous chording is strategically pitched somewhere between Bennink's menacing rattle and Parker's fleeting tonalities. The final track, "Dogmeat", evolves into a bruising guitar/percussion duologue that temporarily elbows Parker out the way. Bennink's steamrolling patterns delineate metre at the same time as questioning the cliché of cyclical rhythmic resolution: Bailey's uncharacteristically four-square rhythms fire Bennink's non-metric patois back as a loaded question.

Paul Rutherford/Derek Bailey/Barry Guy
Iskra 1903: Chapter One 1970–1972
Emanem 3 x CD 2000

The trio Iskra 1903 made explicit the bond between the aspirations of free improvisation and revolutionary politics, but after the lurid blood rush of *Topography Of The Lungs*, the spacious hush of their music is disarming. *Iskra* (meaning 'Spark') was the official organ of the Russian Social Democratic Labour Party prior to the 1917 Revolution: Rutherford added '19' to imply music with specifically twentieth century concerns, while '03' signified that three musicians were playing it.

Iskra was edited by Lenin, and as music acting on the challenges of socialist idealism, Iskra 1903 was exemplary. These musicians considered music making itself to be a worthy goal, and vehemently rejected the idea of music as a 'product'. The acoustical reality of combining trombone, double bass and guitar required a rethink of space, weight and texture, and the trio only existed anyway because three musicians who happened to play those instruments wanted to work together – the power of their individual voices overrode the market requirement for easily assimilated 'classic' ensemble line-ups. But Iskra 1903's revolution was not bloody or violent. Their revolution would be sparked by the intensity of eloquently expressed ideas, outmanoeuvring the status quo through elevated argument.

Rutherford doubles on piano during the earliest sessions, recorded 'live' at the ICA in 1970. His lithe playing is full of surprise, but the contours of the instrument's attack and decay tend to dictate the flow rather too inflexibly. Eighteen months on, however, Iskra 1903 are captured at their peak. Bailey sometimes provokes by not playing anything, and remaining silent for longer than is properly decent. When he does enter, his sparse, scattering note choices are profoundly articulate and unlock deep channels of communication. Commercial music often fetishises carefully manipulated instrumental hooks, but the members of Iskra 1903 transform their instruments into radically refashioned sounding objects. Rutherford's trombone slides between farty rudeness and exquisitely refined sustained lines: Guy sounds as though he is articulating his thoughts with a giant bunch of bananas and a pair of knitting needles instead of his hands and a bow; and where the bass ends and the guitar begins is often anyone's guess. But, just as an audible 'Iskra 1903' identity becomes apparent, that's when Derek decides to bail.

Derek Bailey
Solo Guitar Volume 1
Incus CD 1992, rec. 1971/1978

LACE
Emanem CD 2005, rec. 1989

Any one of Bailey's improvisations on *Solo Guitar Volume 1* contains enough for a lifetime. Some of them are pretty short, too. Not that *Volume 1* feels like an average Bailey album. The original A side showcased composed pieces by Misha Mengelberg, Willem Breuker and Gavin Bryars. A rereleased version in 1978 replaced some of the B side improvisations with others taken from the same session. This CD reissue collates all the above – although Bailey adds droll disclaimers: "My own preference was to make a new solo record", and "as everyone knows, compositions are forever … ".

And the compositions now register as quaint period pieces, while Bailey's improvisations – although obviously of their time – remain mint fresh. "Improvisation No 4" packs an unreal level of detail into its two minute duration. A forcefully plucked twang sets off a sequence of subtone glissandi, like an abstracted steel guitar. Ringing high notes nearly land Bailey on common triads that are abruptly trampled on with a spaghetti rush of broken-up arpeggios. Fiercely whacked notes resonate with the push of pitched drums; that same sound is then overlaid with resonating harmonics. In the midst of all that invention: a single open-string note that reminds the listener about how guitars 'ought' to sound.

Where Bailey begged to differ about how guitars ought to sound was his suspicion that 'good technique' is too often a front for dull – even worse, cynical – standardisation. Composers who notate, say, G sharp to B flat back to F natural need instrumentalists prepared to draw on reserves of technique to dutifully reproduce their intentions, reducing active playing to a reflex impulse. But Bailey had no interest in technique as a catalogue of finger movements that guarantees a specific sound. Technique needed to float between certainties, opening the guitar up to finding what cracks lay between the absolutes he had already established.

The most absolute of all those absolutes was tuning. Bailey rarely strayed from equal temperament, but infinitesimal deviations from the tempered scale, and his keen ear for microtonal elaborations, were enough to shake the system.

The sort of guitar styling advocated by Wes Montgomery or Eric Clapton relies on unambiguously literal tuning – Bailey's blunted beauty stood in direct opposition to the amenable, jaunty brightness of so much 1970s guitar music.

But Bailey's view of technique was even more nuanced than those basic principles. In 2004 he told David Toop, "There are different ways of relating to the instrument, aren't there? I'm a very traditional relater to the instrument. Unless I hold it in a certain way I can't play it." When AMM's Keith Rowe laid his guitar flat on a table, using pickups and 'preparing' the strings with alien objects, his intention was to remove himself from any discussion of traditional technique. If Rowe represents extreme guitar anarchy, Bailey was more of a 'conservative anarchist' who turned technique against itself, but always retained the basic reference point.

LACE is perhaps the definitive Bailey solo record. Recorded in Los Angeles in 1989, he communicates to an obviously bewitched audience with a hitherto unheard directness. Naked, sometimes alarmingly uncomplicated lines are brusquely spun through the inscrutable arithmetic of lopsided symmetries. The richness of Bailey's vocabulary – his forceful blues man's sonorities, a microtonal sieve that adds a koto-like timbre, manic strums, beautifully heard abstract textures – transcends the guitar: this is truly Bailey's bailiwick. "Which bit would you like to hear again?" he deadpans, before delivering an intricately precise encore.

Fairly Early With Postscripts
Emanem CD 1999, rec. 1971–98

Fairly Early With Postscripts is an intriguing pull-together of odds and sods recorded over a 27 year span, including rehearsal material with Anthony Braxton. In an opening set of improvisations, "Six Fairly Early Pieces", Bailey uses a pedal attachment to telescope inside his sounds, colouring individual notes and 'orchestrating' hairpin crescendos in an attractively artificial manner. "In Whose Tradition?" opens with Eddie Lang-like stride guitar that Bailey hilariously decapitates – and then the laughs roll.

Friends relished receiving Bailey's 'cassette-letters' in which he riffed about whatever was troubling him, usually accompanied by a stream of consciousness from his guitar. "Morning!" he barks at Emanem label owner Martin Davidson who, in 1979, was living in the USA: "I don't believe you've heard my kitchen before," he continues as his guitar unleashes a tsunami of clusters. Bailey describes his French windows in knowingly geeky detail, and his Sheffield accent and the wry homespun atmosphere is pure John Shuttleworth. He tunes into BBC coverage of the forthcoming general election: the name "Thatcher" provokes comedy Keystone Cops chase music, while the appearance of Edward Heath's voice makes Bailey yell, with masterful comic timing, "you big twat!" In 1998 Bailey sent Davidson another letter: a different generation of politicians now, but the same sublime abuse: "Tony Blair? He plays guitar, I believe – but who doesn't?"

Derek Bailey & Evan Parker
The London Concert
Psi CD 2005
(orig. Incus LP 1975)
Arch Duo
Rastascan CD 1999, rec. 1980

Evan Parker and Derek Bailey waiting at a bus stop, ostensibly heading in the same direction, but resolutely avoiding each other's gaze – the photograph on the back cover of *The London Concert* says it all. The notorious Parker–Bailey schism is *the* major faultline in British improvised music, but rumours about the true nature of their falling out have often overshadowed the fine music they created before the personal strain became too destructive. In 1975 they played at the Wigmore Hall, London's most august classical chamber music venue, and the performance touched on perfection. In the opening moments, Parker circumnavigates Bailey's sexily elastic microtonal lines before he can spot a convincing way in. As the improvisation evolves, Parker's chirping portamentos both fuse and ricochet against Bailey's microtonal webs to create a broken but holistic two-part counterpoint. The guitar abruptly stops and Parker transforms what were nanosecond sonic flecks into sustained honks. Time elongates. The structure buckles.

Flip five years forward to a gig recorded at 1750 Arch Street, Berkeley, California, released with the cunning title *Arch Duo*, and paths have clearly diverged. Parker's tenor playing unashamedly evokes his instrument's jazz heritage, and Bailey's resolute ungroove is hell bent on unpicking the regenerative patterns flowing from his soprano saxophone. It sounds like they don't even want to communicate any longer. During their second improvisation, Parker drops something that hits the floor with a ricocheting bounce. "Just as well this isn't a broadcast," Bailey goads. Parker winces audibly.

Derek Bailey & Steve Lacy
Outcome
Potlatch CD 1999, rec. 1983

New York-born saxophonist Steve Lacy was saturated in the authentic jazz life. He began playing Sidney Bechet-style classic jazz, before the magical elixir of Thelonious Monk's music drew him in. His very presence at this Paris concert in 1983 ought to have whipped Bailey's anti-saxophone leanings into a frenzy, but *Outcome* is intimately argued and blossoms from a basis of mutual respect – everything *Arch Duo* isn't. Not that Bailey hands Lacy an easy ride. His relentless dumping of rhythmic debris around Lacy's svelte linear inventions is not duo playing as we would normally understand it. Bailey tosses in googlies that unravel Lacy's lines; Lacy lends even the most unlikely of Bailey's juxtaposed textures added harmonic weight. Their brinkmanship is infectiously exhilarating, and both men clearly savour the frank exchange.

Company
Company 6 & 7
Incus CD 1999, rec. 1977
Once
Incus CD 1987

Lacy and Bailey, in fact, had previous. The saxophonist was part of the eye-watering line-up Bailey had assembled for his inaugural Company Week, hosted by London's ICA in May 1977. Joining him on saxophones were Evan Parker, Anthony Braxton and Lol Coxhill: from Chicago came trumpeter Leo Smith; the other musicians were Steve Beresford (piano), Tristan Honsinger (cello), Maarten van Regteren Altena (bass) and Han Bennink. Leo Smith most obviously plays 'free jazz', but the regularity of his phrasing disperses as he zones into the erupting string textures opening underneath him, care of Honsinger and Altena. Braxton tries to overlap the two 'sides', and it's inspiring to hear voices from disparate communities within improvised music knit together while retaining their core identities.

Ten years later Honsinger again played Company Week, in an edition that included Lee Konitz (alto saxophone), Barre Phillips (bass) and Steve Noble (drums). A trio performance by Bailey, Konitz and Phillips reveals something wholly unexpected: Konitz can sound steely and objective within the context of a 'straight' jazz band, but now sounds like he's emoting. He begins with a phrase that evokes jazz balladry. Bailey is ready when the phrase repeats and pounces, gently stretching its phrase lengths and demanding that Konitz bends with him. But Konitz will only be pushed so far – he puts his horn down and plays jazz time on Steve Noble's kit, press-ganging Bailey into charting (relatively) straightahead rhythm guitar. Around such healthy cultural bust-ups were Company Weeks made, as Bailey not only improvised the music – he improvised the thing itself.

Derek & The Ruins
Saisoro
Tzadik 1995
Derek Bailey & DJ Ninj
Guitar, Drums 'N' Bass
Avant CD 1996
Derek Bailey/Jamaaladeen Tacuma/Calvin Weston
Mirakle
Tzadik 2000

Idioms. Hooks. Backbeats. Grooves. All no-nos until now, but as Bailey began to look beyond the familiar orthodoxies of free improvisation, he discovered *playing* could take him places that his *ideas* about music had previously judged off-limits. So Derek Bailey went global, creating a string of albums that showed his purist ideals had relevance beyond the specific concerns and personalities of European improvised music.

When Bailey played with the Japanese post-punk duo The Ruins (Yoshida Tatsuya on vocals and drums, Masuda Ryuichi on bass) in September 1994 he operated as usual: he listened hard, and quickly found himself dealing with the essentials of their language; he embedded self-destruct mechanisms inside their grooves, tugged at their melodic intervals, and lobbed a hyped-up purée of their own idiom back to them, as the duo gorged on his atonal intervals in return. Naturally eyebrows were raised, but *Saisoro* is as incisive a musical triologue as anything by, for instance, Iskra 1903. The albums with Tony Williams and Bill Laswell (Arcana's *The Last Wave*, DIW CD 1996) and Pat Metheny (*The Sign Of 4*, Knitting Factory Works 1997) have dated less well – there's a grim determination about the first, a sense of one idea being stretched too far in the second – but a 1996 collaboration with Birmingham-based DJ Ninj again bore unlikely fruit. This project required subtle repositioning: Ninj's faster than real Junglist breakbeats and his rigidly programmed environment were the antithesis of how improvisors normally seek out space. Bailey seeks out timbral equivalents of Ninj's sounds on his guitar and overlays his beats, transforming them as they happen.

At the end of 1999, Bailey went to New York City to journey deep inside the harmolodic funk of two former Ornette Coleman Prime Time associates, bassist Jamaaladeen Tacuma and drummer Calvin Weston. Tzadik's sleeve blurb ("Intense, fascinating and howlingly funny") stresses the comedic potential: Grandad's dancing at a party – but then you realise he can *move* and, in fact, he's moving with the sharpness of a true motherfucker. Tacuma's lived-in and prodigiously funky basslines embrace the soul of everything that's happened in black music since Louis Armstrong. Manufacturing a tepid cultural fusion-compromise (where neither side ends up sounding like themselves) is not on the agenda: Bailey sometimes snuffs out the groove, but Weston's backbeats and Tacuma's bass always find a way of reasserting the 'one' and drive Bailey onwards. *Mirakle*, indeed.

Derek Bailey/Gavin Bryars/Tony Oxley
Joseph Holbrooke 98
Incus 2000, rec. 1998
Limescale
Limescale
Incus CD 2003

Bailey's long history meant he was not immune from the pressures of nostalgia. A late 1990s revival of interest in The Joseph Holbrooke Trio made a reunion irresistible, and finally it happened in Cologne in October 1998. But it proved that nostalgia ain't what it used to be: Bryars, who hadn't played a note of improvised music for decades, was a hopelessly weak link. His aimlessly sustained notes and the jazz-bounce of his phrasing lack convincing chops, especially as Bailey and Oxley are so deeply tuned into each other.

Bailey was, anyway, more interested in keeping his ear to the ground, as he sought new experiences. In 2004 he recorded with Limescale, an extraordinary new group that paired him with Alex Ward (clarinet), Tony Bevan (bass saxophone) and plunderphonic noise improvisors Sonic Pleasure and THF Drenching. The key to Limescale's music lay in its name. Sonic Pleasure and THF Drenching use bricks, stones and a dictaphone to provide a near-fractal flow of detailed noise, a non-rhythmic underlay that was wholly new to improvised music. Bevan feels liberated by this ultimate non-rhythm and adds strata of stuttering rubble, while Ward's clarinet swoops around the textures, wah-wahing like a baby or sustaining notes that glue the music together. This quicksilver, Quentin Tarantino-like jumpcutting makes free improvisation a young music again.

Derek Bailey
Ballads
Tzadik CD 2002

Bruise
Bruise With Derek Bailey
Foghorn CD 2006

Derek Bailey
Carpal Tunnel
Tzadik CD 2005

Bailey spent his last years in Barcelona, his playing alive with new urgency, and the surprises kept coming. As improbable as a James Last free Improv record, Bailey's 2002 album *Ballads* found him tackling Tin Pan Alley standards, while *Bruise With Derek Bailey* documents a return visit to London during which his performance with Tony Bevan's Bruise ensemble was as airy and roomy as Limescale was hot and febrile. But dark clouds were sadly forming. Bailey was displaying the first signs of the motor neurone disease that would claim his life on Christmas Day 2005. An early manifestation was the crippling hand disorder carpal tunnel syndrome. Typically, Bailey refused treatment, preferring to adapt his playing – and life – around it. *Carpal Tunnel* was recorded as the disease progressed, and each track traces its advance, as Bailey is forced continually to rethink his approach to playing. Remarkably, *Carpal Tunnel* is a witty and optimistic record, and as improvised a statement as is possible: no longer improvising with other musicians, he responds instead to the cruel decay of his own body.

Ornette Coleman

by Barry Witherden

Like the composer Charles Ives, Ornette Coleman has suffered from a commonly held misconception that he is a 'naive artist'. Such an impression is rooted in two anecdotes, neither accurately reported nor understood. When Ornette got his first alto saxophone at the age of 14, he taught himself to play from a piano tutor and mistook C on the alto for A. He eventually realised his mistake, but the misunderstanding made him examine pitch and harmony in a fresh way. Thus began the process which led to an improvising style based on freely moving melody unhindered by a repetitive harmonic substructure, and finally, to his theory of harmolodics – a democratic, holistic organising principle that accords equal weight to melody, harmony and rhythm.

The second fallacy stems from the time Ornette was a member of R&B guitarist Pee Wee Crayton's group in the late 1940s. The group's repertoire was heavily based on blues progressions, and the story goes that Ornette played the blues so badly that he was paid to keep quiet. In fact, he has always been capable of playing blues; he just chose to play something different. Crayton is on record as saying that he was impressed with Ornette's abilities and hired him to play the blues. He told Ornette forcefully to either play

what he was paid to play or keep quiet. So Ornette put up and shut up.

If one believes that Ornette devised his style of playing as a way of concealing his mistake about pitch, and that he couldn't cut it as a member of an R&B band, we get a picture of Ornette as a recalcitrant instrumental incompetent who nonetheless became one of the greatest and most influential musicians of the twentieth century. Surely some anomaly?

Ornette (somehow it never seems right to refer to him as Coleman, or Mr Coleman, which fails to capture either the respect or affection he merits) was born in 1930 in Fort Worth, Texas. He played tenor in his high school band (alongside saxophonist King Curtis, drummer Charles Moffett and flautist Prince Lasha) and in various jazz and R&B outfits around the toughest local nightclubs. He was known as a barwalker and honker, influenced by the likes of Jay McNeely and Arnett Cobb, though when he switched back to alto he favoured Charlie Parker.

Most major jazz innovators kicked the music forward by solidifying ideas already in the air; Ornette knocked it sideways into a new groove. Where once Louis Armstrong supplanted a collective, contrapuntal music with a vehicle showcasing individual genius, Ornette almost reversed the process, democratising the music and its performance by breaking down the hierarchy of tune and accompaniment, of leader and sideman. Ornette's playing is firmly rooted in Charlie Parker's innovations – as later recordings like *Sound Museum* make clear – but in freeing the melody, he jolted jazz out of its 30 year obsession with chords, opening the way to new modes of expression unrestricted by 'unnatural' musical structure.

In his youth, after passing through a succession of touring groups, he found it hard to get anyone to play with him until he eventually hooked up with Crayton, which took him to Los Angeles in 1950. There he made contact with likeminded musicians such as trumpeters Don Cherry and Bobby Bradford, and drummer Ed Blackwell. He also impressed Contemporary Records enough to make his first two albums, *Something Else!!!!* (1958) and *Tomorrow Is The Question!* (1959). Aside from Don Cherry, most of the musicians on the records, including drummer Shelly Manne and bassists Percy Heath and Red Mitchell, were grounded in cooler shades of jazz, somewhat limiting comprehension of Ornette's aims. But their openness and commitment to the music cannot be doubted. Both albums are well worth hearing.

Ornette Coleman
Beauty Is A Rare Thing: The Complete Atlantic Recordings
Rhino/Atlantic 6 x CD 1993
The Shape Of Jazz To Come
Atlantic CD 2005
(orig. Atlantic LP 1959)
Change Of The Century
Atlantic CD 2005
(orig. Atlantic LP 1959)
Ornette!
Atlantic CD 2005
(orig. Atlantic LP 1959)
This Is Our Music
Atlantic CD 2005
(orig. Atlantic LP 1959)

Ornette On Tenor
Atlantic CD 2005
(orig. Atlantic LP 1961)
Ornette Coleman Double Quartet
Free Jazz
Atlantic CD 2002
(orig. Atlantic LP 1961)

The recordings Ornette's quartet made for Atlantic between May 1959 and March 1961 were packaged by the label as revolutionary moments in jazz history (check the futuristic titles) but the music justified the hype. The albums featured unparalleled compositions and performances, among them "Beauty Is A Rare Thing", "Focus On Sanity", "Ramblin' ", "Tears Inside" and the ravishing "Lonely Woman". Whether ballads, blues or something more abstract, the music sounded graceful, meticulous and revitalising. The albums are all available separately, while the superb box set *Beauty Is A Rare Thing* collects every complete track that escaped the fire which destroyed Atlantic's warehouse in 1976, and is unconditionally recommended.

On the first Atlantic release, *The Shape Of Jazz To Come*, a short-haired Ornette is pictured on the red and white sleeve cradling a white plastic alto sax, which looks like it has been sculpted from ivory. Everything about the album is captivating: the jagged unpredictability of the fast tunes; the crepuscular romance of the ballads; the crisp drumming of Billy Higgins; Charlie Haden's sonorous, richly melodic basslines; and Ornette's magnificent alto. As a description of his playing, Val Wilmer's "happy urgency" has never been bettered. These first Atlantic performances demonstrate how well he had learned from his early exercises in song form. There's more than just that singing vitality, though. Ornette's phrasing sounds both asymmetrical and perfectly balanced. His melodic sense is deft and elegant. His tone, though often strident, is capable of darting from shrieking falsetto, to thin, lonely keening, to burred, barrelchested low notes. Its mimicry of human sobs and laughter harks back to worksongs, field hollers and beyond. His playing paints a rainbow in shades of silver and chrome, then explodes into a swathe of crimson velvet.

The following *Change Of The Century* (Atlantic, also 1959) opens with "Ramblin' ", which features one of Ornette's best solos over Haden's Bo Diddley-inspired bassline. *This Is Our Music* (Atlantic 1959 yet again, with Ed Blackwell replacing Higgins) includes the haunting "Beauty Is A Rare Thing", and the group's first and last recording of a standard, the slow deconstruction of "Embraceable You". Scott LaFaro took over from Haden on *Ornette* (Atlantic 1961) and Ornette switched saxes for *Ornette On Tenor* (Atlantic 1961), which had Jimmy Garrison on bass. At the time, the larger sax seemed to make the execution of Ornette's ideas a little cumbersome; but the remastered CD version brings out the rich throatiness of his tenor tone. If his career had ended with these records, his place in the hall of fame would have been assured.

Ornette's Atlantic tenure saw him branch into new ventures. One of them proved a dead end, while the other turned out to be hugely influential. He and Don Cherry were sponsored by the label to attend the Lennox School of Jazz, where they earned the admiration of classical composer/academics like Leonard Bernstein and Gunther Schuller, the main exponent of the fusion of jazz and classical known as Third Stream. In December 1960 Ornette recorded a number of Third Stream compositions with Schuller's orchestra (which included Eric Dolphy, Bill Evans and Scott LaFaro). Third Stream turned into an aesthetic cul de sac, but the sessions, originally released as *Jazz Abstractions*, produced some excellent music. The remastering of the two pieces included on the Rhino box set brings out many unheard subtleties.

The next day, Ornette let loose *Free Jazz*, a "Collective Improvisation" by a specially assembled double quartet, which teamed Freddie Hubbard with Cherry, Ornette with Dolphy, Haden with LaFaro, and Higgins with Blackwell. When the record was released in 1961, the cover featured a reproduction of *White Light*, a 1954 painting by Jackson Pollock, reinforcing the notion that this was the musical equivalent of abstract expressionism's trailblazing modernism. Despite its manifesto title, *Free Jazz*, which consists of a single 40 minute piece, adheres to a fairly conventional structure of solos interspersed with a ragged themed ensemble, but the double quartet format led to some stimulating contrasts. The downside was what it inspired: thousands the world over who thought improvision was merely getting up and blowing all at once.

Ornette Coleman
Chappaqua Suite
Sony Jazz/Columbia 2 x CD 1996
(orig. CBS 1966)

By 1962, Ornette's trio comprised the unique David Izenzon on bass, and Charles Moffett, who, along with Ed Blackwell, has never been surpassed as the best drummer for Ornette's music. A few impressive pieces by the trio, plus string quartet on the chamber piece "Dedication To Poets And Writers", were released as *Town Hall 1962* (ESP-Disk 1962). Soon after, embittered by the lack of commercial headway, Ornette attempted to become his own manager. He refused all engagements that offered less than he thought he was worth (that is, all offers), precipitating a two year 'retirement' from 1963–64, during which he took up trumpet and violin.

In 1965 the trio re-emerged to play New York's Village Vanguard, and in June they recorded *Chappaqua Suite*. It was supposed to be the soundtrack to a movie by Conrad Rooks, but the music resulting from their ten days in the studio was so powerful that the director feared it would overshadow his film. He hired Philip Glass to edit the music, but Glass refused to vandalise what he recognised as an exceptional piece of work. Against Ornette's wishes, Rooks sold the rights to the recording to French CBS, who released an edited version on a double album in 1967 (reissued as a double CD in 1996). *Chappaqua Suite* is nearly 80 minutes of adrenalin pumping, soul stirring, twentieth-century pan-tonal, angular blues, with Izenzon and Moffett in magnificent form, pacing Ornette as he soars, swoops and strafes the brass and string ensemble.

Ornette later claimed that he wanted to be known more as a composer than a saxophone player all along. But his attempts to realise his 'classical' works were frustrated by a perceived stonewalling by both the jazz industry and the classical establishment. (In the case of the epic orchestral *Skies Of America*, however, the problem lay more with the quality of the material.)

Ornette's harmolodic system first made itself evident in classical pieces such as the wind quintet *Sounds And Forms*, from the live album *An Evening With Ornette Coleman* (Freedom LP 1965, Tokuma CD 1997), although its inventor says the system was already there in his music from the 1950s. Much has been written about harmolodics over the years, mostly about how impenetrable the system is for outsiders. But if you listen to what Ornette has to say about it – "I think of communication as a form of energy that allows everyone to be equal. I call it harmolodics" – it seems a wholly benign, intuitive and organic process.

That concert also included the first example of Ornette's trumpet and violin playing. He may not have been fully trained on these instruments, but his adoption of them was part of his search for an instinctive way of playing music, a desire to play "without memory", unrestricted by the baggage of conventional techniques and rules. He has described his work on violin and trumpet as being more "unconscious"; although this concept is rather more plausible for the violin than the trumpet, which requires a certain basic grasp of technique before even the slightest phrase can be produced.

Ornette Coleman Trio
At The Golden Circle Stockholm Volume 1
Blue Note CD 2002
(orig. Blue Note LP 1966)
At The Golden Circle Stockholm Volume 2
Blue Note CD 2002
(orig. Blue Note LP 1966)

Though *Chappaqua Suite* was his first recording with the Izenzon/Moffett trio, the two volumes of *At The Golden Circle*, recorded in December 1965, were released earlier. At the time, bassist Izenzon's remarkable technique – particularly his weird, buzzing, wailing arco work – was applauded, but Ornette's trumpet and violin playing and Moffett's drumming drew critical brickbats. Moffett did not fit any category,

so the simple fact that he was a most flexible, imaginative, powerful and witty percussionist tended to get overlooked. *The Golden Circle* sessions showcase some typically fine Ornette songs, from the nursery rhyme transparency of "European Echoes" and "Dee Dee" to the atmospheric "Dawn". At about this time Ornette's innovations had triggered a strange critical syndrome. Earlier breakthroughs are sympathetically reassessed once something even more difficult comes along: after Archie Shepp, Albert Ayler, Pharoah Sanders and the cataclysmic developments in John Coltrane's later music, Ornette began to sound far more listener-friendly.

Ornette Coleman
The Empty Foxhole
Blue Note CD 1990
(orig. Blue Note LP 1966)
New York Is Now
Blue Note CD 1990
(orig. Blue Note LP 1968)

On *The Empty Foxhole*, recorded in September 1966 – his first studio recording for four years – Ornette showcased a different trio, with Haden back on bass and his ten year old son Denardo on drums. The choice of Denardo was another move in the process of minimising the repressive effect of experience: Denardo was too young to have developed his own clichés and preconceptions. The idea works better on paper than on record. After Higgins, Blackwell and Moffett, Denardo certainly sounds limited, yet he contributes an undeniable freshness and charm to the music. Ornette's trumpet, while still sounding primitive, comes together on "Freeway Express" and the title track. Overall, *Foxhole* is one of his most atmospheric recordings.

Two years later, Ornette enlisted Jimmy Garrison and Elvin Jones, late of John Coltrane's quartet, for *New York Is Now*. After so many years involved in Coltrane's struggle with the potential of chords, the question was how would they adapt to Ornette's melodic approach? After Denardo, Jones's immensely sophisticated drumming could hardly have made a more shocking contrast. Of course, it caused a shift in the balance of the music. The relationship between the front line and rhythm section sometimes edges towards conventional jazz, but these are all musicians who know how to adapt, to interact, to give and take. Dewey Redman on tenor completes the new quartet. His guttural tone, and strange humming and gargling effects, are a fascinating contrast to the bright, darting brass of Coleman's longtime foil, Don Cherry.

The Complete Science Fiction Sessions
Sony Jazz 2 x CD 2000
(orig. CBS LP 1971)

For Ornette watchers, the late 1960s and early 1970s are seen as a period of marking time. Two valuable compilations of unissued Atlantic tracks, *Twins* and *The Art Of The Improvisors*, were issued as stopgaps, including a warm-up version of "Free Jazz" (all these are now included on the Rhino box set). Then, in 1971, Ornette rounded up the usual suspects for *Science Fiction*: Blackwell, Higgins, Redman, Haden, Bradford and Cherry. For the first time, Ornette gave prominence to words and electricity. He drafted in Asha Puthli for the dreamlike (or trip-like) "What Reason Could I Give" and "All My Life", and poet David Henderson for the title track. "Rock The Clock" (the pretext for much heckling, calls for "Lorraine", and diffident pleas from Ornette for the audience to give a fair hearing to new material at the group's 1972 London gig) featured Ornette on trumpet and violin, Redman on musette and Haden playing bass through a wah-wah pedal. The title suggests that Ornette thought the track matched rock's energy. But like the contemporaneous electric music of Miles Davis and Herbie Hancock, nothing on *Science Fiction* sounds compatible with rock's aims, attitudes or intentions, let alone its rhythmic sensibilities. The beat, though louder and more intrusive, remains an integral part of the total structure, rather than part of a rhythm track on which everything else runs.

Body Meta
Harmolodic/Verve CD 1996
(orig. Artists House LP 1976)

Dancing In Your Head
Verve CD 2000
(orig. A&M 1976)

If funk is a basketball thwacked smartly between hand and floor, Prime Time kicked it down a hill and chased after it, sometimes careering out of control in the attempt to catch up with it.

Prime Time was the group Ornette formed in the mid-1970s to carry his harmolodic vision forward using the elements laid down on *Science Fiction*: electric instruments and the mutation of rhythm patterns patented by Hendrix, James Brown and The Grateful Dead. The group would eventually be constituted as a double trio (two guitarists, two bassists, two drummers, all swapping lead and rhythm lines at will, plus Ornette), but its earliest incarnation was a quintet featuring guitarist James 'Blood' Ulmer and drummer Ronald Shannon Jackson. Live, Prime Time was all braying aggression verging on nihilism; it sounded like Ornette was holding up the roof while the others demolished the walls, like more of those hecklers providing a distracting background to a great orator. Whatever the leader's democratic intention, Ornette has always dominated Prime Time, whether because of the relative anonymity of some of the musicians who subsequently came into the group, or because of the way the music is set up, or simply because he is a greater talent than his colleagues. His incisive, elegant alto playing, spooling out endless melodies and spanning tonalities, remained the focus of attention, while the rest of the group busied themselves around him.

Prime Time sounded more cohesive in the studio, where the musicians could be better balanced. The tracks on *Body Meta* and *Dancing In Your Head* were mostly cut at the same session in Paris in December 1975 and were the group's first recordings. Ulmer had left by this point and the records feature the twin guitars of Charles Ellerbee and Bern Nix, their lines entwining each other like rapturous serpents while overlapping with Jamaaladeen Tacumas's finger-popping basslines and Shannon Jackson's parade-ground polyrhythms. Among the five tracks on *Body Meta* are reworkings of two old favourites, "European Echoes" and "Macho Woman". The pattern was set clearly, with Ornette dictating the pace and Prime Time sounding like a big band in revolt in the back of the studio, especially in the early stages of "Home Grown".

Dancing In Your Head includes a brief extract from the recordings Ornette and clarinettist Robert Palmer made with The Master Musicians Of Joujouka in Morocco in 1973 (apparently, about three albums' worth of material was recorded, but has never seen the light of day). The album's two long Prime Time tracks sound relentless and claustrophobic next to the freshness of this meeting of cultures – one characterising twentieth-century jazz, the other representing a tradition which for centuries pervaded and guided the development of music across thousands of miles of Southern Europe, Eurasia, North Africa and India. Yet in both contexts Ornette comes across as adventurous, authoritative and utterly sincere.

Ornette Coleman & Pat Metheny
Song X
Nonesuch CD 2005
(orig. Geffen LP 1986)

Depite his use of electric guitars in Prime Time, which he said could deliver the kind of textures otherwise only available from an orchestral violin section, Ornette's 1986 album with Pat Metheny came as something of a surprise (although in the light of Metheny's apocalyptic meeting with Derek Bailey on the 1997 *The Sign Of 4*, the project appears very benign). Metheny had already played with previous members of Ornette's groups, including Redman, Haden and Higgins, and both Prime Time guitarists had studied under him at Berklee; but the question still remained: why would Ornette choose to record with the guru of jazz-lite, rather than, say, Ulmer, Sonny Sharrock or Vernon Reid? One answer is that it presented a challenge to both musicians. Another might have something to do with the fact that Metheny was signed to Geffen. Although Metheny does most of the adjusting, there is an evident respect for each other's playing and writing throughout; and flanked by Haden, Denardo and second drummer Jack DeJohnette, they exceed everyone's expectations except their own. An expanded version of the album,

containing several previously unissued tracks, was released to mark its 20th anniversary.

To underline the assertion that the principles buttressing Prime Time had been there all along, *In All Languages* (Caravan of Dreams 1987) was subtitled "30 Years Of Harmolodic Music". One disc features a reformed version of the classic quartet, and the other showcases a double trio version of Prime Time. Several themes are common to both records, and the album is an ideal crash course in Ornette's evolution. *Virgin Beauty* (Portrait/Columbia 1988) drew attention by featuring a guest appearance by The Grateful Dead's Jerry Garcia. More crucially, the title track, with Ornette's trumpet floating through a solarised forest of decaying lines and crumbling electronics, was a 'ballad' performance as startling as the 1959 version of "Beauty Is A Rare Thing". Both albums are unfortunately out of print at the time of writing.

Ornette Coleman & Howard Shore
Naked Lunch: Original Soundtrack
Milan CD 1991
Ornette Coleman & Prime Time
Tone Dialing
Harmolodic/Verve CD 1995
Ornette Coleman & Joachim Kühn
Colors
Harmolodic/Verve CD 1998

In the early 1990s Ornette further expanded both the line-up and textural possibilities of Prime Time by adding keyboard player Dave Bryant and tabla player Badal Roy. He also formed a new acoustic quartet featuring M-Base pianist Geri Allen and bassist Charnett Moffett, son of Charles, Ornette's drummer of three decades earlier.

There were other significant developments throughout this period. In 1991 Ornette played the lead role in Howard Shore's soundtrack to David Cronenberg's film of William Burroughs's *Naked Lunch*. The score set Ornette down in a number of scenarios, all of them riveting. The fleet, high energy trio performances with Denardo and bassist Barre Phillips revived memories of the *Chappaqua Suite* sessions; while the combination of Ornette's wounded alto cry and wayward trumpet and violin improvisations with Shore's Hollywood-dramatic orchestrations should never have worked, but proved irresistible. Alluding to Burroughs's own experiences in North Africa, Shore's score even folded in a sample of Ornette's 1973 Moroccan recordings from *Dancing In Your Head*.

Then, three years later, Verve Records bankrolled Ornette to start a new label, Harmolodic. Its first release was *Tone Dialing*, which grew out of a multimedia work premiered at the 1994 San Francisco Jazz Festival. The performance included Prime Time and the new acoustic quartet alongside dancers, poetry, film projections and demonstrations of ritualistic body piercings. ("The whole gamut of feelings humans have was present at that concert," Ornette commented. "It was very healthy. It wasn't about ego or money or sex. It was about democracy and the different things people do to get in touch with their spirituality.")

On *Tone Dialing*, recorded with the new expanded Prime Time, Ornette continued to refine the processes he had begun with *Virgin Beauty*, making the music more harmonically focused and rhythmically tight. The careering ball had been brought in check – a bad move, some thought, akin to Rochester's blinding, or the caging of the Creature from the Black Lagoon. A more balanced view has it that Ornette had assessed his experiments and identified new pathways. He once told Val Wilmer, "When you hear me you probably hear everything I've heard since I was a kid. In fact, it's a glorified folk music." One of his most varied and accessible albums, *Tone Dialing*, is a late demonstration of what he means by that. After half a century of ploughing a very personal furrow with self-immolatory integrity and determination, he has finally relaxed enough to say that his music should not be judged according to whether he can play bebop, blues or 'Cherokee' – he can play them all and a few other things besides. On *Tone Dialing* he ventures into Bach, rap, sound collage, and Latin and Caribbean rhythms with equal conviction.

Ornette's reconciliation with the piano, in the person of Geri Allen, was more surprising. The group on the 1958 *Something Else!!!!* had included a pianist, and the same year

Ornette recorded with Paul Bley, but he did not use a keyboard player again until David Bryant joined Prime Time in 1992. In August 1996, Ornette invited German pianist Joachim Kühn to make an album of duets, which was recorded live at the Leipzig Jazztage and released as *Colors*. If anything, the eight tracks of high octane improvisation stretch Ornette even more than his work with Prime Time. He rises to the occasion magnificently, and prompts Kühn into some of his finest work too. This intense but intimate music sounds far removed from *Tone Dialing*'s sensory overload. But taken together they underline the breadth of vision that characterises all of Ornette Coleman's music.

Ornette Coleman
Sound Grammar
Sound Grammar CD 2007

Ornette's first new CD to appear for nearly a decade was recorded in October 2005 at a concert in Ludwigshafen, Germany, during a European tour. His then-current quartet comprised Denardo and two bassists: Tony Falanga, who played elegant, soulful arco, and Gregory Cohen, responsible for crisp, potent pizzicato lines.

The group's sound evoked the classic trio with Izenzon and Moffatt, though the presence of a second bassist recalled the time when Izenzon and Haden were retained together. (They were the apposite precedent, rather than the paired basses in Prime Time, which created a quite different effect.) Cohen and Falanga made a superb team, in little danger of being eclipsed by comparison with their illustrious predecessors.

This was, arguably, the first time that a new venture by Ornette harked back rather than broke fresh ground. However, if it is true that neither his performance, nor that of the group (either in this form, or in the edition which toured in 2007, augmented by Al McDowell on electric bass, and Charnett replacing Cohen) contained anything that could be described as cutting edge, the music was imbued with a brightness, airiness and open-hearted joy that often seemed absent from his work after the late 1970s.

Nearly two years after this session, Ornette toured with

the five piece version of the group, promoting the CD release. On the Spanish leg of the tour he collapsed with heat exhaustion. He was still in less than robust health by the time they appeared at London's Royal Festival Hall in July 2007 but, once he began to play, his corporeal frailty was forgotten, utterly belied by the strength of spirit and imagination of his improvising. A fine melodist himself, Ornette rarely quotes other composer's tunes, but on "Turnaround" on *Sound Grammar* he threw in unexpectedly substantial quotes from "If I Loved You" and "Beautiful Dreamer" before toying with their melodies throughout the track and, startlingly, at the Royal Festival Hall concert he quoted the opening bars of "Just a Closer Walk With Thee" on all but one number. Alongside *Sound Grammar*, this tour confirmed that he remains a lively, communicative and exhilarating player, still with much to say.

Fire Music

by David Keenan

"God," affirmed the legendary Russian ballet dancer Vaslav Nijinsky, "is a fire in the brain." And the ecstasy of free jazz (aka energy music and ecstatic jazz, but whose immolating force is best served by the rubric of Fire Music) manifests in flame-ravaged synapses, sense-destroying celestial communion. Ripping away from the chordal structures and harmonic complexities that had held jazz in a vice-like grip since before the war, Fire Music was, and still is, a freely improvised, spiritualised, resolutely militant jazz of wall-destroying force. Donald Ayler, Albert Ayler's trumpeting brother, summed it up when he announced that "it's not about the notes anymore". Instead, Fire Music was an attempt to break on through to something primal, sensually liberating and consciousness-expanding: to create a total music unmediated by the mind. As Albert Ayler, Fire Music's most charismatic preacher, declared: "We are the music we play. We keep trying to purify our music, to purify ourselves so that we can move ourselves – and those who hear us – to higher levels of peace and understanding." And anyone who has spent serious time with these records will know that there are moments of genuine transcendence that can go off like a bomb.

Emerging during a time of crisis for America (Vietnam, race riots, student sit-ins), Fire Music positioned itself alongside the Black Arts and Black Power movements as a catalyst for change: social, political and spiritual. It remains primarily a African American artform, which is why there is no European representation in this Primer, despite the fact that Fire Music often had more support outside of the USA (in the early 1970s the flame was kept alive largely through the patronage of great Euro labels such as BYG, Shandar and Center Of The World). Musicians such as Peter Brötzmann, Alex von Schlippenbach and Evan Parker were undoubtedly the European response to Albert Ayler, Cecil Taylor and John Coltrane, but they have developed a sufficiently idiosyncratic direction of their own to demand separate coverage.

It is a myth that this music is impossibly difficult; in fact, it impacts at uniquely physical and emotional levels. Although the players can really rip it out at times, most of their music is still very much inside the tradition. These were musicians with a great love of venerable idioms like gospel, blues and New Orleans jazz (inspired rereadings of old spirituals dot most of these discs). They believed they were furthering black music by opening up the range of 'legitimate' sounds and techniques it could draw on, in an effort to communicate beyond words (or notes) the contents of their souls. Albert

Ayler put it in perspective when explaining the logic leaps of his new music: "I feel that I've lived more than I can express in bop terms alone." At its best, Fire Music galvanises the intuitive, unconscious energy of folk art with hyper-advanced techniques. It is both exhilaratingly primitive and satisfyingly cerebral.

John Coltrane
Ascension
Universal/Impulse! CD 2000
(orig. Impulse! LP 1965)
Meditations
Universal/Impulse! CD 1999
(orig. Impulse! LP 1966)
Interstellar Space
Universal/Impulse! CD 2000, rec. 1967
(orig. Impulse! LP 1974)

Recorded in the summer of 1965, *Ascension* is the most important record John Coltrane ever made. It marked such a violent severance with his past that many critics thought he had lost his mind. The meditative classic *A Love Supreme* had been released at the beginning of the year to almost universal praise, but Coltrane was a restless and brave artist, seemingly motivated solely by his inner voice, and by June the same year he was some other place entirely. His appearance in March at a benefit concert for Amiri Baraka's Black Arts Theatre at New York's Village Gate, alongside Albert Ayler, Archie Shepp and Sun Ra, was symbolic of the growing solidarity he felt with the "New Black Music", as the concert was titled.

For *Ascension*, he called in ten of the hottest talents in town for a mass levitation, a primal evocation of hurricanes, volcanoes and storms. At certain points, the 40 minute collective improvisation sounds like a dense war cloud. According to saxophonist Marion Brown, during the session "the people in the studio were screaming. I don't know how the engineers kept the screams out of the record." Even so, the piece has a familiar structure, starting with the same slow-sunrise vamping that characterised *A Love Supreme*, with each player stepping forward to take a solo – each strikingly different –

before being engulfed in the maelstrom. Coltrane's is big-bodied and sensual, bluesy at first before bursting and ripping like a pack of wolves catching the scent of its prey; both John Tchicai on alto and Archie Shepp on tenor blow passages full of sadness. But it is Pharoah Sanders who really succeeds in raising the spirits, with one of the most mindblowingly 'out there' solos ever committed to tape. Starting with high register squeals and screams, he descends into lawless, raging grunts and hollers. The group actually recorded two takes of *Ascension*. The latest CD edition compiles both, but there is not much between them, apart from some elemental tweaking with the order of soloists.

Meditations, recorded five months later, sees Coltrane's regular trio of bassist Jimmy Garrison, drummer Elvin Jones and pianist McCoy Tyner augmented once again by Pharoah Sanders and second drummer Rashied Ali – much to the chagrin of the rest of the group. Jones felt that Ali was playing against him rather than with him, while Tyner was becoming increasingly bemused by the lack of tunes. It was not long before both players jumped ship, but not before they helped cut the greatest session of Coltrane's career. It's a gospelised suite influenced by the mutant folk strains Albert Ayler was experimenting with. The wild flights of the ecstatic "The Father And The Son And The Holy Ghost" contrast with moments of humbling quietude during "Love-Consequences-Serenity". In the interstices of these two performances you sense what Amiri Baraka means when he was compelled to make his dramatic exegesis of Coltrane's music: "[It] is the absolute open expression of everything … a direct route into God."

Coltrane's use of two drummers was the most visible example of his attempt to develop new rhythmic vortices, from which his own playing could levitate into the stratosphere. According to Rashied Ali, "He was in a drummer thing. There has been times I played with Trane, he had a battery of drummers … about three conga players, guys playing batas, shakers and everything". And for Coltrane, Ali was "one of the great drummers … He's laying down multidirectional rhythms all the time." *Interstellar Space* is the most dramatic symptom of Coltrane's self-professed "drum fever" (as well as his immersion in astrology: the tracks are named after signs of the zodiac). It features the saxophonist and Ali going head to head without any kind of harmonic base, as though they're taking a tightrope walk. The perilous act precipitates some of their most inventive playing, with each of them carving and shaping naked sound, all colour and motion.

Cecil Taylor Jazz Unit
Nefertiti, The Beautiful One Has Come
Revenant 2 x CD 1997

(orig. Fontana LP 1962)

Cecil Taylor Unit
It Is In The Brewing Luminous
hatOLOGY CD 2001, rec. 1989

Cecil Taylor was the first of the new jazz musicians to make expressive use of atonality, and many of the major Fire Musicians cut their teeth with him at some point, among them Albert Ayler, Sunny Murray, Charles Gayle and David S. Ware. Jazz has not yet come to terms with his unique conceptions, making it impossible for any contemporary player to approach the jaws of the piano without feeling his hand on their shoulder.

Taylor famously described his vision of the piano as "88 tuned drums". His sound is primarily percussive, dominated by jarring note clusters and abstract, dancing patterns. There is so much movement in his music that the first-time listener's attention seems pulled in contradictory directions all at once. His work needs to be heard as one massive, looming organism, constantly pushing forwards and further out, a music of continuous symphonic expansion.

Nefertiti is still a great introduction, especially in Revenant's beautiful edition. A fairly lo-fi and fuzzy recording, it was nonetheless a breakthrough set. Made by the world-beating trio of Taylor, alto saxophonist Jimmy Lyons and drummer Sunny Murray in Copenhagen in 1962, it starts off hilariously loose and unimposing, with Taylor tinkling schmaltz over the bored mutter of cafe punters. Thirty minutes later, the trio is absolutely raging in front of what must have been an utterly bemused audience. A stunning drummer, Sunny Murray is a constant presence throughout the history of Fire Music, but we'll get to him later. Jimmy Lyons is really Taylor's best man, an altoist capable of gurgling lava just as easily as squeezing the subtlest nuances from a starlit ballad. He's still there in 1980, playing alongside Murray, second drummer Jerome Cooper, violinist Ramsey Ameen and bassist Alan Silva on the ravenous *It Is In The Brewing Luminous*. The title, like the music within, makes perfect sense until you attempt to pick it apart, at which point it disintegrates into chaos. Though superficially heavy, the various elements of Taylor's music are connected with thin, silvery webs of dream logic, which dissolve if tugged too hard. A continuous 70 minute concert performance, *Brewing Luminous* is, like all works of great beauty, perilously fragile.

Albert Ayler Trio
Spiritual Unity
ESP-Disk CD 2006

(orig. ESP-Disk LP 1964)

Albert Ayler
Lörrach/Paris 1966
Hat HUT CD 2003, rec. 1966

Live In Greenwich Village: The Complete Impulse! Recordings
Universal/Impulse! 2 x CD 1999

(orig. Impulse! 2 x LP 1967)

Albert Ayler is the most important and influential player in the Fire Music canon. His unique synthesis of marching band melodies, folk songs, mutant national anthems and black church music, all rendered via the most terrifyingly possessed tone of any saxophonist, continues to resonate benign waves into the future. Most of the musicians he worked with speak of him in awed terms, some relaying mysterious tales of supernatural abilities. Trombonist Roswell Rudd called him "a phantom". Drummer Milford Graves claims to have seen him blow a hole in a concrete wall with sonic force, while poet/activist Amiri Baraka once told me that Ayler's albums are only 'rumours', and that no recording was capable of truly capturing the awe-inspiring sound of his horn. As for Ayler himself, he saw his music as an instrument of divine revelation and deliverance. Towards the end of his life, he took on the mantle of a biblical prophet, haunted by visions. Prophesying the coming of a New Jerusalem, it had been revealed to him, he announced, that he and his brother Donald "had the right seal of God Almighty in our forehead". That he died in mysterious circumstances in 1970, aged 34, with so much left to do, only served to perpetuate the myth. But his music stands as one of the most challenging and spiritually rewarding bodies of work of the twentieth century.

Many of the new musicians, from the mysterious saxophonist Giuseppi Logan to The New York Art Quartet, got their first recording contract thanks to Bernard Stollman's ESP-Disk label. Fittingly, Ayler's epochal *Spiritual Unity*, cut with Sunny Murray and bassist Gary Peacock in 1964, was ESP's first release. To all intents and purposes, the opening "Ghosts" has become Albert's theme song, a big pumping slice of joy that sounds deceptively straightforward until Ayler starts quaking with inspiration, erupting into a fantastic gurgling solo.

Ayler's music is virtually the opposite of Cecil Taylor's, although the two did work together in the early 1960s. Whereas Taylor is expansive, Ayler is always wrestling with his sound in a bid to reduce it to its most primal phonetics. He revolutionised the tenor saxophone and, through him, it became the greatest conduit for the souls of African American musicians. Ayler often played harrowing phantom scales unreachable by fingering alone. That the most avant garde saxophonist of his generation chose to frame his playing in structures that often sounded archaic, sepia-tinted or sentimental only added to the controversy and bewilderment his music generated, in the process underlining the problematic nature of his quest to forge a universal music.

Nineteen sixty-six was Ayler's year, and the atmosphere during that autumn's European tour with a new group is by all accounts comparable to what Bob Dylan's electric band faced night after night a few months earlier. In London the BBC filmed one performance, only to destroy the tape after judging

it too far out to broadcast. The *Lörrach/Paris* album catches a classic Ayler line-up live in France and Germany: Albert on tenor, Donald on trumpet, bassist William Folwell, drummer Beaver Harris and the phenomenal Dutch violinist Michel Sampson. Here the group is at its most celestial, with the strings echoing and rephrasing the rollicking brass, and the rhythm section rocking the house. By this point Albert sounds like a channel for some unearthly energy, and his solos are like ultra-focused beams of light, piercing even the thickest of skulls.

Back in New York, Ayler signed to Impulse! at the behest of John Coltrane. The concerts captured on *In Greenwich Village* amplify the orchestral power of the European group by adding a second bassist, either Henry Grimes or Alan Silva, and cellist Joel Friedman. The results are devastating. On "For John Coltrane", over a string quartet that lurches from soul-melting lyricism to modernist scrapings Ayler blows a series of alto solos full of sobbing legato arcs, while the rendition of "Truth Is Marching In" sounds like the fanfare for the Day of Judgement. *In Greenwich Village* forms just part of the *Complete Impulse! Recordings* set. Although taped at the same gigs, the extra material tends to diminish the impact of these amazing perfomances, and the sleeve art – featuring a papier maché puppet of Ayler – is horrendously inappropriate.

Archie Shepp
Mama Too Tight
Universal/Impulse! CD 1998
(orig. Impulse! LP 1967)
Blasé/Live At The Pan-African Festival
Charly/BYG Actuel 2 x CD 2004
(orig. BYG 1969/BYG 1969)

To steal a phrase from Miles Davis, Archie Shepp was a motherfucker. One of the meanest, suavest, hippest of the new players, and possessor of the blackest of tenor tones, he was Fire Music's greatest theorist and polemicist, coining the very term on a 1965 album. While that record didn't really live up to its branding, his late 1960s sides are all titanic, genrestraddling classics. *Mama Too Tight* is the best record he cut for Impulse!, with a group that included Ayler's drummer

Beaver Harris, bassist Charlie Haden and trombonists Roswell Rudd and Grachan Moncur III. According to Shepp, "A Portrait Of Robert Thompson (As A Young Man)" was meant to couple "the poignancy of the blues and the jubilant irreverence of a marching band returning from a funeral", so no wonder it carries echoes of Ayler. Although still structured, it constantly threatens to explode with exuberance. "I play music out of an overwhelming need to play; to make the rains come; to abolish wars," claimed Shepp in a noble piece of hyperbole gracing the LP jacket.

Live At The Pan-African Festival, which the CD reissue couples with the 1969 Paris studio date, *Blasé* was recorded in Algiers in 1969 at a festival organised by the country's FLN (National Liberation Front). The two long tracks elevate the New World Music of John Coltrane's "Om" and Pharoah Sanders's Impulse! albums to higher peaks of intensity, as Shepp, Moncur and cornet player Clifford Thornton blast their way through a desert storm of clattering percussion and massed, ululating pipes played by an orchestra of Tuareg musicians. During "We Have Come Back", someone (possibly poet Ted Joans) declaims: "Jazz is a black power! Jazz is an African power!" By this point, Fire Music was already returning to the future, from whence it had originally come, and tribal dress, beads and afros now replaced the musicians' sharp Italian suits.

After Algiers, a photographer from French magazine *Actuel*, Jacques Bisceglia, invited most of the participating musicians to Paris to meet his editor Claude Delcloo, who was also an A&R man for new French label BYG. The offer came just in time; with the death of Coltrane in 1967 and the resultant petering out of major label sponsorship, New Black Music's moment in the American spotlight was effectively over. From here on in the musicians would have to rely increasingly on fans like Fernand Boruso, Jean Luc Young and Jean Georgakarakos, the men behind the legendary BYG/Actuel series.

Various
Jazzactuel
Charly 3 x CD 2001

Alan Silva & The Celestrial Communication Orchestra
Seasons
Get Back 3 x LP 2001
(orig. BYG/Actuel 3 x LP 1970)
Frank Wright
One For John
Abraxas LP 2002
(orig. BYG/Actuel LP 1969)

BYG Actuel is the most consistently great underground jazz label. As well as releasing some of the best sides by Sun Ra, The Art Ensemble Of Chicago and Don Cherry, it documented many lesser known players, giving them studio time and space to develop their ideas. The label had a strong uniform look, thanks to Claude Caudron's sleeve designs, which undoubtedly contributed to making it insanely collectible. However, the situation has improved for more impoverished fans, thanks to a vinyl reissue programme instigated by the Italian Get Back label. That said, the best overview of the label has to be the triple CD box set *Jazzactuel*, compiled by Byron Coley and Thurston Moore. It opens with a ferocious cut from Sunny Murray's *Sunshine* and proceeds through more wild performances, including tracks by such long lost Fire Musicians as intense altoist Arthur Jones and Jamaican tenorist Kenneth Terroade. It also culls a 20 minute wall of black noise from pianist Dave Burrell's *Echo* album.

Most of the recordings here were cut in one extended session during the Parisian summer of 1969 by a revolving cast of musicians; indeed Alan Silva's monstrous triple album, *Seasons*, features every musician who was in town at the time. If the legendary status of *Seasons* is partly due to its rarity, it is mostly down to the breathtaking and genre defying nature of its racket: bassist Silva leads an orchestra (including the whole Art Ensemble Of Chicago!) through six sides of squawking brass, heavy percussive lumbering and heavenly mutated choirs. The final movement, also available in the *Jazzactuel* box, is the single most intense piece made by any of the participants before or since, with Silva dropping some electroacoustic 'inventions' just when the group is ready to levitate. It sounds like Merzbow, illuminated by angelic light.

The self-styled Reverend Frank Wright was a wild tenor player and a teenage buddy of Albert Ayler's, whom he followed to New York from their hometown of Cleveland. Although his style embraced primitive street-noise and vocal barking, he was equally at home blasting out brassy Coltrane-like testimonials. A big-hearted sound dominates his two ESP Disks, but his really wild side was nurtured at Europe's ever-loving bosom. *One For John*, dedicated to Coltrane, show-cases a great quartet, in which the Reverend is joined by more Americans on the run: altoist Noah Howard, pianist Bobby Few and drummer Muhammad Ali, Rashied's brother. The four of them, alongside Alan Silva, went on to form the Center Of The World collective, running a DIY-type label to showcase their stellar wares.

Noah Howard
The Black Ark
Bo'Weavil CD 2007
(orig. Polydor/Freedom LP 1969)
Sonny Sharrock
Black Woman
Water CD 2005
(orig. Vortex LP 1969)
Frank Lowe
Black Beings
Get Back CD 2008
(orig. ESP-Disk LP 1973)

Before Noah Howard left America for Paris to join the BYG blowout, he cut *The Black Ark* early in 1969. It's a vicious album: Howard's tenor sound is tradition-soaked and often ferocious, but one of the main reasons for the record's legend-ary status is the presence of Arthur Doyle on tenor saxophone. Doyle takes off from the flesh-rending sound of Coltrane-era Pharoah Sanders and moves further out, often singing, screaming or weeping into the horn. He is very much at the centre of *The Black Ark*, breathing molten fire over the others.

Sonny Sharrock was a self-taught guitarist who came to Fire Music straight from the blues. As a result his conceptions are always earthily satisfying and firmly anchored by meaty note runs, sandwiched between ever-flowing walls of feed-back. He appeared on saxophonist Marzette Watts's 1966 self-titled ESP album and later played on Miles Davis's *Jack Johnson*, but it was his two albums with Pharoah Sanders, *Izipho Sam* (Strata East 1969) and, especially, *Tauhid* (Impulse! 1966), that cut a huge, smoking afro into the map. He recorded a great session for BYG/Actuel, *Monkey Pockie Boo*, with his wife, the Yoko Ono-like vocalist Linda Sharrock (a track is included in *Jazzactuel*), but the 1969 *Black Woman* is his finest moment. Beneath blurred, speeding chords, Linda splits the skies with formless shrieks and hollers. Elsewhere Sonny settles into rootsier territory on tracks like the solo acoustic "Blind Willy". But "Portrait Of Linda In Three Colours, All Black" is the one that really burns, with a hilarious attempt by Milford Graves to limit himself to a standard 4/4 beat. By this point, Graves's meta-conceptions of time were so advanced that such caveman demands made little sense.

In the late 1960s saxophonist Frank Lowe was briefly a member of a group led by John Coltrane's wife, Alice. He was also a Vietnam veteran. "I brought some Coltrane records with me to Vietnam and I listened to them con-stantly," he once said. "His music was like life to me, and death was just down the road." All of his albums are worth tracking down, especially *Black Beings* – a "hardcore record", as Lowe accurately described it. See also the smoky late-night stylings of the one-sided *Out Of Nowhere* LP (Ecstatic Peace! 1992), which caught him in the middle of a Lester Young trip.

William Parker
Through Acceptance Of The Mystery Peace
Eremite CD 1998
Various
Wildflowers: The New York Loft Jazz Sessions
Knit Classics 3 x CD 2000, rec. 1976
Arthur Doyle
Alabama Feeling
DRA CD 1998
(orig. Ak-Ba LP 1978)

Plays More Alabama Feeling
Forced Exposure LP 1993, rec. 1990

The mid- to late 1970s through the early 1980s are commonly characterised as barren years for freedom in general, but the flame was still burning bright. Only it was hidden away in countless artist-run lofts. With the music now deemed commercially unviable, the musicians took to supporting themselves and each other, establishing an informal network of performance and meeting spaces in New York's East Village. Bassist William Parker, nowadays the Lower East Side's very own lightning rod, bass player with David S. Ware and leader of ensembles like In Order To Survive and Little Huey Orchestra, made his first recordings during this period. *Through Acceptance Of The Mystery Peace* is a compilation of performances from throughout the 1970s. Such loft scene regulars as the flighty post-Ornette altoist Jemeel Moondoc, multi-reedist Daniel Carter and drummer Denis Charles put in appearances across a series of stately, precisely plotted compositions that burn with evangelical fervour. Parker combines the authentic wood and wire feel of bassist Jimmy Garrison with an esoteric, poetic approach to ensemble writing that encourages highly individual voicings and interpretations. In a way, he has taken up Coltrane's mantle of getting players gigs and deals, and keeping them philosophically strong and focused. His workshops are legendary, more like mystical-philosophical pow-wows than practice sessions.

For a broad overview of the entire loft scene, the *Wildflowers* series is essential. Originally spread across five LPs and now available as a triple CD box set, it documents the Wildflowers festival staged by Sam and Bea Rivers in their Studio Rivbea loft in May 1976. As an aural snapshot of a once in a lifetime moment in jazz, it's unbeatable. It catches first-generation players like Jimmy Lyons, Sunny Murray, Marion Brown, Anthony Braxton and Roscoe Mitchell rubbing shoulders with representatives of the new breed such as Julius Hemphill, Oliver Lake, David S Ware and David Murray. Murray's subsequent trajectory has been unpredictable. He started off as a riproaring Ayler acolyte but subsequently drifted into more traditional areas where, arguably, he found

his own unique voice. On *Wildflowers* he leads a quartet through a ghostly dirge, tracing hollow, groaning circles around Olu Dara's (Donald) Ayler-esque trumpet. David S Ware makes an early showing as part of drummer Andrew Cyrille's Maono, but here Ware is really toeing the line, giving few hints of the huge impact he would make later on.

If it's impact you're after, then Arthur Doyle's your man – at least if you're still talking late 1970s. *Alabama Feeling* was originally released on Charles Tyler's tiny Ak-Ba label. It's a terrifying mess, a blast of proto-No Wave noise that is at once purgatorial and punk as all hell. The same goes for *Plays More*. Another one-sided disc, recorded on a walkman in Doyle's front room, it consists of two tracks, "Hao", a Doyle original, and a deranged cover of "Nature Boy" – Doyle abandons his horn completely and starts shrieking and babbling in tongues, stomping up and down the room. The lo-fi sound lends this one the shamanic, ritualistic air of an urban field recording.

Charles Gayle
Homeless
Silkheart CD 1988
Booker T Trio
Go Tell It On The Mountain
Silkheart CD 1988
Sonny Simmons Quartet
Judgment Day
CIMP CD 1996

Active since the 1960s, tenorist Charles Gayle was homeless in New York for a long spell, but recent years have seen him flourish, and *Homeless* is the perfect introduction to his wonderfully monomaniacal soundworld. He hits at 100 miles per hour and accelerates from there, overloading the senses with so much movement and noise that everything seems to still and freeze. On *Homeless*, he is joined by bassist Sirone and drummer Dave Pleasant. But Gayle isn't really about group interaction: rather, he seems immersed in total war. On almost all his records, he leaves the other musicians to puzzle over his tyretracks while he ascends, solitary, through the rapture. Gayle's playing has its lyrical side: he shares the Fire

Musicians' penchant for spirituals and church music. His beautiful reading of "Lift Every Voice" effectively puts to rest the one-dimensional caricature of this music being all bluster and no heart.

However, the most charismatic of the newer players is New York tenorist Booker T Williams. Although active since the 1970s, his discography is shockingly scrappy: this trio set with bassist Saheb Sarbib and drummer Andrew Cyrille, and one other. Williams is unwilling to play in venues where people smoke and drink, and tales abound of a strange entourage of fans and religious oddballs (including, at one point, the Reverend Frank Wright) that regularly travel with him. Most of *Go Tell It On The Mountain* is given over to traditional, sanctified folk songs like "What A Friend We Have In Jesus". But unlike Gayle, Booker T is more measured and less fevered in his approach, less Ayler and more Coltrane, his every note heavily weighted and full of breath.

Simmons is yet another marginalised figure in the Fire Music pantheon, even though he was in there at its birth: in 1963 he appeared on *Illumination* alongside Jimmy Garrison and Elvin Jones, and in 1966 he recorded two sessions for ESP, *Staying On The Watch* and *Music Of The Spheres*. During the last 30 years he has disappeared off the radar for long periods, but in the early 1990s he was briefly signed to Qwest/Reprise, for whom he taped two records of undiminished power (*Ancient Ritual* and *American Jungle*). On *Judgment Day*, drummer Charles Moffett pushes the music forward with the same kind of kinetic motor that he used to drive Ornette Coleman's mid-1960s trio. Despite being in poor health at the time, on the title track and "The Call For Old Sirus" Simmons blows like a man possessed – by apocalyptic visions and a raging, indignant anger, as is made transparent in the unequivocal sleevenotes: "The world will be judged by the Sound of Holy Music, which we here represent," Simmons writes, before adding: "It has been said, among some musicians, I can't play the tenor saxophone. So I am settling the score to silence these egotistical bastards for all time."

David S Ware
Third Ear Recitation
DIW CD 1993
Godspelized
DIW CD 1996
Surrendered
Columbia CD 2000
William Parker/In Order To Survive
The Peach Orchard
AUM Fidelity 2 x CD 1998

David S Ware is the undisputed modern heavyweight champion, a tenor player with a tone of honeyed depth. His various quartets have singlehandedly raised the legacy of John Coltrane and Albert Ayler to another plane. Ware's world is underpinned by a complex mytho-philosophical system, claiming to draw inspiration from "the eternal storehouse of music", a place where all rhythm and harmony is happening at once. That is why, he once explained, his music is multi-rhythmic – he is trying to replicate a music that he has so far only glimpsed in visions.

It doesn't hurt that Ware's quartet includes Matthew Shipp and William Parker, two contemporary masters of their respective instruments. Parker talks of the double bass as containing within it every other stringed instrument, from the sarangi to the violin, and he has developed corresponding techniques to free its many voices. His arco work is particularly heartbreaking, although he is often best in Ware's group when he is picking out a big strutting beat. Often assuming an anchoring role in Ware's music, Shipp's playing is much more melodically epic than, say, Cecil Taylor, with whom he is inevitably compared.

Third Ear Recitation is a great place to start with the quartet, as it showcases most of Ware's exploratory methods. He loves to demolish schmaltzy old standards, such as "Autumn Leaves" here, breaking on through to the elemental folk truths deep inside them. Drummer Whit Dickey keeps everything flying, often driving tracks in double time, way ahead of the rest of the group. *Godspelized* is his most Ayler-esque set to date, the title track especially, where Ware blows a reverent spiritual built on the lick from Ayler's "Angels", while the rest of the group, this time with Susie Ibarra on drums, dance like dervishes around him.

In 1998 Ware signed to Columbia, and for a moment it felt like Fire Music had come full circle, back on a major and once again making inroads into the popular consciousness, thanks in no small part to the evangelical work of the likes of Sonic Youth, who invited Ware to open for them at a show in New York. Ware's first Columbia album, *Surrendered*, is his boldest to date. He has cut out some of the endless trilling and frilly punctuation of old and nailed a set of roaring uptempo pounders, most successfully in "Glorified Calypso", a tumbling mix of world rhythms and possessed testifying. He has inevitably attracted snipers from the many fanboys who interpret the fact that he is no longer making albums full of paint-peeling squall as a compromised stance towards melody. But such a reaction not only reduces the musicians to caricatures, it misses the point entirely. Fire Music has always been about urgent communication, getting the message across. It is an open music, not a hermetic artform that speaks in harsh, indecipherable code solely to the initiated.

In any event, the deal with Columbia lasted for just two albums, and Ware signed to AUM Fidelity, which is where William Parker's *The Peach Orchard* comes in. Anyone intent on setting off into these seemingly perilous waters is recommended to start here. The quartet of Parker, drummer Susie Ibarra, altoist Rob Brown and pianist Cooper-Moore play with such a burning sense of mystery and wonder, as if they are creeping through the twilight in search of adventure, that it can't fail to sear you. And once you've been burned, there is no going back.

Sun Ra

by John Szwed

Sun Ra – Herman Blount, Le Sony'r Ra, philosopher, poet, self-proclaimed space alien, free jazz innovator, traditionalist, prophet, cosmic joker, messenger for the Creator – had many names and many callings. But he had even more records – well over 100 – and it is by his records that we shall ultimately know him. And this is as it should be, for records held special importance for Sun Ra. He spent hundreds of hours listening alone – the only way to hear them, he said – two people of different spirits listening to the same record can cause problems for the music. And he was a pioneer in creating his own record company, controlling every aspect of production, becoming a sonic auteur.

By the time his El Saturn label output began to appear in the 1950s, commercial record companies had already perfected a style which assured that the recording process itself would be invisible, the machinery of phonography being used as a picture window through which an illusion was created of 'being there' with the musicians. But Sun Ra consistently violated this convention by recording live at strange sites, using feedback, distortion, high delay or reverb, unusual microphone placement, abrupt fades or edits, and any number of other effects, noises or accidents which called attention to the recording process. (On some records you can hear a phone ringing, or someone walking near the microphone.) It was a rough style of production, an anti-style, which anticipated both free jazz and punk production to come, but also reflected a shrewd sense of how one could shape album-sized works out of hours of rehearsal recordings and at the same time make the studio a part of the performance.

The process by which Saturn records came into existence and were distributed was as mysterious as the rest of Sonny's life. The albums were assembled and sequenced by an obscure syntax, often mixing together recordings done on different occasions, at rehearsals and in the studio, then labelling them all with the same date, or with the wrong personnel, so that The Arkestra might appear to be playing in widely divergent styles on a single occasion; 45 rpm singles of a given composition might or might not contain the version which appeared on the LPs with no mention that they had been issued before. Many of the records had hand-drawn covers and labels, the wrong titles or no titles at all. Sometimes they were labelled as being in "Solar High Fidelity" or were registered with "Interplanetary BMI". Sonny called the Saturn releases his "avant garde" records: "Whatever I think people are not going to listen to, I've always recorded it."

There was no conventional advertising for El Saturn records, no promotional copies for review, and no distribution channels except mail order, hand delivery to a few record shops, and sales from the bandstand after performances. Orders sent to the El Saturn address might or might not get a response, and when a record came, it might be a different one than ordered. For years it was only possible to locate Sun Ra's recordings with the help of those wired into the record underground. Only in the 1990s did the vaults of Saturn finally begin to open.

Sun Ra
The Singles
Evidence 2 x CD 1996

The Singles are among the rarest of the Sun Ra oeuvre, ranging from his mid-1950s doo-wop experiments to bizarre R&B, such as singer Yochannan's "The Sun One" – a blasting riff tune with cosmological overtones, wherein the Sun King emerges as a mack man – and "Message To Earthman", a short account of an alien invasion set against swirling horns. There are alternate takes from Saturn LPs, chanted poems like "The Bridge" and some 1982 parlour piano. Since *The Singles* is organised chronologically, this would seem to be the place for the beginner to start, but Sun Ra's music follows no easy progression, and many later recordings sound as if they should be the earliest. This set purports to contain all known Saturn singles by Sun Ra (some of which exist in only one copy), but who can be sure?

Sun Ra And His Arkestra
Sun Song
Delmark CD 1991
(orig. Transition LP 1957)

This, the first Sun Ra LP (originally titled *Jazz By Sun Ra*), was recorded in Chicago by the legendary African American producer Tom Wilson, who in 1956 was busy organising the first recordings of Cecil Taylor, John Coltrane and Sun Ra as leaders, and later went on to produce Frank Zappa, Nico, The Velvet Underground and Bob Dylan's first electric group.

Though nothing here is especially startling, *Sun Song* gives us a hint of what earlier Ra groups must have sounded like, especially Ellingtonian pieces like "New Horizons", the theme song for Ra's first Chicago big band. "Fall Off The Log" in turn recalls a chorus-line dance step from his days as pianist with Fletcher Henderson's group at the Club DeLisa. But other compositions offer subtle clues of things to come: "Possession", for instance. This was a waltz written by British composer Harry Revel for *Perfume Set To Music*, a suite of tunes originally arranged and recorded by Les Baxter with lush string writing, harp, oboe, theremin and Novachord organ. Though Sun Ra's version is straightforward, the choice itself tells us something about his listening habits at the time and his vision of the future.

Le Sun Ra And His Arkestra
Super-Sonic Jazz
Evidence CD 1992
(orig. Saturn LP 1957)

Super-Sonic Jazz is the first LP on Saturn, Sun Ra's own label. These 1956 recordings included "India" and the two-part "Sunology (A Suite Of Philosophical Sounds)". "India" was built on a single chord, and was laden with percussion; "Sunology" was rightly described by Sonny as "a different kind of blues". Chicago was a source of inspiration for many compositions here, as some of the titles reflect, though the connection was never simple. "El Is The Sound Of Joy", for instance, honours the Canaanite God, but also signifies on Fletcher Henderson's 1934 recording, "Hotter Than 'Ell", as well as being a praise song for the elevated trains which connect all of Chicago and ran past Sun Ra's apartment. This was part of a "Chicago Suite", which also included "Springtime In Chicago" and "Street Named Hell". On "Springtime" Sonny plays a piano so out of tune it sounds 'prepared', altered for percussive effect. And the electronic delay used on this cut was so extreme that it reverberates like a King Tubby dub.

Most of these pieces have some family resemblance to the music of the era – clipped post-bop touches, funk gestures, Latin affectations. But acoustic and electric piano alternating within the same solo, the presence of an electric bass, otherwise evocative melodies decentred by unexpected accents and intervals, swing rhythms punched up with heavy timpani accents – none of these quite fit the profiles of either swing or bebop, and manage to make both styles seem slightly strange.

Sun Ra And The Arkestra
Sound Of Joy
Delmark CD 1994, rec. 1957
(orig. Delmark LP 1968)

Supposed to be *Jazz By Sun Ra Vol 2* on Transition, *Sound Of Joy* did not appear until 1968, retitled. With two baritone saxophones and bass and timpani now in the group, "Two Tones", "Ankh" and "Reflections In Blue" have an enormous bottom sound. "Overtones Of China" extends the orientalism of some earlier jazz with gongs and woodblocks, asymmetrical themes and the feel of shifting time; and two pieces ("Paradise" and "Planet Earth") are given idiosyncratic Latin rhythms. Running through all of them are unusually conceived background riffs, multi-thematic melodies (each having different rhythms and different keys), timpani solos and surprising counter-melodies.

Though this sequence of tunes approximates what Sun Ra was playing at clubs, it must have seemed unusual at the time, evoking its sources but never surrendering to them. It was music which could drift past without notice, which could even be danced to, but nonetheless was uneasy listening. Nothing was quite what it seemed.

Sun Ra And His Arkestra
Jazz In Silhouette
Evidence CD 1991
(orig. Saturn LP 1958)

Silhouette was a major statement by The Arkestra, helped by the addition of Hobart Dotson, an exceptional trumpet player who later worked with Lionel Hampton and Charles Mingus. Dotson's composition "Enlightenment", the first of The Arkestra's 'space marches', became a nightly staple for the next 36 years, a vehicle on which the whole group stood or

marched or sang in unison. It loped along like some cartoon animal theme, but quickly transformed itself by turns into a hard bop anthem and a rhapsodic theme cut by cha-cha, march and 4/4 swing rhythms, all of it accomplished without the melody repeating itself. "Ancient Aiethopia" calls up the spirit of Ellington's programmatic 'African' themes like "Pyramid" or "Melenik". But what The Arkestra achieved on this piece was unprecedented in jazz (though Ravel's *Bolero* might be claimed as a distant relative): by means of the simplest of structures (a single chord and a crisp but subtly shifting 'Latin tinge' rhythm) The Arkestra is set free from the conventions of the pop song and its grip on the swing era, but also liberated from the beboppers' appropriation. Once the ensemble states the melody, two flutes improvise collectively; a poised Dotson solo takes full advantage of the harmonic freedom which a few years later would be called modality; Sun Ra plays with the bass tones of the piano, ringing out rhythmically against the drums; musicians blow through mouthpieces without their horns; and two singers intone words so softly and independently that their parts cancel each other out. But improvised and open as "Aiethopia" is, there is an inexorable sense of direction, a destiny about the piece. And as with all of Sun Ra's work, pieces as prophetic as these coexist on the same record with slightly outré two-beat compositions like "Hours After". The cover proclaims that "This is the sound of silhouettes, images and forecasts of tomorrow disguised as jazz", and who could deny it?

Sun Ra And His Solar Arkestra
Secrets Of The Sun
Atavistic Unheard Music Series CD 2008
(orig. Saturn LP 1962)

In the early 1960s The Arkestra lifted off from their experimental test pad in Chicago on a mission to relocate to New York. Gaining unlimited free access to a rehearsal space known as the Choreographer's Workshop allowed the group to progress and push forward Ra's new, bolder music that, although still steeped in bebop, was slowly edging towards something completely new. *Secrets Of The Sun* was one of the first transmissions from the Big Apple: the opening "Friendly Galaxy" is unusual in that Ronnie Boykins's bass and Tommy Hunter's drum rhythms are more of a futuristic Techno lope than anything to do with jazz. This backing track is further fleshed out by Ra's erratic piano groove and Calvin Newborn's free electric guitar contortions, all of which gives the music an 'interstellar exotica' feel. "Solar Differentials" is even stranger, with saxophonist John Gilmore offering up muted 'space bird sounds' while the rest of the group bleed off into echoing dissonance. This mixture of experimentation and altered state modern jazz makes *Secrets Of The Sun* one of the most compelling and listenable albums in Sun Ra's fathomless discography. The spliced sliver of rocketship tape collage at the beginning of extra track "Flight To Mars" teasingly suggests that Ra was aware of Stockhausen and other electronic music pioneers, and was keen to incorporate 1960s electronica into his own equally futuristic compositions.

Sun Ra And His Myth Science Arkestra
Cosmic Tones For Mental Therapy/Art Forms Of Dimensions Tomorrow
Evidence CD 1992, rec. 1963/1961–62
(orig. Saturn LP 1967/Saturn LP 1965)

With The Arkestra now located in New York City, and recording everything they played at rehearsals (they had few public appearances for several years), *Cosmic Tones* was made in 1963. "And Otherness" is a small group study of the lower tones – bass, bass clarinet, bass trombone, baritone sax – the chamber-like quality of the piece bolstered by bassist Ronnie Boykin's richly bowed passages. On "Thither And Yon", oboe, bowed bass and drums are overwhelmed by such reverberation that it now seems to anticipate psychedelia two years before the fact. Other pieces on this record were recorded live at ten in the morning at The Tip Top Club in Brooklyn when it was possible to borrow their Hammond B-3, the organ of choice in the 1960s; but instead of using it for obvious funk purposes, Sun Ra employed it for its tonal colours.

Art Forms Of Dimensions Tomorrow was recorded earlier. "Cluster Of Galaxies" and "Solar Drums" are early experiments with the studio; rhythm exercises with such strange reverberations that the instruments' identities begin to disappear and turn the music into low budget musique concrète. On "The Outer Heavens" Sun Ra used no rhythm section at all, just a chamber group of Ra's piano and a quartet of reeds and a trumpet, each player developing his own lines with relative independence. But "Infinity Of The Universe" is nearly all rhythm section, built around a centre established by a repeating rumbling figure deep in the bass of the piano, with trumpet and bass clarinet joining only at the end. From the very first, then, the New York Saturn recordings suggested that every record would be idiosyncratic, as if they had been made by different groups.

When Angels Speak Of Love
Evidence CD 2000, rec. 1963
(orig. Saturn LP 1966)

When Sun Ra landed in New York City in the early 1960s, he began rehearsing and recording at the Choreographers' Workshop at 441 West 51st Street. Engineering these rehearsal sessions was drummer Tommy 'Bugs' Hunter, who accidentally created the famous echo effect on *When Angels Speak Of Love* by connecting the tape recorder's output back to its input. When a live microphone was plugged into the recorder's other input and adjusted accordingly, however, Hunter turned the machine into a primitive effects box that could be operated while The Arkestra were playing. It is this reverberating sound that gives *When Angels Speak* its futuristic feel – an amalgam of modern jazz, interplanetary field hollers (on the lengthy "Next Stop Mars") and early experimental and electronic composition. With molten Fire Music saxophone solos from core Arkestra members John Gilmore, Marshall Allen and Pat Patrick – together with their leader's equally outré rumbling piano explosions – the entire vibe of the recording is (literally) echoing with Ra's brave new vision of how his music should sound now – and in the future.

When Sun Comes Out
Evidence CD 1993
(orig. Saturn LP 1963)

A rehearsal recording from 1962–63, *When Sun Comes Out* appeared in blank or handwritten covers. There were still backward-looking atmospheric flute solos and bolero-like drums, and "Circle" had a wordless vocal which suggested the Duke Ellington of "Creole Love Song". But innovations were everywhere else on the record: three years after the first version, a new treatment of "We Travel The Spaceways" shows Sun Ra's piano becoming increasingly atonal, suddenly erupting into double-double time figures; on "Calling Planet Earth" Pat Patrick tests the physical limits of the baritone saxophone and strays freely from Sun Ra's persistent mining of a single tonal centre on the piano. And behind most of the pieces, breaking up the beat, unsettling the expected groove, is Clifford Jarvis, the most tempestuous and sophisticated drummer Sun Ra would ever have.

Sun Ra And His Solar Arkestra
Other Planes Of There
Evidence CD 1992, rec. 1964
(orig. Saturn LP 1966)

In 1964 Sun Ra shifted his methods once again. The title piece is a major work, and a departure from everything he had done before. At 22 minutes, it took up one whole side of an LP, and was one of the longest pieces ever recorded by a jazz group at the time. Despite being collectively improvised, it is astonishingly coherent and organic: there are 12 instruments, though very few play at the same time; soloists appear and disappear quickly; a trombone trio seems to rise from nowhere and lay a foundation for the other horns to enter. At times the piece threatens to become conventionally rhythmic in a jazz sense, but never yields to the temptation, and the drums continue to play texturally, almost melodically. Sun Ra's piano weaves through it all, linking the parts together, until at the end they all rise inevitably together.

The Magic City
Evidence CD 1993
(orig. Saturn LP 1966)

The Magic City, a direct reference to Sun Ra's terrestrial 'home town' of Birmingham, Alabama, was collectively improvised in 1965 and lacks a fixed theme as such, though individual statements and isolated tones flow together to form an incremental melody. Like many of his compositions from this period, it was sketched out with only a rough sequence of solos and a mutual understanding which came from gruelling daily rehearsals. Sun Ra gave it order by pointing to players, by signalling with numbers which referred to prepared themes and effects, and by hand gestures to direct the musicians on what to play – what composer Butch Morris would later call "conduction".

Sun Ra simultaneously plays piano and Selmer Clavioline, usually in conjunction with Ronnie Boykins's bowed bass, but also at times with Roger Blank's reverbed drums, Robert Cummings's bass clarinet or Marshall Allen's piccolo. It ebbs and flows, with duos and trios appearing and disappearing, yet always returning to Ra's quietly gyrating keyboards and Boykins's singing basslines. Almost three-quarters of the way through, saxophones begin to enter in various configurations, followed by a sudden ensemble cry, and a quiet return to Ra and Boykins. There had been other grand attempts at collective improvisation – Ornette Coleman's earlier *Free Jazz* and John Coltrane's contemporaneous *Ascension* – but none had the seamless quality of *The Magic City*; nor its secret formalism (if anything, *Magic City* is closer to Karlheinz Stockhausen's completely annotated *Zeitmasse*, composed in 1955–56). It was never played again after 1965, saxophonist John Gilmore said, because it was "unreproducible, a tapestry of sound".

The Heliocentric Worlds Of Sun Ra Vol 1
ESP-Disk CD 1992, rec. 1965

Heliocentric was the second in a series of extraordinary recordings made in 1965. The title piece, like all of the works on Ra's mid-1960s albums, builds its melody cumulatively through collective improvisation. Some might claim that "Helio-centric" lacks a melody, but they would surely recognise its motives, like the staggered entry of three trombones (which oddly suggest the "Kane" motive at the opening of *Citizen Kane*), a figure which also occurs in "Outer Nothingness" and "Of Heavenly Things". Melody or no, Sun Ra maintains interest by contrasts of register and texture, piccolo against bass, timpani, trombones and bass marimba. 'Outer Nothingness' follows a similar pattern, and might even be another take of "Heliocentric". "Other Worlds" pits Sun Ra's furiously atonal piano (sometimes played simultaneously with celeste) against the rest of The Arkestra.

Sun Ra And His Arkestra
Nothing Is
ESP-Disk CD 1992, rec. 1966

(orig. ESP-Disk LP 1970)

In May 1966 The Arkestra went on a one week tour of New York State colleges sponsored by the ESP label's Esperanto Foundation, and *Nothing Is* offers a glimpse of The Arkestra live on the road, suggesting that they were attempting to do as much as possible within a limited time on stage. Sun Ra can be heard cueing the group to what composition is coming next, moving from abstract piano openings to recognisable melodies, and compressing both "Imagination" and "Rocket Number Nine" into 1 minute and 44 seconds. It also shows that The Arkestra could improvise collectively live, even under the pressure of time.

Sun Ra And His Astro Infinity Arkestra
Strange Strings
Atavistic CD 2007

(orig. Saturn LP 1966)

For *Strange Strings*, Sun Ra insisted that The Arkestra should down horns and improvise on exotic stringed instruments instead. Although none of the ensemble had played any of these before, the exercise produced some of Ra's most astonishing and experimental music. Reinforced with flashes of 'lightning sheet' metal percussion and Thlan Aldridge's (aka

Art Jenkins) eerie space vocal, The Arkestra screeched their way through a set of echoing improvisations that force the various players to communicate with each other using a foreign creative language – seemingly without guidance from or consultation with their leader. *Strange Strings* lives up to its title, and remains one of the most curious Saturn releases.

Equally curious is the jawdropping bonus track, "Door Squeak", included on Atavistic's reissue. Sun Ra can be heard playing a door with squeaking hinges – accompanied by various zithers, hand drums and percussion. In the spirit of French musique concrète composer Pierre Henry's earlier *Variations For A Door And A Sigh* (1963), Ra plays this wooden instrument with all the excitement and thrill of discovery that he would later display with his first Minimoog synthesizer.

Atlantis
Evidence CD 1993, rec. 1967–69

(orig. Saturn LP 1969)

Recorded at Nigerian drummer Olatunji's cultural centre in New York City in 1967, "Atlantis" is a 21 minute epic, with Sun Ra on Gibson organ (a Farfisa knockoff) and Clavioline. It begins ominously with sonar beeps from the organ; then, as it develops, he rolls his hands on the keys, presses his forearm along the keyboard and plays with his hands upside down, spinning with his arms, windmilling the keys – a virtual sonic representation of the flooding of Atlantis, a great smear of a solo, Sun Ra's "Toccata And Fugue".

My Brother The Wind Volume II
Evidence CD 1999, rec. 1969–70

(orig. Saturn LP 1971)

By the late 1960s the audience for live jazz had diminished considerably. To survive (without compromise), Ra once again harnessed his music to the future and incorporated synthesized sounds into his performances and recordings. This selection of loosely structured Arkestra ensemble pieces are separated by their leader's electronic synthesizer sketches. The laidback space age bachelor pad rumba of "Somebody Else's World" (with exotic vocalising by June Tyson), and the thrilling reed exchanges on the opening "Otherness Blue" that stylishly prevent the album from just sounding like another modern jazz date. The other factor is Ra's Minimoog: these five tracks (with such cosmic titles as "The Wind Speaks" and "The Design – Cosmos II") are adventurous abstract explorations, gloriously devoid of rhythm or melody, yet not without a finely tuned sense of composition. This evolving technique would be expanded on later recordings, especially on the still to be excavated *Space Probe (A Tonal View Of Times Tomorrow Vol 1)* – a ferocious Minimoog live solo recording, released on Saturn in 1974, which is the Sun Ra equivalent of Lou Reed's *Metal Machine Music*.

Sun Ra And His Intergalactic Infinity Arkestra
Night Of The Purple Moon
Atavistic CD 2007
(orig. Thoth Intergalactic LP 1970)

Often referred to as Sun Ra's Roksichord (sic) album, this astonishing recording starts off enjoyably enough with a couple of small group Arkestra outings with John Gilmore and multi-reed player Danny Davis alternately blowing up the occasional freeform gale or demurely keeping time on a set of traps, while electric bassist Stafford James provides a minimal backbeat. The majority of the set, however, is dominated by the presence of Sun Ra's mighty Roksichord electronic keyboard (the 'c' removed from the manufacturer's original brand name for cryptic or cabbalistic reasons), which he backs up with two Minimoog synthesizers. In his solo passages he explores every musical nuance of his new toy, tweaking and pushing its dual rock organ/harpsichord sound into darkened alleyways of abstracted rhythm and fractured harmonics, veering from vaguely recognisable snippets of jazz tunes and blues dirges to gobbets of modern composition that are still forming within Ra's teeming sound cosmos.

Bonus tracks include a beautifully sparse alternate take of "Love In Outer Space", together with three home recorded examples of Sun Ra playing Wurlitzer electric keyboard, where he manages to make the instrument sound like an electrified thumb piano.

Sun Ra And His Intergalactic Solar Arkestra
Soundtrack To The Film Space Is The Place
Evidence CD 1993, rec. 1972
Sun Ra
Space Is The Place
Impulse! CD 1998
(orig. Blue Thumb LP 1973)

"Space Is The Place" is Sun Ra's signature song, an interplanetary anthem that urges his audience to break free from the petty restrictions and artistic/racial prejudices of Planet Earth and join him on his mission to discover unknown worlds. Some (but not all) of these ideas were transplanted onto the original soundtrack to the 1974 film *Space Is The Place* (available on Plexifilm DVD 2005), California-based film producer Jim Newman and director John Coney's planned 30 minute documentary on Sun Ra and The Arkestra which eventually evolved into a surrealistic trip, part low budget science fiction, part blaxploitation flick, part revisionist Biblical epic.

Flushed with spiritual success from their recent tour of Europe and Egypt, the group were keen to hone their improvisational skills, and the film provided the freedom to spread their collective creative wings and soar. Containing such solar spirituals and moon marches as "Calling Planet Earth", "Outer Spaceways Inc" and "Satellites Are Spinning", the songs on the *Space Is The Place* soundtrack (and on the subsequent live revue that went under the same title) are radically reassessed and given looser and more energetic treatments.

Originally released on Beefheart producer Bob Krasnow's Blue Thumb label in 1973, Impulse!'s *Space Is The Place* is a completely different album from the OST, with production by Alton Abrahams and Ed Michel. The highlight of the set is a 21-minute-plus version of the title song, a full-blown gospelling meltdown replete with barking horns, a winding Tyson-led chorus and some of Ra's finest Farfisa space organ squiggles.

Sun Ra And His Arkestra
Media Dreams
Art Yard 2 x CD 2008
(Saturn LP 1978)
Disco 3000
Art Yard 2 x CD
(Saturn LP 1978)

Following a similar path to the one that Miles Davis had travelled six years earlier on the revolutionary albums *On The Corner* and *Big Fun*, Sun Ra turned his attention to the new wave of dance music vibrating through the streets. Recorded in Italy as part of a European tour, *Media Dreams* scales down The Arkestra to a quartet, with Ra on various keyboards, John Gilmore on tenor saxophone and drums, drummer Luqman Ali, and new recruit Michael Ray on trumpet. Beginning with a low bass roar from Ra's synthesizer on the opening "Saturn Research", the album soon gets into its stride with a Latin feel (led by Gilmore and Ali), over which is sprayed Michael Ray's scorching trumpet, Ra's erratic keyboard clustering and Gilmore's confidently charged saxophone gusting. Elsewhere, on the less structured "Of Other Tomorrows Never Known", Ra unleashes an untamed piano solo where his full range and knowledge of the instrument is allowed to break free.

The same group (plus vocalist June Tyson) is also responsible for the even funkier freefall, *Disco 3000*. Recorded at Milan's Teatro Cilak in January 1978, the full performance is a spectacular display of the quartet's concentrated playing power. Art Yard's beautifully packaged and carefully compiled reissues of *Media Dreams* and *Disco 3000* return to the original tapes – restoring extra, previously unheard, material to the mix in order to create definitive versions of these rare recordings.

Sun Ra
Lanquidity
Evidence CD 2000
(Philly Jazz LP 1978)
Sun Ra And His Intergalactic Myth Science Solar Arkestra
Sleeping Beauty
Art Yard CD 2008
(Saturn LP 1979)

Back in Philadelphia (his operational base since 1968), Sun Ra teamed up with Tom Buchler's Philly Jazz label to create *Lanquidity*. The album was recorded at Blank Tapes studio in downtown Manhattan, and the captivating blend of modern jazz signatures and shuffling funk riffs could be described as cosmic disco. Shot through with Ra's Fender Rhodes keyboard, and electric guitar contributions from Dale Williams and the mysterious Disco Kid, The Arkestra's hypnotic big band sound became elasticated, only to snap back again in a flurry of free jazz that was tinged with traces of Philly-styled funkadelia.

Recorded a year later, *Sleeping Beauty* (aka *Door Of The Cosmos*) can be seen as a companion piece, only this time a more soulful groove pulses through its three long, drifting tracks. Complete with whispered female vocals, vibes and tinkling electric piano, there is a worldly warmth to the music that makes it feel more like a Strata-East release than one from Saturn.

Both *Lanquidity* and *Sleeping Beauty* would become especially popular with dance club DJs, a factor that brought Sun Ra's work to the attention of an entirely new audience, many of whom were hearing his music for the first time – and were astonished by what they heard. (*Edwin Pouncey*)

Modern Composition

John Cage

by Louise Gray

Born in Los Angeles in 1912, John Cage exerted a profound influence on the course of modern music, yet his ideas and writings are often held to be more interesting than the sound of his music. The son of an inventor who eventually went bankrupt, Cage took on the role of inventor-composer at a time when art, history and recording technology could intertwine with extraordinary results. He received a formal training in the 1930s under the composers Henry Cowell and Arnold Schoenberg, but was never seduced by the latter's 12 tone (or serialist) compositional methods. Instead his early works, including some of the first ever compositions for percussive ensemble, display an interest in textural inventiveness, space, and the flow of time itself.

Three meetings in the 1940s and 1950s were crucial in propelling Cage beyond 'ink and paper' composition. In 1942 he wrote his first music for choreographer Merce Cunningham, beginning a close partnership, professional and personal, that lasted until the end of his life. Between 1945–47 Cage attended classes under the Zen Buddhist writer and teacher DT Suzuki, and his involvement with Zen seemed to clear his head of the prejudices that go with the territory in the classical music establishment. Finally, in 1950, Cage met

pianist David Tudor, with whom he devised some of his most enduring and paradigm-shifting works.

As a non-militant anarchist, Cage began searching for a music which would integrate people with the sounds that surround them. He opened up his work to include tuned radios, noise, electronics, lumps of wood and stone, overlaid multiple tapes, and, most famously, the environmental sound that lies in the background of silence. He developed typically (and beautifully) loose strategies for creating new texts or pieces, allowing each work to mushroom into shape like the fungi he studied avidly. These chance (or, as Pierre Boulez termed them, aleatoric) operations, involving flipped coins, star maps, the I Ching (the Chinese Book of Changes which had been introduced to him in the early 1950s), esoteric numerology, Tarot cards and magic squares, became the basis of Cage's indeterminacy, and had a lasting impact on his working practice. Writing in his book *Experimental Music: Cage and Beyond* (originally published in 1974; second edition Cambridge University Press 1999), Michael Nyman links such chance operations to Cage's "deepening attachment to the Zen philosophy of non-involvement", while drawing a distinction with his pre-indeterminacy method of "letting the sounds be themselves". By the time of his death in 1992, aged 80, Cage was acknowledged as a composer of overarching authority and remembered as the man who had given subsequent generations the permission to continue. "Art", Cage had once written, "is a sort of experimental station in which one tries out living."

John Cage
The 25-Year Retrospective Concert
Wergo 3 x CD 1994, rec. 1958

This is a whackingly long recording, spread over three CDs, of a 1958 New York concert put together by jazz producer George Avakian in honour of Cage's 45th birthday. More to the point, it's a good collection of Cage's early works, including *First Construction In Metal* (1939) for percussion and *Six Short Inventions For Seven Instruments* (1934). The latter was a riposte to Schoenberg's 12-tone technique: Cage crams 25 notes – not 24! – into two octaves. But the recording has further significance. Bringing together compositions ranging from *Imaginary Landscape No 1* (1939), various short songs and, most memorably, the 1952 *Williams Mix* (the first piece of magnetic tape music made in the USA), the discs represent Cage's continuing search for new compositional methods. These works contain the germ of all his later work, ranging from technical aspects to the use of silence and chance operations. It is good recording which picks up both enthusiastic applause and – especially on *Williams Mix* – some vigorous dissenting noises.

Good sleevenotes, too: Cage's short *The Future Of Music: Credo*, written in 1937, is remarkably prescient of a future that would become our present, anticipating the rise of electronic synthesis, sampling and ambient sound: "I believe that the use of noise to make music will continue and increase until we reach a music produced through the aid of electrical instruments which will make available for musical purposes any and all sounds that can be heard."

Sonatas And Interludes For Prepared Piano
Naxos CD 1999

Take one grand piano, a screwdriver, several screws, bolts and nuts, a handful of pencil erasers. Open piano lid and, following the score's instructions, screw, bolt, position the above articles in stipulated places. Cage began working with prepared pianos as early as 1940 (on *Bacchanale*), and, in the following 15 years, wrote a slew of pieces for them, and, on occasion, for toy pianos as well.

The 20 *Sonatas And Interludes*, a kind of twentieth century retort to Bach's *Well Tempered Clavier*, are dated 1946–48. Influenced perhaps by Cowell and Conlon Nancarrow's alternative approaches to piano playing, Cage's metapraxis – using the piano outside the logic of a piano – was to affect subsequent generations of composers profoundly. On this excellent, budget-priced recording, performed by the Russian pianist Boris Berman, the resulting sounds are subtly managed. With the piano's natural harmonics dampened, Cage could concentrate on its rhythms. "A mysteriously lucid score" is how one writer described it. Nevertheless, this offers a fresh, zesty listening experience, with some dramatic moments in the sonatas. Arnold Schoenberg was once asked if he had had any interesting students among his American pupils at UCLA. He mentioned Cage, who had become his student in 1933. "Of course, he's not a composer," Schoenberg continued, "but he's an inventor – of genius."

Befitting the status of the *Sonatas And Interludes* as among Cage's pivotal works, there have been numerous recordings over the years, including ones made by Maro Ajemian (to whom they are dedicated) originally on Composers' Recordings Inc in 1950 and now New World (2007); Philipp Vandré (Mode 1994), Joanna MacGregor (SoundCircus 1998) and Margaret Leng Tang (Mode 2003). It is worth singling out for special mention John Tilbury's 1974 recording of Cage's *Sonatas And Interludes For Prepared Piano* released on LP in 1975 by Decca and rereleased on CD in 2006 by Explore. Being one of the most significant interpreters of avant garde music (as well as an accomplished improvisor with AMM), Tilbury brings out the percussive rhythms of Cage's pieces with dramatic effect. Completists should consider searching out two currently unavailable recordings of *Sonatas And Interludes For Prepared Piano*: Joshua Pierce's 1994 recording for Wergo and David Tudor's recordings, lamentably unavailable for years.

Music Of Changes Books I–IV
Wergo CD 1999, rec. 1988

Indeterminacy
Smithsonian Folkways 2 x CD 1992, rec. 1958

(orig. Folkways LP 1959)

Preceding the notorious 'silent' piece by one year (see below), *Music Of Changes* (1951), a piano work written for Cage's new collaborator David Tudor, constitutes the composer's first foray into full indeterminacy. Cage generated numbers by throwing three coins six times, and used the results to write the music. As a historical document, this version by Herbert Henck is invaluable, as is *Indeterminacy*, a recording from 1958 with the rather withering subtitle *New Aspects Of Form In Instrumental And Electronic Music Ninety Stories By John Cage, With Music*. Here Cage reads his own texts and Tudor plays prepared piano, amplified objects, and manipulates prerecorded tapes which Cage had produced in the electronic Studio di Fonoglia in Milan earlier the same year and which made up the original version of *Fontana Mix* (see below). The wit and humour that always accompanied the composer is evident in this series of one minute stories, which emerged from the 'lectures' Cage had then been giving for over 20 years. Hold on to the humour aspect: it's important, because for all the complexities inherent in his sometimes manifestly simple music, Cage has often been accused of elitism.

4'33"
Floating Earth CD 1991

Depending on your point of view, this composition, premiered in 1952, is either the biggest statement of musical liberation ever made, the ultimate piece of conceptual art or the biggest con ever. Either way, *4'33"* is, without contention,

Cage's greatest claim to fame/infamy in the world outside experimental music. Numerous versions exist; this one happens to be for piano (although Cage did not stipulate that instrument in the score), and 'performed' by Wayne Marshall. As the three movements of the piece require, Marshall (and piano) are silent for the requisite 4 minutes and 33 seconds. (The duration of the piece isn't entirely arbitrary: 4 minutes and 33 seconds adds up to 273 seconds, and –273 degrees Fahrenheit is absolute zero, the state at which all matter ceases to exist. A further twist: in our world, absolute zero, like total silence, is unattainable.) Towards the end of this performance, a few distant noises can be heard – proof that no studio sound can ever be as inertly still as the Harvard anechoic (echoless) chamber that supposedly provided Cage with the partial encouragement for the composition. While the piece stated a truism – that a performing silence doesn't exist, and that the ambient sounds surrounding it also constitute the event – which many found baffling, or deeply unmusical, later generations of musicians have spoken with gratitude of the permission to attempt anything that is Cage's legacy.

Iconoclastics aside, *4'33"* has its antecedents in Cage's own influences: Olivier Messiaen's pan-global harmonies, Erik Satie's furniture music, Schoenberg's serialist structures and Cowell's crashing piano techniques. The presence of Marcel Duchamp (New York's dadaist in residence after 1920, later befriended by Cage) is also never far away. The piece is perhaps the most obvious manifestation of Cage's immersion in Zen Buddhism and the I Ching: certainly the simplicity of *4'33"* opens numerous dialogues, not least its knowing repudiation of the composer's control. (Incidentally, in 1962 Cage wrote a work called *0'0"*, scored for any number of players using any sounds or instruments.) Cage's music has often been described as head music rather than ear music, meaning it's easier to think about than listen to. But maybe *4'33"* is best described as heart music. Built on the concept that nothing is repeatable (tell that to the minimalists), its deepest foundations, far away from Cage's manifest humour, are of sadness and ineffable melancholy. The title of this piece is often confused with *Silence*, the name of an anthology of Cage's writings from 1939–61.

Imaginary Landscapes
hat[now]ART CD 1996, rec. 1995

Imaginary Landscapes comprises six pieces, dating from 1939–85, and ranging in their sounds from shortwave radio to crashing thumps of gamelan-like percussion. In these proto-musique concrète works, a sense of location, structural or otherwise, is hard to fix. The *Landscapes* are nevertheless important and fascinating recordings, spanning Cage's development from early post-serialist work to fully formed indeterminacy. Although Cage was never a serialist, it took him some time to move from his own alternative structure to something altogether more fluid. If nothing else, these percussion pieces stress the paramount importance of rhythm in Cage's music.

Concert For Piano And Orchestra/Atlas Eclipticalis
Wergo CD 1993

"By the time Cage got around to writing orchestral scores, he had stopped writing scores", begin the sleevenotes, in suitably gnomic fashion, to The SEM Ensemble's digital recording of Cage's best known orchestral compositions. Under the baton of Petr Kotik, they are particularly dynamic pieces, twisting and turning through changes in pitch, volume and rhythm. The 1958 *Concert* began life as a solo piece for David Tudor, with additional musicians being added later. There is literally no score: just 63 pages to be played, in whole or in part, in any sequence. The conductor was instructed to represent a chronometer of variable speed: an example of the composer relinquishing control on a grand scale.

Atlas Eclipticalis (1961), commonly regarded as the *Concert*'s companion piece, has similar origins. Written for 86 instrumental parts to be played in whole, or in part, with any duration and with or without the inclusion of *Winter Music*, an indeterminate piece dating from 1957, it was 'written' by placing the transparent manuscript paper over star maps and logging the constellations as notes. Cage has linked *Atlas* to his Buddhist studies, although it could be pointed out that the idea of mapping a 'music of the spheres' followed a European musical tradition that began with the ancient Greeks. How does it sound? Weird and pendulous. When, a few years later, Leonard Bernstein included *Atlas* in a New York Philharmonic season, in which it was to be conducted by a slow-motion clock, it provoked mutiny among the orchestra's ranks and the public voted with their feet in a landslide stampede for the bar.

EMI Classics' 2008 release of a 1971 recording of *Concert For Piano And Orchestra*, by Ensemble Musica Negativa under conductor Rainer Riehn, is worth checking out. This CD comes with a bundle of other Cage compositions, including *Music For Amplified Toy Pianos* (wrongly listed on the sleeve as *Suite For Toy Piano*) and *Music For Carillon Nos 1–3*, recorded here by the rarely heard Gentle Fire, the live electronic group led by Hugh Davies during the early 1970s – well worth hearing, too.

Fontana Mix
hat[now]ART CD 1992

Fontana Mix (1958) again demonstrates the 'no-will of the composer' principle Cage had absorbed from his Zen studies. Dedicated to the white paintings of his friend, conceptual artist Robert Rauschenberg, the directions for *Fontana Mix* were thus: "To be prepared from the score for the production of any number of tracks of magnetic tape, or for any number of players, any kind and number of instruments." The score, such as it was, was ten sheets of transparent paper featuring various measurements and points. This version is led by flautist Eberhard Blum, who superimposes three taped parts of the mix. The effect gives one the hallucination of listening to a three-dimensional map. Not so much a transitional piece – Cage had made earlier forays into electronic and tape music – as a work which describes well the sheer density of the Cagean soundworld. It's interesting to compare this work with some of the mixed media pieces among the *Imaginary Landscapes*, and the 1960 *Cartridge Music*, scored for amplified phonograph cartridges, which, in the hands of the right performer, usually David Tudor, could describe a spectral world of unknowable noise.

Cartridge Music
Mode CD 1991, rec. 1988

Cage's *Imaginary Landscapes* variously involved the use of variable-speed phonographs, frequency tones, a giant metal coil electronically amplified by a phonograph cartridge, 12 radios, and sounds drawn from 42 LP recordings to be cut up and re-organised on magnetic tape. Arguably, *Cartridge Music* (1960) was an even more radical step. On this 1988 realisation, Cage and David Tudor attach contact microphones and phonograph cartridges to various household objects – furniture, ladders, waste baskets – and replace their needles with wire, matches, pipe cleaners, feathers and the like. By physically handling all these objects, they invent a spontaneous, indeterminate, live form of musique concrète. Notwithstanding Cage's graphic instructions to focus the performers on their task, the procedures produce mostly minuscule percussive sounds that resemble incidental activity more than music making.

Sixty-Two Mesostics Re Merce Cuningham
hat[now]ART 2 x CD 1991

"I have become interested in language without syntax," Cage said in 1971, the year he completed *Sixty-Two Mesostics*. "One of the things that separates the people of the world is not only the various cultures, but the different languages; and we see already that the development of language is graphic – anyone can understand it, regardless of where they come from. This has become necessary through travel by air. I noticed in the plane I took to San Francisco recently that it didn't say 'No Smoking'. Instead it had a picture of a cigarette with an X across it … I have noticed that people are looking at these things I am doing, instead of following a line, begin jumping over a page, inventing words that I don't even know are there; and that is what I wanted to do with music – to let people hear it in their own way."

Cage's interest in non-syntactical language manifests itself in his mesostics, a method of 'writing through' a pre-existing text. Constructed like a horizontal acrostic, the mesostics follow a vertical rule, only one which runs down the middle as opposed to along the edge. For instance, the opening mesostic of *Writing For The Fourth Time Through Finnegans Wake* picks James Joyce's first name in its vertically arranged clusters of letters.

Cage wrote hundreds of the things, and this CD features Eberhard Blum 'reciting' 62 that spell out the name of Merce Cunningham. Reproduced on the sleeve in varying typefaces, they often look as wonderful as Cage's graphic scores. Usually unintelligible to listeners without the requisite code-breaking apparatus, here they seem to follow a rhythm all their own, becoming a series of richly dense 'poems'.

Roaratorio
Wergo 2 x CD or Mode 2 x CD 1992, rec. 1979

Contrary to expectation, much of Cage's vocal music is delicate and exploratory. *Roaratorio: An Irish Circus On Finnegans Wake* (1979) is Cage's playful concession to a form at the heart of the traditional music canon. Scored for voice (here, Cage's own) and a small ensemble of traditional Irish musicians (including singer Joe Heaney, Uilleann piper Seamus Ennis and flute player Matt Molloy); sounds include snatches of Irish jigs and a tape montage of horses neighing, street noises and crashes. Its 2293 sounds were located in the score with the help of the I Ching. Its text is presented as mesostics. Cage himself sings in a fragile, surprisingly high, yet lulling voice.

Ryoanji
hat[now]ART CD 1996, rec. 1995

A Zen-dedicated piece had been in the pipeline ever since Cage became involved with Buddhism. Begun in 1983, this piece refers back to a visit, made in 1962, to the Zen sand and rock garden, Ryoan-Ji (Peaceful Dragon) in Kyoto. Based on a series of drawings, aspects of which were then subjected to a random number sequence, this is the result. For a small ensemble, dominated here by Eberhard Blum's flute and John Patrick Thomas's voice, it is a sparse, elegant and inevitably meditative work.

The Seasons
ECM New Series 2000, rec. 1997

Led by a performance of *The Seasons*, an orchestral work that Cage had written in 1947 for a one act ballet, choreographed by Cunningham, for New York's Ballet Society, this CD, featuring the American Composers Orchestra, offers some wide-ranging musical moods. Two orchestral versions of *Seventy-Four* (1992) are also present, as are two recordings of *Suite For Toy Piano* (1948), both performed by Margaret Leng Tan; both pianists and orchestra combine on the 20 minute *Concerto For Prepared Piano And Chamber Orchestra* (1950–51).

Anyone expecting terse and atonal statements in *The Seasons* is in for a surprise: Cage uses his debut as an orchestral writer to produce a lush and expansive score, strong on harmonies and also their antitheses. Individual voices – piano, flute – are clearly audible as motifs are stated, taken up, inverted. But although *The Seasons* at first hearing can sound almost conventional (at least in a post-Stravinsky soundworld), it really isn't: chance operations are placed at its heart by opportunities to improvise, and its structure is underpinned by Cage's increasing interest in Eastern philosophies. Change and cyclical ideas are being worked out. The *Toy Piano* suite (here in both its solo and its 1963 orchestral form, the latter by Lou Harrison) is both playful and, in all the limits imposed by the octaves available, seriously inventive.

Cage Performs Cage
Mode CD 2009, rec. 1991

This is one of John Cage's very last recordings and his whispery voice, duetting with Yvar Mikhashoff, on *Empty Words* (1973–74) betrays a fragility that his music has often embraced. Recorded at Buffalo State University, this spoken word piece is performed by Cage himself, and was recorded one year before his death. Very much a work where the two vocalists bounce off each other in their soundings, it is also, as critic Dan Warburton has noted, a "musical affair … Cage singing more than speaking, stringing together his disjointed conso-

nants into a kind of ultraminimal folk song from some hitherto undiscovered country."

Also there is a very different piece – *One*[7] (1991), here performed for solo voice, recorded live by Cage. Written in a flexible time bracket, the performer has the freedom to feature a number of sounds of his or her own choosing. Pianist Mikhashoff, the dedicatee of *Europera 5*, is also present to deliver *Music For Piano* (1952–56), a work of great delicacy, with little sonic drops of piano sounding and fading away.

Various
A Chance Operation – The John Cage Tribute
Koch International Classics 2 x CD 1993

In which a whole bunch of individuals and ensembles come together to perform John Cage works or do pieces inspired by him. Released after Cage's death, Koch's double album is a wonderful celebration of Cage's art, and its ethos is characterised by the permissibility that emanates from the composer's example. Michael Fine, Koch's vice president at the time, was a former administrator of Merce Cunningham's studio, and well positioned to bring off such a tribute. In his sleevenotes, Fine writes that Koch handed all the artists contributing to the album a 'blank cheque' – they could do what they wanted. The list of musicians involved in *A Chance Operation* is akin to a roll-call of the international avant garde: The Kronos Quartet, Takehisa Kosugi, John Cale, Christian Wolff, Yoko Ono, Ryuichi Sakamoto, David Tudor, Robert Ashley, Meredith Monk and James Tenney are all present and correct in their admiration of things Cagean. So too is Laurie Anderson, whose *Cunningham Stories* sets to her typically atmospheric soundscapes texts that Cage had spoken during performances of Merce Cunningham's dance *How To Pass, Kick, Fall And Run* in the late 1960s. Frank Zappa delivers a version of *4'33"* more restless than that of Wayne Marshall, and the set concludes with just over a minute's worth of ambient noise recorded outside Cage's former apartment in New York City. Cars hoot and brake, voices murmur, there's a near-constant shimmer of sound. It is a very Cagean tribute.

Morton Feldman

by Philip Clark

As dogs resemble their owners, composers are supposed to look and behave like their music: not so the larger than life Morton Feldman. His pungent personality and guttural Brooklyn accent positively bounced off the walls. He dressed shambolically and moved awkwardly, yet he loved the rapid and ever changing pace of New York life. By contrast, his music turns up the quiet, as impulsive patterns and hushed harmonies gently lap to and fro over the long durations of his pieces. Feldman could move easily between quiet, intense environments such as art galleries or Zen gardens, and noisy, acrid burger joints. He was known for his razor sharp, ego-deflating wit, and even had a reputation among certain contemporaries for bloody-mindedness and arrogance. Yet Feldman engendered tremendous loyalty and affection from his colleagues, who included musicians, painters, poets and filmmakers like Jackson Pollock, John Cage, Earle Brown, Frank O'Hara and Philip Guston. And behind the thick glasses and mass of greasy hair was the mind of a sensitive aesthete who produced some of the most delicate, visionary sounds in twentieth century music.

Feldman simply heard things differently. Just like Beethoven in the early nineteenth century and Stravinsky in the early twentieth century, Feldman unpicked the very fabric of sound and discovered new subclauses in musical language. After Stravinsky's *Rite Of Spring* (1913), composers had to work with altered notions of rhythm, or write themselves into obscurity. Likewise, Feldman's contribution has been to concentrate the mind on soft sounds and the demands of long-duration listening, where there's a blurring of the edges between melody and harmony, and the subtlest shift in orchestration feels like a gargantuan musical statement. Feldman discovered that his pared-down sound needed ever longer time spans to work itself out. "Up to an hour you think about form, but after an hour and a half it's scale," he said.

Born in 1926 in New York, Feldman acknowledged his childhood piano teacher Madame Press for teaching him to appreciate what constituted a "beautiful sound". But his later composition lessons with serialists Wallingford Riegger and Stefan Wolpe were often stormy. In 1950 Feldman went to hear a performance of Webern's *Symphony Op 21* by The New York Philharmonic, and met John Cage when they both fled the Rachmaninov piece that followed. Cage's methods encouraged Feldman to reject systems and write instinctively; this valuable lesson made Cage the most important teacher he never had. Even when composing his extended late pieces, Feldman would finish a page, flip his pad over and not look at it again. Once his shackle to tradition was loosened by Cage's homebaked approach to the act of creation, Feldman's works became exercises in streams of consciousness.

Through Cage, Feldman plugged into a wider milieu encompassing avant garde artists, writers and the musical circle now known as the New York School. The abstract expressionist paintings of Mark Rothko, Philip Guston and Robert Rauschenberg all had a tremendous impact on his music. He found their work refreshingly free from signification, and believed it grew directly from a tactile relationship to the medium. This experience further divorced him from musical conventions. Instead, Feldman concerned himself with the nature of musical material, like a painter scraping or smoothing oil paint onto a canvas. Generic titles such as *Violin And Orchestra*, *Piano And String Quartet* or *Voices And Instruments* echo Mondrian's *Composition With Red And Black* and Rothko's *Red And Maroon*, and stemmed from a similar impulse. Feldman wanted to strip away layers of 'learnt' and conditioned musical expression and start with a clean sheet.

Much of Feldman's music has no point of reference outside of itself. In his early piano pieces, grace notes and disembodied chords hang off empty staves. There's no narrative development. Instead, with their hazy use of only a few colours, these musical 'objects' dangle in space like the fields of colour in Rothko's canvases. Their attraction is precisely that they express nothing extra-musical, but draw the listener in through their cool and sensuous soundworld. Later pieces like *For John Cage* and *Crippled Symmetry* continue this childlike fascination with the simplest compositional building blocks, but there are darker and more disturbing presences in such pieces as *String Quartet And Orchestra* or *For Samuel Beckett*. Feldman spoke about the melancholy in his music relating to his Jewishness and the pain of the Holocaust. Themes of death and claustrophobia became increasingly important, as they had with Mahler and Schoenberg before him.

Similar preoccupations drew Feldman to the great Irish playwright and novelist Samuel Beckett. Their collaborative works *Neither* and *Words And Music* reveal how much the two men had in common. The suffocated woe of Beckett's obsessive texts finds a seamless counterpart in Feldman's music. He poured scorn on 'professional' American composers who chose to ignore the pioneer spirits of Ives, Cowell and Varèse in order to write cod-European music. Feldman himself found a more fertile springboard in such disparate artists as Rothko, Pollock, Beckett and Franz Kline than the music of Aaron Copland, Roy Harris or Morton Gould.

Feldman's music is often described as a precursor to minimalism, but his intuitive scores are surely the antithesis of the systems-based music of Steve Reich and Philip Glass. The fascination with Feldman's music is precisely that he hovered above systems. The music is in a continual state of unpredictable regeneration – a state the composer once described as always being "on camera". Feldman had a passion for the shifting patterns that characterised oriental carpets. For him, they represented the products of a cultivated society: highly ordered but infinitely flexible. Feldman's music similarly embodied such discipline and unaffected refinement.

Morton Feldman
First Recordings: 1950s
Mode CD 1999, rec. 1950–53

This Mode set, played by pianist Philipp Vandré and Frankfurt's Turfan Ensemble, is the most comprehensive collection of Feldman's early music. The score he wrote for Hans Namuth's famous 1950 documentary film on Jackson Pollock was his 'opus 1', and demonstrates that even at this stage Feldman's music was highly disciplined. It's a valuable historical document, with the high pitched, angular music for two cellos providing a perfect counterpoint to Pollock's drawling commentary. The remainder of the CD chronicles Feldman's steep learning curve as he absorbed the ideas of new mentors like Cage and Rothko. The pieces for solo piano – including his early 1950s *Intermission* series, the *Nature Pieces* and the *Variations* (both 1951) – show how well Feldman had adapted abstract expressionist ideas to music. Static harmonies hover in the air, contrasting with the stirrings of gentle, lapping melodies. Interestingly, the two pieces for violin and piano sound less Feldmanesque and more like distant memories of Webern. Indeed, he did once admit that "my music sounds like Webern, except longer". Feldman's only electronic piece, *Intersection* (1953), is something of a dog's dinner in comparison, suggesting he did well to leave that medium to others.

Durations I–IV/Coptic Light
CPO CD 1997

A CD that compares and contrasts Feldman's earliest ensemble scores with late masterpieces. He famously told Earle Brown that his works were as good as finished once he had chosen the instrumentation. In *Durations* (1961) he transferred his graphic notation experiments to larger ensembles. Players are given a set of specific pitches which they can choose to play at their own tempo. But Feldman sets the instrumentation, while demanding that the pulse be slow and the dynamics hushed. Beyond that each performance will provoke its own quasi-improvisational feel, as the uncoordinated parts throw up coincidences of harmony and line. Under the influence of Pollock's action paintings, Feldman was aiming for a less predetermined structure.

Feldman's final orchestral score, *Coptic Light* (1985), was inspired by his love of the fastidious, interwoven patterns of early Coptic carpets. Believing that these artefacts conveyed something of the sophisticated nature of the society they came from – Egypt in the early Christian era – he went on to write one of his lushest and most celebratory scores. He liked Sibelius's comment that, unlike the piano, the orchestra doesn't have a sustain pedal. In *Coptic Light* he creates a shimmering orchestral underlay, in which sounds are allowed to breathe naturally while flowing against one another.

Rothko Chapel/Why Patterns?
New Albion CD 1992

Rothko Chapel (1971) forges a connection between Feldman's Jewish roots and his desire to write a music that stripped away layers of conditioned expressivity. The chapel in Houston, Texas contains 14 massive Mark Rothko canvases; Feldman was commissioned to write his piece while attending the opening ceremony. Rothko wanted his chapel to be a place for contemplation and meditation for all faiths, and Feldman's piece was designed to 'fill the edges' of the room, just as Rothko's clouds of colour often drift towards the edge of his canvases. The piece contrasts meditative, poised writing for solo voices and chorus with beautifully turned viola melodies, delicately accompanied by percussion and celeste. Near the end, the viola makes a direct allusion – rare for Feldman – to a quasi-Hebraic theme he wrote when he was 15. The 'intrusion' of a conventional melody would be shocking if it wasn't so simple and touching. Perhaps he had rediscovered the uncomplicated melody of a child through the prism of his late friend's vision.

Why Patterns? (1978) introduces an instrumental combination that Feldman would return to in later works: flute, piano and glockenspiel. He wanted the piano's resonant bass to act as a gravitational force, anchoring the high flute and glockenspiel sounds. Rather like an update of his *Durations* pieces, most of the score has the different instruments moving independently, requiring the players to listen closely to one another to achieve the most sensitive interweaving of the three instrumental colours. California EAR Unit get straight to the heart of this problematic score. The 'patterns' of the title again refer to Feldman's fixation with oriental carpet designs.

Piano And Orchestra/Flute And Orchestra/Oboe And Orchestra/Cello And Orchestra
CPO 2 x CD 2000

The sheer length of Feldman's pieces makes collecting CDs of his music an expensive business. Here's a budget alternative: two CDs for the price of one, featuring excellent performances, directed by German conductor and Feldman champion Hans Zender, of four imposing orchestral scores from the 1970s. Feldman's dislike of polemic meant he was never going to lapse into the conventional concerto format, where soloist and orchestra traditionally struggle for supremacy. Instead he either queries the distinction between background and foreground, or he arranges matters so that soloist and orchestra show mutual respect for one another's material, sharing ideas and gestures.

Cello And Orchestra (1972) and Flute And Orchestra (1977–78) definitely fall into the latter category. The cello piece has an ecstatically charged solo part pitched at the top of the instrument's range, and it's given a glowing cantabile performance here by the legendary Siegfried Palm. Piano And Orchestra (1975) is an unusually austere and schizophrenic piece for Feldman. The calm is disturbed by a rambunctious choir of oboes and the score even includes chords marked 'fff' (that is, to be played very loud) – an incredibly rare event in Feldman's late music. The performance – with Roger Woodward – appears again on another mid-price CD on Col Legno, coupled with Coptic Light.

Three Voices
Col Legno CD 2006
Only: Works For Voices And Instruments
New Albion CD 1996

Feldman wrote Three Voices for vocalist and composer Joan La Barbara in 1982, using (rather than 'setting') a text that poet Frank O'Hara had dedicated to him. The score calls for two giant loudspeakers, representing the tombstones of O'Hara and Philip Guston, to project prerecorded layers of the piece along with the live vocalist. Thus he established "an exchange of the live voice with the dead ones". In the opening sections, Feldman uses sounds abstracted from O'Hara's poem as pure 'objects' before adding sections of the actual text. He memorably paints the whirling motion of falling snow, an image from the poem, as delicately tumbling chromatic figures of increasingly rhythmic complexity. Feldman confessed that he himself was surprised by the "sensuous, if not 'gorgeous', sound of most of it. I never expected it would go that way." La Barbara's version has been released by New Albion, but Marianne Schuppe's more recent performance on Col Legno is more determinately anti-ambient, as she makes Feldman's notes dissolve into seemingly infinite permuta-

tions of generating cells. For a piece concerned with death, the sense of perpetual rebirth is curiously touching.

If Three Voices creates an instrumental ensemble from vocals, then La Barbara sets out to explore the kernel of this idea in Only, her recital of Feldman vocal works on New Albion. As she explains in her sleevenote, the meshing of close intervallic tunings of the three lines in Voices And Cello (1973) predates the soundworld of Three Voices, while the very early For Franz Kline (1962) is an attempt to transform his painterly textures into sound. However, the most immediately striking piece is Pianos And Voices (1972), for five pianos (one doubling on celeste) and as many voices. The five keyboard parts allow Feldman to build harmonies and textures of extraordinary sonority out of which pure vocal tones can flow.

Complete Music For Violin And Piano: For John Cage/ Piece For Violin And Piano/Projection 4/Extensions 1/Vertical Thoughts 2/Spring Of Chosroes
Mode 2 x CD 2000
Piano And String Quartet
Elektra Nonesuch CD 1993

Though Feldman admired Edgard Varèse, unlike the older composer he retained a natural affinity with string instruments. If the viola encouraged his most lyrical and nostalgic side, the string writing in his orchestral works often acts as a harmonic pivot around which everything else spirals. For John Cage (1982) is his most idiomatic string composition, in which the piano's well-tempered tuning system clashes with the more malleable sliding tones of the violin. It is another example of Feldman entering into a tactile dialogue with his medium, creating an unstable microtonal haze by severely restricting his palette to the notes C-A-G-E, which waft in and out of focus and imperceptibly expand outwards to chromatic intervals of increasing richness. The psychology of Feldman's pieces became increasingly complex in the 1980s, and For John Cage is at once elusive and intriguing. The tremendous composure of Marc Sabat and Stephen Clarke's performance reveals a deep understanding of the anti-systematic nature of Feldman's organising strategies.

Highly inventive and understated string writing is also a feature of *Piano And String Quartet* (1985), performed with great refinement by its dedicatees, pianist Aki Takahashi and The Kronos Quartet. The strings hold sustained chords which occasionally resolve into unisons, while the pianist concentrates on exotic arpeggiated chords. This subtle tension underpins the piece for nearly 80 minutes as lopsided canons, derived from a fragmentary motif in the cello, float into and out of the texture. The pianist holds down the sustain pedal throughout, and the only variation in the string texture are pizzicatos which appear after about 50 minutes.

Crippled Symmetry
Bridge 2 x CD 1999
For Philip Guston
Wergo 4 x CD 2008

Crippled Symmetry (1983) and *For Philip Guston* (1984) both develop the flute piano glockenspiel ensemble first introduced in *Why Patterns?* In *Crippled Symmetry*, Feldman has each player double on another instrument – the flautist and pianist also play bass flute and celeste, while the percussionist doubles on glockenspiel and vibraphone. The result is a mellower ensemble, with a greater variety of tone colours, which Feldman fully indulges over a 90 minute span. If *Why Patterns?* was about generating interlinking musical shapes, then *Crippled Symmetry* builds similar patterns only to subtly deconstruct ('cripple') them. Rather like *For John Cage*, Feldman lets the instruments themselves dictate the parameters of the composition process. He started by considering how long a flautist could physically sustain a note, contrasting the long durations with the staccato, percussive quality of the flute's high range. He experimented with colouring the glockenspiel with the tinkling quality of the celeste, while wondering how the mellifluous quality of the vibraphone might interact with the flute. *Crippled Symmetry* is one of Feldman's most mesmerising pieces, played here by the highly authoritative California EAR Unit.

Having wrapped up a 90 minute piece for an unconventional instrumental grouping, most composers would be desperate to move on to something else. Not so Feldman. *For Philip Guston* is four hours long, and adds marimba and tubular bells to the percussion battery. Feldman insisted that the increasing length of his works was necessary to support the pared-down nature of his material. He famously said, "I need at least 45 minutes of a work before I can begin to know what it is about". Elsewhere he elaborated, in his typically graceful and enigmatic prose style: "It seems that scale is not given to us in Western culture, but must be arrived at individually in our own work in our own way. Like that small Turkish 'tile' rug, it is Rothko's scale that removes any argument over the proportions of one area to another … The sum of the parts does not equal the whole; rather, scale is discovered … It is not form that floats the painting, but Rothko's finding that particular scale suspends all proportions in equilibrium."

The similar thought processes at play in the tiny melodies and jingling sounds of *Crippled Symmetry* and *For Philip Guston* might seem naive or insignificant over a short timespan. Listeners need time to live with its slow tempos and carefully considered timbres, so they can gauge how it evolves into an overarching 'statement'. In an audio clip on the enhanced CD accompanying this set, Feldman describes how he's upset that postmodernists think about art only in terms of style and not content or 'facility'. He then mournfully describes how he fell out with Guston: "He asked me what I thought of his canvas. I asked him, 'Let me look for another minute', and our friendship was over. We fell out over an issue of style." *For Philip Guston* tackles these issues through the ebullient confidence of Feldman's own language. It had become so personal and distilled that mere issues of style were rendered impotent. The trio of Julia Breuer (flute), Matthias Engler (vibraphone, marimba) and Elmar Schrammel (piano, celeste) create a balmy default tone. Wergo's fastidious miking creates the illusion of a single voice, as flute and glockenspiel overtones entwine, while also having proper definition. Perfection.

String Quartet No 2
hat(now)ART 4 x CD 2001
String Quartet No 2
Mode 5 x CD 2002

The big one – Feldman's *String Quartet No 2* (1983), is his most notorious piece. Not that many people had actually experienced it: because it lasts some six hours, record companies had baulked at the prospect, but the two versions appeared in quick succession, beginning with The Ives Ensemble in 2001. A few months later, the New York-based Flux Quartet offered another view on Mode. As composer and Feldman colleague Christian Wolff points out in his sleevenote, Feldman may well have been provocative, but he provokes with sounds that are "exquisitely beautiful" and "seductive". The Flux Quartet take this paradox and run with it gleefully. They deliver a more determined and deliberate performance than The Ives, and their slower tempo unearths a greater spectrum of detail. The difference is audible from the start, as pizzicato stabs punch above their weight, cutting through the diaphanous seesawing of the upper strings. Tremulous, dissonant outbursts rub furiously against the prevailing delicacy, and The Flux's achievement in realising these inner structure tensions over such an immense span is exemplary. Extremes of scurrying harmonies sound more like human breath than instrumental timbre, and there's a telling moment on disc four as Feldman's patterns coincide as though they're about to quote Schubert. The Flux don't overplay this moment – they just let it be.

For Bunita Marcus
MDG CD 2008
For Bunita Marcus
hat(now)ART CD 2009, rec. 1990
Aki Takahashi Plays Morton Feldman
Mode CD 1999

The piano remained central to Feldman's music, with a scattering of important works through the 1970s and 1980s, climaxing in the awesome *For Bunita Marcus* (1985), dedicated to one of his pupils.

From a barren opening, *For Bunita Marcus* builds into a dense network of quasi-canonic structures, as page after page deals with a mere three notes. This section has a joyful, dancing quality about it that slowly subsides, as Feldman reins things in and winds down the music. Achieving a Bach-like purity, the piece is profoundly affecting. Hildegard Kleeb's magical 1990 performance on hat(now)ART is one of the most intellectually discerning and meticulously beautiful Feldman recordings that ever was, and is no longer available in a fresh remastering. Her near-implausibly muted touch and an alive rhythmic bounce make for an exacting blueprint. German pianist Steffen Schleiermacher's alternative account for MDG is floatier, but more self-consciously nuanced.

Bunita Marcus herself commissioned Feldman to write a piano piece in 1986, with the stipulation it should only be ten minutes long. In the event the piece that resulted, *Palais De Mari*, came out twice that length and, like *Bass Clarinet And Percussion*, it feels like an extended piece over a short duration. As Feldman explained to the German composer Walter Zimmermann, "Turkish carpets are knit so that the finished part disappears downwards and does not remain visible, so what can be controlled visibly is transferred to the memory." *Palais De Mari* plays similar tricks with memory as musical paragraphs are wrapped around one another and material is constantly reordered and sorted. Aki Takahashi's appropriately ethereal and airy version is one of the most beautiful recordings in the Feldman catalogue. In contrast, the violent progress of the 1977 *Piano* is quite a revelation. Where some interpretations crash like Thelonious Monk into the still moments, Takahashi is more controlled and refined.

Triadic Memories
Mode CD 2004
Triadic Memories
MDG CD 2008

Triadic Memories (1981) is undoubtedly Feldman's most ambiguous and problematic piano composition. Lasting anything between 80 minutes to 2 hours, its knotty clusters and sometimes monumental piano writing appear to contradict

Feldman's demands that the dynamics should range between 'ppp' and 'ppppp' (that is, extremely quiet to practically inaudible). As the title suggests, the tiniest suggestions of earlier piano harmonies gently metamorphose into a piece with an unusually wide variety of gestures. Steffen Schleiermacher's tone, on MDG, is pinched and his progress relatively swift – he shaves 13 minutes off nearest rival Marilyn Nonken's 2004 Mode version. Nonken is recorded more intimately and, within Feldman's constraints, brings a wider range of dynamics and timbral strata. But their greatest divergence is rhythm: Nonken counts out Feldman's asymmetrical patterns with mathematical precision, while Schleiermacher floats on a carpet of supple but discernable rubato. Schleiermacher is wholly admirable, but it's Nonken who penetrates more keenly into Feldman's inscrutable patterns. Just short of two hours, the vast span of her recording allows Feldman's piece to speak as he intended. As he said, "Art is a crucial, dangerous operation we perform on ourselves. Unless we take a chance, we die in art."

Neither
Col Legno CD 2000
Words And Music
Montaigne CD 2001

Feldman's first meeting with Samuel Beckett in 1977 started badly. Blinded by the lights in the theatre, Feldman shook the Irish playwright's hand and fell off the stage. He had requested a text from Beckett, who replied that he hated opera and didn't like having his words set to music. Feldman assured him that he too had little time for opera and had no intention of tampering with one of Beckett's existing texts. Rather, he was looking for something he described as a "quintessence, something that just hovered". As it turned out, Neither was indeed described as an 'opera', and it premiered at the Rome Opera in 1977. Yet it has nothing to do with operatic convention. A lone soprano voice intones Beckett's metaphysical text over orchestral writing of intricate beauty. There's no plot or narrative, but the dialogue between 'self and unself' alluded to in Beckett's text is contained in the purely musical relationship between soprano and orchestra. Depending on your point of view, Neither is either 'anti-opera', or one of a handful of late twentieth century theatrical works that achieves a genuine fusion of intention between music and text.

Words And Music (1987) is something of an oddity in the Feldman discography. Beckett wrote the text as a play for radio in 1961 but was dissatisfied with the first production. His script includes numerous musical directions, and when the play was revived in 1986, Beckett proposed that Feldman should provide a new score. Even though the piece's demands for short, self-contained bursts of music ran against Feldman's current concern with slowly unfolding organic forms, such was his respect for the writer that he readily agreed. The transformations of Beckett's compulsive text are met by Feldman, as he put it, "half way in the sentiment. I don't write in terms of literary images, though 95 per cent, 98 per cent of the world's music is in literary images ... I took it to the quintessence of it." In doing so, Feldman also reached the quintessence of his own aesthetic. Words And Music manages – in another Feldmanesque paradox – to be both typical and untypical.

For Samuel Beckett
Kairos CD 2000

Feldman's final composition, completed a few months before his death in September 1987, feels like a fully realised version of the musical seeds he had planted in Words And Music. The orchestral writing has a lazy urgency about it, as though struggling to contain all the strands of its tightly packed material. The scorched, suffocated textures and sourer than usual harmonies are eerie, especially compared to the lush and shimmering sound of the previous year's Coptic Light. Given Feldman's distrust of 'learnt' musical expression, is it possible that he had written a late, mournful masterpiece? It seems unlikely, yet it has an undeniable twilight quality, as palpable as anything in late Schubert, Mahler or Nono. More likely, his immersion in Beckett's writing allowed Feldman to tap into more universal feelings of isolation and frustration. Because he spent his working life attempting to eliminate style and affectation, such natural human responses could be expressed in a highly personal and uncluttered form.

Roland Kluttig's performance with The New Music Chamber Orchestra Of Berlin on CPO is fantastically detailed and sonorous, but Sylvain Cambreling's Kairos version with Klangforum Wien is a more daring attempt to realise the score's deathly chill. At 54 minutes, it's closer to the composer's preferred duration of one hour, making it a Feldman interpretation of the highest order.

Musique Concrète & Early Electronic Music

by Art Lange

Imagine music made solely from the sound of trains. It's an idea straight out of dada, or Jules Verne. When Pierre Schaeffer broadcast his *Étude Aux Chemins De Fer* over French radio in October 1948 as part of a *Concert De Bruits* (*Concert Of Noises*), he caused shockwaves of disbelief, humour and outrage. Hearing it today, it sounds less daunting. It's not as if non-musical sounds hadn't been heard in European concert halls before – think of Leopold Mozart's eighteenth century *Toy Symphony*, the typewriters in Erik Satie's *Parade* (1917), the aeroplane engines heard in George Antheil's *Ballet Mécanique* (1924), not to mention Luigi Russolo's Futurist noise extravaganzas. But instead of introducing his sounds as novelty elements, Schaeffer intended his painstakingly produced tape constructions of found objects and distorted instrumental tones to be taken seriously – not as music, but as musique concrète, a radically new aesthetic of sound divorced from any literal, musical or symbolic identification. They were meant to be heard in the spirit of Gertrude Stein's prose and Kurt Schwitters's collages, as abstract art offering its own meaning and motivation.

But despite his wishes, Schaeffer's brief reconfigurations of found sound became another piece of the larger puzzle of twentieth century musical modernism and, with Schoenberg's serial procedures, Cage's indeterminacy and chance operations, and many others, eventually effected a fundamental change in our way of listening to and defining music. The ramifications of musique concrète are everywhere today, not just in electronica, dancefloor or Ambient musics, but in acoustic and digital improvisation, rock, film and television soundtracks, and even – especially – advertising. After Schaeffer, melody, supported by some system of harmonic validation, was no longer the only game in town. Focus shifted to event attached to event, based on the quality and characteristics of the sound itself, creating its own tension, flow, rhythm, shape, movement. Schaeffer may not have been a musician, but he was something more important: the inventor of a new form, a poet of radical perception.

In 1951 he established the Groupe de Musique Concrète (later changed to the Groupe de Recherches Musicales) and founded a studio that soon attracted longterm GRM collaborators like Pierre Henry, Luc Ferrari and Iannis Xenakis. It was also visited by composers like Olivier Messiaen, who arrived with his pupils – including Pierre Boulez and Karlheinz Stockhausen – and Edgard Varèse, who worked on *Déserts* there. Eventually, they all grew disenchanted with the hours of hands-on effort entailed in working with vinyl recordings and magnetic tape, and moved onto other things. Even Schaeffer gave up music for good in the 1970s, dying, disillusioned, in 1995.

Similar ideas quickly spread like wildfire, however, and studios opened in Milan (1955), Tokyo (1956), Warsaw (1957), London and Stockholm (1958), each experimenting with new and better equipment as it became available. Varèse composed his *Poème Électronique* for the Brussels World's Fair in 1958, attracting the kind of attention that established electronic music in the consciousness of the general public. In America, in 1959, the Columbia-Princeton Electronic Music Centre boasted the room-sized RCA Synthesizer, while the Bell Telephone Laboratories in New Jersey began programming their computers with musical capabilities in order to allow composers a level of precision far beyond human control. Then, in 1964, Robert Moog invented the Moog synthesizer, reducing the size of sound-generating systems and simplifying their use, thereby opening a new chapter in electronic music. But that is another story.

Since this Primer first appeared, many more recordings of vintage electronic music have come to light. Compilations of particular note are the historic five CD box set *Archives GRM* (INA 2004), which includes pieces by almost anyone who used the French facilities, including a number of previously neglected women composers; and *OHM: The Early Gurus Of Electronic Music 1948–1980* (Ellipsis Arts 2000), a highly eclectic collection which traces academic electronic music's journey into sound art and the experimental rock and pop of Brian Eno, Holger Czukay and Laurie Anderson. Sub Rosa's *Anthology Of Noise & Electronic Music* series of double CDs, which began in 2002 and has run to five volumes at the time of writing, are "A-Chronologies" that excavate historic and lost pioneering works, setting them alongside a diverse range of experimental music, electronica, avant rock and improvised sounds, in an act of sometimes wistful retrieval. The full story is still being told, but this is where it starts.

Pierre Schaeffer
L'Oeuvre Musicale
INA 3 x CD 1998

Schaeffer's complete musical output – not counting the revisions he made of several works a decade or two after the fact – takes up less time than a performance of Mahler's ninth symphony. But its historical impact may equal that of another 'miniaturist', Anton Webern. Precisely because he was not a trained musician or composer, Schaeffer was able to work with sounds under unorthodox, non-musical conditions, injecting them with philosophical ideas in the process, while developing many techniques that anticipated subsequent musical practices.

Using lathe-cut vinyl discs and tape machines, Schaeffer devised a number of procedures to alter the basic parameters of a sound beyond recognition – speeding it up or slowing it down, playing it backwards, cutting off its point of attack, extending its resonance or chopping it short, superimposing it over other sounds. In *Étude Pathétique* (1948) the quick-taped repetition of voices 'sampled' from discs anticipates the hiphop scratch mix. In the "Rigodon" movement of his *Suite Pour 14 Instruments* (1949) he subjects the recycling of Stravinsky-like neoclassical music to electronic distortion and pushes it into a postmodern future. His *L'Oiseau RAI* (1950) was conceived before Messiaen's transcriptions of bird calls. Most importantly, his methods of organisation presupposed an acceptance of abstract – that is, non-literal or symbolic – sound patterns with an emotional, and not just intellectual, response. So in the infamous *Étude Aux Chemins De Fer* (1948) he can use non-musical resources, altering pitch, regulating rhythm and creating a sound design that achieves a 'concrete', if not a musical, logic. The roughness and inelegance of the results are a tactical advantage, distancing the sounds from conventional music.

His collaboration with Pierre Henry, *Symphonie Pour Un Homme Seul* (*Symphony For A Man Alone*, 1950), is a masterful sequence of small études which paint a psychological portrait of an individual's moods and humours, drawn from recognisable and unrecognisable sound sources, using discontinuity as a tool. Working with Henry over the course of the 1950s may have suggested to him the value of a musical aesthetic, so Schaeffer's later works seem more accessible. A piece like *Étude Aux Sons Animés* (1958) now sounds perfectly natural: compact gestures, well constructed, attractive tonal qualities, and tension that builds in such an organic way that it paradoxically sounds improvised. The five-part *Études Aux Objets* (1959) reveals a similar assurance of purpose: these are no longer random experiments with unpredictable results, but tightly constructed assemblages displaying wit and drama. Schaeffer's ingenuity in sculpting the shape of sonorous materials made traditional musical training unnecessary.

Pierre Henry
Le Microphone Bien Tempéré
Doxy LP 2009 (rec. 1950–51)

Mix 04.0
Universal 4 x CD 2004

Variations Pour Une Porte Et Un Soupir/Voile D'Orphée
Harmonia Mundi CD 1994 (rec. 1963/1953)

Pierre Schaeffer's and Pierre Henry's divergent personalities set them on a collision course. The older man had settled, within a state corporation, to a lifetime's work of coolly quantifying a new alphabet of sounds. Henry, 17 years his junior, was temperamentally opposite: a visionary firebrand demanding as early as 1950 that "all music should be destroyed". The materiality of musique concrète offered modern music the chance to climb down from its intellectual remoteness to bathe in the realm of living senses and emotions: "cries, laughter, sex, death. Everything that puts us in touch with the cosmic, that is to say, with the living materiality of planets on fire …"

Using material no more or less exotic than Schaeffer, Henry is an alchemist of sonorities, with a ruthless attitude towards sound in his quest to create a new aural substance. The ultra-low fidelity of his earliest pieces, made between 1950 and 1958, lessens their impact only slightly. Previously

collected on the now deleted triple CD *Des Années 50* (Mantra), these early experiments are currently divided between a vinyl-only release and the fourth of Philips's ongoing *Mix* series of Henry's oeuvre. *Le Microphone Bien Tempéré* includes the surrealistic free association of prepared piano, voices, xylophone, thunderstorm and other sounds distorted beyond recognition in *Fantasia* (1950); and the sustained energy music, approaching Varèse's power, of the tam-tam studies (*Tam-Tam I–IV*, 1950, which Stockhausen would later borrow from for his two *Mikrophonies*). In *Micro Rouge* (1951) he extended the resonances of a piano into tones resembling organ, bells and chimes: a volatile cocktail of illusory environmental sounds in the manner of Luc Ferrari's imaginary landscapes. In its microscopic view of acoustic detail, *Dimanche Noir* (1951) anticipates the work of Hugh Davies and two generations of British improvisors. The piano repetitions in *Tabou Clairon* (1951) plough similar ground to that of Conlon Nancarrow's player pianos; the seeds of John Zorn's 'slash and stitch' montage technique appear in *Antiphonie* (1951).

The marvellous works of this period are mesmerising and prophetic, loaded with unnerving sonorities and ghostly presences – notably the "Cinquième Mouvement" from *Musique Sans Titre* (1950) and the insectoid, blustery wilderness noises of *Spirale* (1955), both collected on *Mix 04.0*. By the mid-1950s Henry began exploring long forms, at first in the cinematic Greek tragedy *Voile D'Orphée* (1953), and later in the flow and development of harshly treated voice recordings in *Haut-Voltage* (1956). *Coexistence* (1958) displays his remarkable vision intact, with a delicacy of tonal qualities and organisation, subtle relationships between sounds and events, and the first stirrings of extended ambient sound.

Henry parted company with the GRM in 1958, removed his tapes from their archive (a bone of contention to this day), and set up his own Studio Apsome at his home. A year later he was calling his work "Nouveau Réalisme Musical"; in 1962 he created a masterpiece worthy of the name. That summer, at a dilapidated Carcassonne farmhouse, Henry installed microphones around the building and surrounding landscape, with a mixing desk on the ground floor. He was particularly exercised by the squeaky hinges of an attic door, and *Variations Pour Une Porte Et Un Soupir* (*Variations For A Door And A Sigh*) is the result of hundreds of minuscule tape splices of his virtuosic manipulations of the door, from sawtoothed, buzzing groans to high-pitched explosive squeaks. The 'sigh' was a literal exhalation, plus percussive strikes on a flexible saw. Occasional offstage noises intrude: Henry blocked the stream to heighten the sound of rushing water, starved the pigs to make them squeal, rampaged after clucking chickens, recording all the while. The final mixdown was conducted in the resonant acoustic of the church of Saint-Julien-le-Pauvre in Paris in June 1963. The genius of the work lies in the enormous distance between the finished article and its prosaic source material: this is sonic alchemy reaching an expressive peak.

Various
Acousmatrix 6: Cologne-WDR – Early Electronic Music
BVHaast CD 2005
Various
Pioneers Of Electronic Music
CRI CD 1991

A dramatic opposition to Schaeffer's methods appeared in Cologne, where in 1951 the Westdeutscher Rundfunk (West German Radio) started an electronic studio with equipment – primitive by today's standards – designed to allow composers the ability to control completely all aspects of musical production. The main difference introduced at WDR was the use of serial procedures to organise the musical parameters and the source material itself. Instead of pre-existing sounds, the Germans began with 'pure' electronic tones originated by sine-wave (a tone containing no overtones) generator, a white noise (a tone containing all frequencies) generator, filters to separate the frequencies, and tape machines to capture and modify the sounds.

The studio drew in composers like Karel Goeyvaerts, Gottfried Michael Koenig, Giselher Kiebe and Karlheinz

Stockhausen, who wished to experiment with synthetic sound-generating equipment aligned with (at least at first) strict serial procedures. Interestingly, in the earliest pieces, like Herbert Eimert's two *Klangstudien* (1952) and the Eimert and Robert Beyer collaboration *Klang Im Unbegrenzten Raum* (1952), the serial methods are completely masked by the timbral and textural fabric – artificial wind sounds, echoes, percussive clicks, glissandi, tonal distortion. Goeyvaerts's intense focus on pitch selection, for example, limits his timbres to organ tones (albeit of a spacy, Sun Ra variety) and exposes his minimalist roots.

Some of these sounds and procedures seem simplistic or banal today, the editing crude and the ideas one dimensional. But their creators were working in the dark, often with equipment they knew little about, and every step was a discovery. In a few short years, they tended to lose their obsession with serialism, and instead explored imaginative alternatives based on sound production itself. Thus Henri Pousseur's *Seismogramme I + II* (1955) and Bengt Hambraeus's *Doppelrohr II* (1956) break free of pitch dependence in order to explore the manipulation of timbres; Franco Evangelisti's aggressive collision of sounds on *Incontri Di Fasci Sonore* (1957) and the playful patterns of György Ligeti's *Artikulation* (1958) set electronic music on a new course.

The CRI disc contains the first experiments of Vladimir Ussachevsky and Otto Luening, the most important figures in early American electronic music. Their approach was to manipulate tapes of live instruments, usually played by themselves. Possibly because they did not wish to obscure the musical values of the acoustic instruments, their earliest pieces, like Ussachevsky's *Sonic Contours* (1952) and Luening's *Invention In Twelve Tones* (1952), sound naive and even childlike compared to the abstract experiments of Schaeffer and Henry from the same period. However, by 1956 Ussachevsky's *Piece For Tape Recorder* resulted from a collage-like method of construction that was more dramatic and varied. The collection then fast-forwards to the late 1960s and early 1970s, when composers like Bulent Arel and Pril Smiley, working on advanced equipment with more sophisticated techniques, developed new procedures, often combining tapes of instruments with synthetic sounds in a manner that became identified as American. From here, in the hands of composers like Mario Davidovsky, such attitudes evolved in a more electroacoustic direction, using electronics to accompany live instruments.

Luciano Berio
Momenti/Thema-Omaggio A Joyce/Visage
BVHaast CD 2005

Luciano Berio (1925–2003) worked on electronic music projects in the early 1950s, and cofounded Milan's Studio de Fonologia with Bruno Maderna in 1955. *Momenti* (1960) is a rough, aggressive, frictional fantasy dedicated to speed, with electronically generated sounds stretched slowly or subjected to hyperwarp acceleration. But Berio's true love was the human voice, and both *Thema-Omaggio A Joyce* and *Visage* (1961) reduce language to its smallest components, phonemes, and adds non-verbal vocalese – moans, laughs, sighs, cries, coos – in an almost embarrassingly exhibitionist display. The homage to James Joyce (1958) uses excerpts from *Ulysses*, and Berio mirrors Joyce's own manipulation of language by transforming Cathy Berberian's voice into a chorus, or siren song, or an indefinable sound of nature. This disc includes two pieces by Berio's colleague Maderna, including his masterpiece, *Le Rire* (1962), a dramatic, improvisational manipulation of vocal, synthesized and concrète sources.

Luc Ferrari
Petite Symphonie/Strathoven/Presque Rien Avec Filles/Hétérozygote
BVHaast CD 2005
Henri Pousseur
Scambi/Trois Visages De Liège/Paraboles-Mix
BVHaast CD 2005

Originally a composition student of Arthur Honegger and Olivier Messiaen, Luc Ferrari (1929–2005) joined up with Schaeffer in 1958, and was one of the cofounders of GRM. Influenced by the freedoms espoused by John Cage, however,

Ferrari began to incorporate into his extended pieces 'real' taped sounds unblemished by musique concrète procedures. An early work like the long *Hétérozygote* (1963–64) mingles fragments of taped voices, street sounds and nature noises in an abstract, non-referential collage. Eventually Ferrari took Cage's idea of 'imaginary landscapes' literally, and sought to evoke visual imagery (or soundscapes) by integrating the realism of environmental sounds with studio electronics. In the *Petite Symphonie* (1973) he adds a synthetically engineered flute melody to the tape of wind, dogs, birds and so on, until the scenery is swarming with relentless percussive electronics. By the time of his *Presque Rien Avec Filles* (1989), the environmental tapes are edited and either sped up or slowed down, but otherwise left alone. That is, all the sounds are natural but, as in the cinema, real time is compressed into artistic time, on a scale that focuses our perception on gradual changes and small details.

Henri Pousseur (1929–2009) worked in Cologne in 1954 and Milan in 1957, and then helped establish an electronic studio in Brussels. *Scambi* was created in Milan, though it clings to the 'purist' Cologne philosophy, using serial techniques to modify the frequencies in a band of white noise. *Trois Visages De Liège* (1961), a mixture of environmental and synthetic sources, is the closest Pousseur came to Ferrari's kind of soundscape, though the 'real' sounds are not so easily recognised. In addition, Pousseur likes to paint a big picture with large gestures – manipulating sounds with spatial and contrapuntal effects, using instruments to suggest an ambience the way Bernard Herrmann did in his music for the film *Psycho*, erupting into the calm with huge Sun Ra-like organ chords, and thickening the textures to a symphonic complexity. *Paraboles-Mix* (1972) is more characteristic; Pousseur created eight separate 30 minute tapes of 'études paraboliques' (real time electronics, no tape manipulation), which may be variously mixed in live performance to bring out different details or combinations. The version heard here is a continually shifting fabric of synthetic sound, shaped via rhythmic and dynamic variables and the changing intensity of white noise effects.

François Bayle
Motion-Emotion/Les Couleurs De La Nuit
INA/Magison CD 1998 (rec. 1985)

Bernard Parmegiani
De Natura Sonorum
INA CD 2001, rec. 1975

Both François Bayle and Bernard Parmegiani were among Schaeffer's earliest and most loyal collaborators, joining GRM in the late 1950s and remaining longer than most. Each, however, devised a personal compositional strategy. In *Motion-Emotion* (1985) Bayle questions the philosophical complexities of the grey area between passive and active states of awareness. By this time, his palette of orchestral sounds, flutes and inside-piano scraping combined with electronic tones could be considered a cliché, save for the skill with which he manipulates them into alternating passages of movement and repose. The speed of his variable syntax, as well as its clarity and colour, comes from newer technology based upon musique concrète procedures. His Bartókian evocation of night sounds has an intensely tactile quality – grainy and rough, elastic and spongy – and is organised with a poise that sounds composed, not improvised.

There is a dual meaning suggested in Parmegiani's title *De Natura Sonorum* – not only the sounds of nature, but the nature of sounds. Parmegiani works like a scientist, analysing and isolating the particular effect which certain procedures derive from a sound source, and setting up the sound fields accordingly. But, with the perception of an artist, he can draw music out of that analysis. The results can be full of dreamlike ambiguity and allusion, if his sounds are heard as symbolic or referential. Often his drones are not merely drones; they are reminiscent of harmonic lines in Stravinsky's *Firebird*, or Strauss's *Also Sprach Zarathustra*, or Penderecki's *Dies Irae*. What with his saxophone inflections and resonances, the sounds of fire and water, and glittering electronic rhythms that we may relate to other experiences, Parmegiani gives his music not just life, but reason.

Rune Lindblad
Death Of The Moon: Electronic & Concrète Music 1953–60
Pogus CD 1997

Living and working in Sweden, Rune Lindblad (1923–91) was not caught in the controversy between Paris and Cologne factions, so he could borrow freely from either technology. But, except for a single concert in 1957, his work went mostly unnoticed until the 1997 release of *Death Of The Moon*. It's a major discovery: it reveals a composer expanding the available technology to express his imaginative ideas. *Party* (1953) synthesizes all the prevalent conditions of sound production – instrumental sounds, radio broadcasts, location recordings, oscillators – with common techniques like speeding up, layering, mixing tones, crosstalk, and source material secretly recorded from a concealed machine in a cocktail waiter's trolley. By way of contrast, the three *Fragments* (1955–56) drift in and out of ethnic-flavoured percussion and flutes, using tape splicing to suggest ritualistic moods and large-scale form. However it may be constructed, *Optica 1* (1959–60) gives the impression of a new manner of instrumental synthesis, one that creates its own rhythms from the melodic contour rather than the physical parameters of the sounds themselves.

James Tenney
Selected Works 1961–69
New World CD 2003

Tod Dockstader
Quatermass/Water Music
Starkland CD 2000, rec. 1964/1963

James Tenney (1934–2008) was an ideas man, who in his electronic and instrumental music sought to develop the open-ended concepts of Ives, Varèse and Cage in his own fashion. During the 1960s he worked at Bell Labs with the equipment and computer programs devised by Max Matthews, which helped give shape to Tenney's mathematical and indeterminate theories. *Collage #1* (1961) approaches musique concrète with a characteristically American swagger using Elvis Presley's "Blue Suede Shoes" as material to transform.

But Tenney's breakthroughs came in computer-generated forms, such as the complex relationships formulated in *Phases (For Edgard Varèse)* (1963), where the proportions and relationships sound so exact as to represent the inaudible inner workings of nature or a Mozart adagio, and the lucid yet indeterminate *Ergodos II (For John Cage)* (1964). *Fabric For Ché* (1967), influenced by Xenakis's stochastic theories, sounds like the inside of a hurricane, while *For Ann (Rising)* (1969) is the musical equivalent of an Escher drawing: an aural enigma.

Like Pierre Schaeffer, Tod Dockstader is an outsider without musical training, who sought to free the "sounds trapped in everything" and thus conceived what he preferred to call "organised sound" from simple materials and hands-on tape manipulation, which he learnt while working as a film editor and sound engineer in the 1950s. (In silent acknowledgment of Dockstader's cinematic techniques, extracts from his early *Eight Electronic Pieces* (1960) were selected by Federico Fellini for the soundtrack of the 1969 *Satyricon*.) *Quatermass* (1964) is a masterpiece of extended sound production and drama: balloons sound like massed Tibetan horns; adhesive tape pulled off cymbals could be the sound of shooting stars; and the cries of whales and foghorns in the distance are evoked. Yet it's the musical logic that makes it work as a whole, rather than as a collection of sound effects. In five longish movements, *Quatermass* is a mysterious, remarkably concise and focused musical entity that extends the earliest experiments of musique concrète into quasi-cinematic environs far beyond the original intent of Schaeffer. That's not to say it's an improvement, more an unavoidable evolutionary step.

BBC Radiophonic Workshop
A Retrospective
Mute/BBC Music 2 x CD 2008, rec. 1958–97

In the field of contemporary music Britain may not have produced a Stockhausen or a John Cage, but the music created in a dusty, airless room at the BBC's Music Studios in West London is among the most inventive and vertigo-inducing electronica since the war. The BBC Radiophonic Workshop was set up in 1958 to supply incidental music and sound effects for the corporation's drama department. Its employees, an assortment of technicians, composers and inventors, were left largely to their own devices in the early days – devices including tape machines, editing facilities, soldering irons and all manner of household objects, which they transformed into sound cues of considerable wit and ingenuity, such as Daphne Oram's music for *Amphitryon 38* and Dick Mills's explosive "Major Bloodnok's Stomach", from *The Goons*. The success of Desmond Briscoe's uncanny effects for the sci-fi series *Quatermass and The Pit* (1958–59) paved the way for the Workshop's most famous product, the theme for *Doctor Who* (1963), by visionary new recruits Delia Derbyshire and Brian Hodgson, who scraped keys across a broken piano's bass strings to achieve the familiar vacuum-sucking judders.

Derbyshire's interest in Pythagorean mathematics and electronic synthesis made her the unit's most intriguing member, although on this set she's represented by several of her more prosaic talk show theme tunes. Nevertheless, this set fairly represents the high proportion of women Radiophonic composers: Oram, Derbyshire, Maddalena Fagandini, Bridget Marrow, Elizabeth Parker. The clunky analogue synthesis utilised by Paddy Kingsland, John Baker and others from the mid-1960s has come to be viewed as the epitome of a certain British low budget sci-fi aesthetic, and the Workshop's achievements stand as a rare example of early electronic music that actually registered with a mass audience. This double CD contains 100 tracks from Auntie Beeb's sound lab, right through to the Workshop's last official project in 1997.

Morton Subotnick
Silver Apples Of The Moon/The Wild Bull
Wergo CD 1994 (rec. 1967/1968)

New ideas result in new technology, which results in new ideas. Working at the San Francisco Tape Music Center in the early 1960s, Morton Subotnick, Ramon Sender and Donald Buchla created the Buchla Series 100: a modular, voltage-controlled synthesizer which allowed the user to predetermine and program aspects of the compositional structure, patch together several different modules with varying characteristics, repeat prerecorded sections with sequencers, and spontaneously modify various sound parameters. The relatively easy operation of this "Electric Music Box", as opposed to the painfully slow cut and paste methods of tape composition, or the multiple layerings of awkward computer/synthesizer programming, gave Subotnick a new fluidity of organisation which no doubt influenced the music he composed on it. *Silver Apples Of The Moon* (1967) was the first electronic composition specifically commissioned by a record label (Nonesuch). Today, its 'blip and bleep' sound palette might seem a bit dated, but Subotnick overcomes the timbral limitations with a sense of continuity and a lyrical attention to shape, dynamics and textures, the music often flowing in and out of open, rubato passages. The sequencers highlight repetitious episodes and regular, pulse-driven rhythms (the second part locks into a groove that's even danceable – by a robot, perhaps). Though of a more sombre mood – well, it was inspired by an ancient Sumerian poem about death – *The Wild Bull* essays an even wider expressive range, including some obsessive rhythmic episodes, forlorn 'cries' and mournful backgrounds. Both works have mysterious and meaningful moments, even if the large-scale form isn't always convincing.

David Tudor
Rainforest (Versions I & IV)
Mode CD 1998, rec. 1968/1973

David Tudor (1926–96) was a brilliant pianist and conceptualist, without whom many important scores of the 1950s and 1960s would neither have been composed nor realised. But he gave up the piano in order to concentrate on his own electronic compositions, most of which used sound systems that he devised or modified (as heard on the Lovely Music reissue of *Three Works For Live Electronics*). *Rainforest* is an exception, borrowing John Cage's idea of attaching microphones and cartridges to unconventional objects and then treating the amplified sounds with his own electronic system. This CD carries two of the four existing versions of *Rainforest*: *Version I*, for Tudor's and Takehisa Kosugi's live electronics, and *Version IV*, a recording of an installation where audience members interact with sound-generating objects, creating an alien landscape that rumbles, hums, groans and whines. You could be listening to a three-dimensional sculpture garden, or be in the pit of Moby Dick's stomach.

Karlheinz Stockhausen

by Barry Witherden

Karlheinz Stockhausen (1928–2007) fulfilled a seminal role in twentieth century music, and will doubtless be equally revered and vilified in the twenty-first century and beyond. Starting out from Teutonic serialism, he fashioned a soundworld uniquely his own: magical, mystical, uncompromising. His philosophical beliefs fed obtrusively into his art. He insisted he was merely the channel for music, while accepting the kudos due to a creator. That underlying conflict runs through his work. He eagerly employed chance and performer discretion in his compositions, yet set strict limits, specific guidelines which ensured that the product was unmistakably Stockhausen. Apparently secure in certainty, his business was paradox, and the reconciliation of supposed incompatibilities. He invented a genuine World Music, or what he liked to refer to as "Universal Music": in *Kurzwellen* and *Hymnen* he literally plucked sounds from the air, drawing, from the celestial sphere of shortwave transmissions, essences of most cultures with access to radio. In the stunning *Telemusik* he went beyond collage to meld music from countless traditions into a startling, unique, fertile hybrid.

His music, theory and personality lay at the centre of European music for six decades. He studied with Olivier Messiaen and Pierre Schaeffer; taught Cornelius Cardew, Hugh Davies, Jon Hassell, Helmut Lachenmann, Tim Souster, Kevin Volans and La Monte Young; influenced Miles Davis, Anthony Braxton, The Beatles (he appears on the sleeve of *Sgt Pepper*), Philip Glass, Can and Björk; magnetised, fascinated and/or exasperated Berio, Boulez, Cage, Copland, Kagel, Ligeti, Maderna, Nono, Penderecki, Pousseur ... the list is endless, the selection arbitrary.

Karlheinz Stockhausen
Chöre Für Doris/Choral/Drei Lieder/Sonatine/ Kreuzspiel

Stockhausen-Verlag CD 1992, rec. 1975/1973/1976
(orig. Deutsche Grammophon LPs 1973/1975/1976)

Kontra-Punkte (1952) is Stockhausen's official opus 1, but in the early 1970s he admitted a number of earlier works into the authorised canon. All of the pieces on this CD, from 1950–51, predate *Kontra-Punkte*. *Sonatine* for violin and piano pays homage to Arnold Schoenberg. *Chöre Für Doris* and *Choral* would not obtrude at a Three Choirs Festival. The song texts in *Drei Lieder* are by Stockhausen himself. Already the composer inhabits his own mythology, as he would, more dramatically, in *Licht*. *"The String Man has torn his hand … has already sat a long time in the rain … his ear perceives … the never played."* Stockhausen's is not the human-centric universe of the Romantics, where even the natural elements are projections of human passions. As early as *Kreuzspiel*, he was looking into the cosmos, reflecting the stars in the use of 'sound-points', but perhaps the main significance of this piece lies in its reaching towards total serialism, systematising sets of pitches and durations.

Elektronische Musik 1952–60
Stockhausen-Verlag CD 1992, rec. 1952–60
(orig. Deutsche Grammophon 10" 1959/LP 1962)

Kontakte
Wergo CD 1992, rec. 1968
(orig. Vox LP 1968)

Stockhausen was quickly drawn to the idea of total control of all aspects of the compositional process, which was made easier and more comprehensive by electronics. His first attempt was *Étude* (1952), made in Paris by manipulating piano tones from a 78 rpm disc. Preferring electronic synthesis, because it allowed him to determine all parameters of the sound and its organisation from scratch, he created *Electronic Studie I* (1953) and *II* (1954) at the WDR Studio in Cologne. With these pieces he attempted to apply serial principles to timbre and frequency, areas which resisted control in instrumental music. From this perspective their success was limited but, as music, *Studie I* at least is a triumph. Despite the straightjacket of serial methodology, this alien song from a mistakenly imagined future blooms richly and freely out of the ether.

On the highly regarded *Gesang Der Jünglinge* (1955–56), he combined musique concrète principles and electronic synthesis. An excerpt from the biblical Book of Daniel, sung by a young boy on tape, is reduced to phonemes and tonal fragments, or built up into choral masses, with an electronic component that acts as counterpoint to and continuation of the transformed vocal point.

If music exists only in time, sound inhabits space. In *Gesang* Stockhausen experimented with placing and moving sounds. It had been done before, of course, not least by the Venetian Renaissance masters, but electronic technology gave Stockhausen a freedom that went beyond hocket and antiphonal devices, beyond echo and stereo effects, moving a single sound as it happened. He designed the piece for five channels, with the boy's voice assigned to its own overhead speaker. The ingenuity and intricacy of the sounds, and the dramatic thrust of the music, forced composers and listeners alike to take the medium seriously. After *Étude* a rift had developed between Stockhausen and Schaeffer, polarising electronics between Paris and Cologne, sounds found or sounds synthesised. *Gesang Der Jünglinge* reconciled the methodological and philosophical dichotomy, knitting electronic and natural elements into a strange, exultant hymn praising God and celebrating the purity of the human voice, despite the electronic manipulation.

Kontakte (1959–60) is an example of Stockhausen's 'moment form', with which he 'verticalised' time to emphasise temporary, flexible, changing relationships rather than conventional formal structures, and where each sound event, though part of a structure or process, is viable in itself, not dependent on that process or structure for its validity. It also exploited the differing ways in which rhythms are perceived depending on the speed at which they are presented. This Verlag release has the original version for tape, without the live piano and percussion parts Stockhausen later added. This latter version is on the Wergo CD, with David Tudor on piano, Christopher Caskel on percussion, and Gottfried Michael Koenig assisting the composer with the electronic manipulations. Other performances with piano and percussion soloists reacting to the taped elements are available on another Verlag CD, paired with *Zyklus* and *Refrain*.

Carré/Gruppen
Stockhausen-Verlag CD 1993, rec. 1960/1965
(orig. Deutsche Grammophon LP 1965)

Between 1955 and 1957 Stockhausen tried similar spatial tricks with live performers in *Gruppen* (1957), where three independent, equal (but not identical) orchestras fire flak at the listener. The subsequent *Carré* (1959–60) has four orchestras with added mixed choruses using phonetic sound differentiations. The conductors face inwards, and the audience was meant to be ranged diagonally across a square auditorium. As in *Kontakte*, Stockhausen employs moment form. *Carré*, he said, "does not carry you along but leaves you in peace". The listener can elect to make the journey or simply enjoy the ever renewed present. The music is not as meditative as this may suggest. There are violent outbursts, though nothing as intense as the most turbulent passages of *Gruppen*, which predict the textures of Ornette Coleman's *Free Jazz* (1960) and John Coltrane's *Ascension* (1965). Significantly, having broken off from *Carré* to compose *Kontakte*, Stockhausen left composer and sometime AMM member Cornelius Cardew to work up the score from sketches and instructions. During the 1960s and early 1970s he would increasingly relinquish direct control over the details of his music.

Given the crucial importance of the spatial relationships between each group of performers and the audience, both these works present major realisation problems. It was relatively easy for taped electronic sounds to be projected around an auditorium, with the speakers more or less surrounding the audience, but for *Carré* and *Gruppen*, Stockhausen somehow needed to get the same effect with orchestras. The solution was a spherical performance space, with the audience suspended in the middle. His dream was briefly fulfilled in Osaka, Japan, where a suitable hall was constructed for the 1970 World's Fair.

Klavierstücke I–XI/Mikrophonie I & II

Sony Classical 2 x CD 1993, rec. 1965
(orig. Deutsche Grammophon LPs 1965/1966)

In the notes for this set, containing 1965 performances of the *Klavierstücke*, Stockhausen – who evidently believed that your art's what you eat – gives a detailed report on every meal, snack and drink taken by pianist Aloys Kontarsky during the days of the recordings. The first cycle, numbers *I–IV*, are ascetic miniatures written in Paris in 1952–53 when Stockhausen was studying with Messiaen. During this time he was evolving from 'point' music to 'groups' (Gruppen). *VI* exploits factors largely outside the control of composer or musician, its overall structure governed by the natural periods of sound decay and reverberation. *XI* displays Stockhausen's first thoroughgoing application of aleatory principles (involving a degree of chance for both composer and performer) with the score comprising irregularly distributed groups of notes which the pianist plays randomly within certain parameters. The pianist decides what order to play the groups in, but the score contains instructions in each group which affect the way that the next, whatever it might be, is realised.

Performances of the two *Mikrophonie*, composed in 1964–65, are created in real time, in front of an audience. The mechanics of sound production and transformation became integral to the performance. In *Mikrophonie I* two tam-tams are agitated by one set of musicians, while a second set monitors the results through hand-held microphones and a third modifies the sounds with filters and potentiometers. *Mikrophonie II* involves similar procedures but uses a chorus as the main sound generator, and patches in samples from earlier works. The results are electric.

The evolution from strictly notated scores to music which could only exist in performance was already discernible in the *Klavierstücke*, but with *Mikrophonie I & II*, Stockhausen had no choice but to fuel in-flight. Forsaking serialist discipline, he strove to "mediate between organisation and non-organisation". Characteristically, having set up a situation accommodating performer choice, Stockhausen modified the score during rehearsal because the interactions were unpredictable. His practice of controlling the mixing and projection of live sounds was to cause conflict with some of his interpreters, who felt that it was tantamount to using the musicians as puppets.

Telemusik/Mikrophonie I & II

Stockhausen-Verlag 1994, rec. 1966
(orig. Deutsche Grammophon LP 1966)

Along with *Hymnen*, *Telemusik* was my visa to Stockhausen's empire, still provoking a special nostalgia. I first heard it on a radio broadcast which was also the first time I had heard Stockhausen speaking, introducing and explaining his work. *Telemusik* is quite capable of exerting its spell through sound alone, but the conditions and method of its creation intensify the awe it provokes. All his previous electronic works, except *Gesang Der Jünglinge*, were sourced entirely from synthesized sound, but *Telemusik* used found sounds, taking recordings from Japan, China, Spain, the Amazon, the Sahara, Hungary and elsewhere. It's a work whose fundamental concept would have been unrealisable, perhaps even inconceivable, in any previous century. The electronic analysis of sound waves allowed Stockhausen to take elements of the sampled music which could not be isolated in any other way and mix them into a previously non-existent sound. In that radio talk, he described how he modulated the melody of one recording with only the rhythm of another and the dynamic intensity of yet another, further modulating these with the harmony and timbre of synthesized sounds, finally processing the five elements through ring modulators to create something entirely new and – if you like – alien. In the composer's own words, he felt it his recurring dream of "a music of the whole world, of all lands and races" a step closer.

Hymnen

Stockhausen-Verlag 4 x CD 1995, rec. 1965–67
(orig. Deutsche Grammophon 2 x LP 1967)

Like a number of Stockhausen's other works, *Hymnen*, completed in 1967, exists in more than one form. It can be 'performed' purely on tape as well as with soloists, when the problems of exercising control while using aleatoric and improvisatory elements rise again. Both versions are included here. This monumental ceremony, comprising four "Regions" totalling some two hours, also exists in a version with an orchestral third Region.

In the light of contemporary sampling and sequencing capabilities, *Hymnen* may seem technically primitive and clumsy, but it's still a remarkable experience emotionally, an imaginative expedition which has no parallel. Where

Telemusik and *Gesang Der Jünglinge* were compacted, their components smelted and transmuted into a dense conglomerate, *Hymnen* lays out its processes and constituents. Stockhausen builds the work from national anthems, banal tunes snatched from less than respectable employment and pressed into utopian service. He wants them to fetch all their disreputable baggage so that he can empty it out, mixing it with natural sounds, electronic interventions and the reactions of live performers, his citizens of Harmondie. Stockhausen's comment on *Carré*, quoted earlier, seems better applied to *Hymnen*. Listeners have to be content with being on the train: with its slow pace, extended transformations, passages of near-silence and shortwave static. *Hymnen* requires you to meditate on your journey's purpose rather than fret about arriving, while an insistent, rather sinister voice asks you to place your bets. Stockhausen puns with sound – as when crowd noises mutate into swamp-ducks – and a Brechtian (or proto-postmodern) episode lets us eavesdrop on a conference from the recording sessions themselves.

Stimmung (Collegium Vocale Köln)

Stockhausen-Verlag 2 x CD 1995, rec. 1969/1982
(orig. Deutsche Grammophon LP 1969/Harmonia Mundi 3 x LP 1982)

Stimmung (Singcircle/Gregory Rose)

Hyperion CD 1986, rec. 1983

Stimmung (Theatre Of Voices/Paul Hillier)

Harmonia Mundi CD 2007

If *Hymnen* isn't quite Stockhausen's masterpiece, *Stimmung* (*Tuning*), a choral work composed in 1968, must be. Written during a frozen Long Island winter, *Stimmung* incorporates erotic poems written for his wife together with a selection of the many names of God, but its foundation is a specified series of overtones on B flat. The notes are to be sung softly, without vibrato, resonating only in the cranial spaces, but bringing out the overtones as strongly as possible. The work comprises 51 'models' which Stockhausen brilliantly binds into a single, inexorably unfolding organic entity, creating a wonderland of floating, drifting, ebbing and flowing sound. *Stimmung* was to become a significant influence on the 'spectralist' composers: although most of those labelled as such reject the name, they would admit Stockhausen's influence.

Live performances of this piece, around an hour and a quarter long, can be utterly bewitching, with the singers ranged in a semicircle in the gloom. The chanted vowels and phonemes swirl in a twilight of consequential chords, with occasional, fully formed recognisable words darting out to illuminate the mists from within. The shifting textures suggest images which would later be given substantial form in the most effective scenes of *Donnerstag Aus Licht*. Play this through headphones and slide into an alien but protective realm.

The Verlag album contains two recordings of the piece, made 13 years apart by Cologne's Collegium Vocale, who commissioned and premiered the work. In 1983 the British ensemble Singcircle recorded it for Hyperion. It's a superb performance, and the quality of the recording is clear, tightly focused and up-front, but this gives a quite different experience from a live performance. In his 2007 edition, recorded for Harmonia Mundi, Paul Hillier (a former member of Singcircle) set out to more accurately realise the effect of the piece in concert, and he succeeded admirably: for once, surround sound was more than a gimmick. The dazzling realisation by Hillier's Theatre Of Voices – known as the "Copenhagen Version" – is a companion rather than a rival to the earlier recordings. Nonetheless, there is no substitute for the ritualistic enchantment of a live performance in a darkened auditorium with candles or a centrally placed illuminated sphere.

From The Seven Days

Stockhausen-Verlag 7 x CD 1996, rec. 1969
(orig. Deutsche Grammophon 7 x LP 1969)

Aus Den Sieben Tagen (extracts)

Harmonia Mundi CD 1988, rec. 1970
(orig. Harmonia Mundi LP 1985)

The circumstances which triggered the creation of this monumental sequence – 15 works on seven CDs in the Verlag version – were exceptional, as were the results. In May 1968 Stockhausen's wife Mary was due to return, with their children, from a holiday in America. Instead she sent a letter ending their relationship. Stockhausen pleaded by telegram and, when she did not reply, determined that he did not wish to go on living. He began a hunger strike, designed to bring Mary home, and starved himself for seven days. Towards the end of the second day, he wrote a text, verbal instructions for improvisation, except that he prefers the term 'intuitive music'. After four days without food, he went to the piano and played a single note. "How this note shocked me ... for days on end I had heard nothing but birdsong ... I played another note [and heard] an inner life such as I had never heard before." Gathering together a number of close associates and empathetic performers, he set out to realise a series of compositions based entirely on texts rather than conventional or even graphic musical notation. Finally he had let go, leaving performers to interpret his words through the intermodulation of their own personalities and experiences. Yet the regime was punishing: "Goldstaub", for example, calls on the players to fast for four days "in complete silence ... sleep as little as possible ... close your eyes/just listen." From the distress of his personal situation came a catharsis which would shape his output for years to come. The full, exhausting seven CD set of *Sieben Tagen* is expensive. Neophytes might be better off (in more ways than one) going for the budget priced Harmonia Mundi CD, which features two extracts, "Fais Voile Vers Le Soleil" and "Liaison", giving an excellent representative flavour of the whole work, and features Stockhausen and several of his regular collaborators, including Aloys Kontarsky (piano), Rolf Gehlhaar (tam-tam), Michel Portal (reeds) and Harald Boje (electronium). "Goldstaub" ("Gold Dust") is also available separately, on a Verlag CD (formerly DG LP).

Trans

Stockhausen-Verlag 1996 CD, rec. 1971/1973
(orig. Deutsche Grammophon LP 1973)

So many of Stockhausen's compositions call for a degree of theatrical realisation that it should have been no surprise when, in 1977, he eventually announced that everything he wrote in future would be subsumed into the massive opera, *Licht. Trans* (1971) has only been performed twice in Britain in anything near its intended form: at a student concert at the Royal College of Music and in 2008 at London's Southbank. The piece came, virtually fully formed, in a dream. Stockhausen saw vertical ranks of string players bathed in a reddish violet light; they moved stiffly, mechanically, abruptly changing the musical material as the sound of a massively amplified loom shuttle leapt over the audience's heads. From some concealed place behind the strings, wind and brass, other instruments could be heard. Stockhausen hints at another world behind the everyday, and has alluded to the Tibetan Book of the Dead, believing that this music may help guide a newly dead soul on its journey. This CD includes the world premiere concert performance, opening with a gasp from the audience as the eerily-lit strings appear, as well as a studio recording. Both versions are spellbinding.

Sternklang

Stockhausen-Verlag 2 x CD 1996, rec. 1975
(orig. Deutsche Grammophon 2 x LP 1975)

Conceived in 1969, *Sternklang* (*Star Sound*) was premiered in June 1971 at the English Park in Berlin. It is subtitled "Park Music For Five Groups" and provides another example of that theatricality – or, perhaps it is more accurate to say, ceremonial or ritual quality – so often present in Stockhausen's work. The composer directs that the five groups of musicians are separated as far apart as the dimensions of the venue will permit. All singers and players are individually amplified over loudspeakers. Runners transport musical 'models' from one group to another, where they are taken over and integrated. At ten points during the piece a centrally positioned person signals a common tempo, so that all five groups synchronize.

There are certain similarities with *Stimmung*. *Sternklang* is based on five eight-note chords, tuned as overtones in pure tuning. The chords have only one note in common. All the musical models represent the classical star constellations, either through rhythm, timbre, or pitch intervals. Stockhausen

proposes that, on clear nights, star constellations can be directly read from the sky and integrated as musical figures where the score prescribes. In the score Stockhausen expressly states that this is sacred music, and the intention of performing in the open air, under the open sky with (all being well) the stars clearly visible, exemplifies the composer's ongoing fascination with the eternal and infinite cosmos. For the recording, made in a Paris studio, the five groups were separated by soundproof walls, with the percussionist, although located in a separate booth, able to make visual contact. The percussion sounds were transmitted into the studio at a level that was audible to the musicians.

Ylem

Stockhausen-Verlag CD 1996, rec. 1973
(orig. Deutsche Grammophon LP 1973)

Developing from the technique – the gamble – pioneered in *Sieben Tagen*, *Ylem*'s 1972 score comprises a short text, a skeletal blueprint for a piece that always surprises by the similarity of each realisation. Again, though Stockhausen is content to offer verbal recommendations rather than the strict instructions of his fully notated scores, musicians have commented on how strong and unavoidable they find the guidance. *Ylem* was inspired by the oscillation theory of the origin of the universe. The process used in the piece is a loose parallel to that of the very early *Kreuzspiel*. The players, clustered in a group around the keyboard, are invited to play a note from the centre of their instrument's range. They then move gradually outwards, pitch-wise and physically, spreading out into the audience and towards the edges of the performance space until, at a shouted syllable, the expansion halts, and the contraction back into the point of genesis begins.

Stockhausen had now become a facilitator, an initiator, rather than a maker. The technique would be developed and varied in such pieces as *Atmen Gibt Das Leben* (1974), but by the end of the decade the trend would be reversed and, with the complex projects making up *Licht*, the composer would become architect, ringmaster, priest and court jester to a distinctive visual as well as aural universe.

Donnerstag Aus Licht
Stockhausen-Verlag 4 x CD 1996, rec. 1980–82
(orig. Deutsche Grammophon 4 x LP 1982)

The entire *Licht* was planned as seven nights of music theatre and, from 1977 until the cycle was completed, whenever anyone commissioned a work from Stockhausen they had to accept that it would be incorporated into *Licht*. Nonetheless, right from day one, as you might say – *Donnerstag* (*Thursday*) – it was clear that many scenes would be able to stand on their own and, indeed, often worked better as freestanding works, if only because they thus became more accessible in the concert hall and on record. As the Days drew on, it was sometimes difficult to avoid the impression that the composer recognised, at least subconsciously, that he had made a rod for his own back: certainly he readily permitted, and indeed, supervised, recordings and performances of individual sections from the overall work. By the time it was completed with *Sonntag* (*Sunday*) in 2004 – the last scene, "Light Pictures", was premiered in October of that year – *Licht* totalled some 29 hours of music.

Donnerstag was the first day to be completed (in 1981) and staged. The composer's personal mythology was complex, abstruse, mystical and in many ways naive, redolent of the most optimistic and gentle elements of 1960s hippy philosophy. Thursday's opera involves a dry-ice rainbow, a runaway toy lorry, a remarkable shadow-show reminiscent of Indonesian puppets, an entirely wordless act comprising a trumpet concerto representing the Archangel Michael's circumnavigation of the Earth, and a bag-lady who asks audience and performers, "*Why don't you all come home?*" Early reviews of the first days in the cycle inferred that, in *Licht*'s cosmology, Stockhausen himself could be identified with the Archangel Michael, if not with the Almighty, but the composer was adamant that this was not the case and, indeed, could never be. In amongst all the miracles and wonders, the music itself was probably the most conventional that Stockhausen had ever written or inspired, and the echoes of Wagner, though distant and distorted, were not confined to the colossal scale or the cast of archetypes. Amongst these were Eve, Lucifer and, of course, Michael, who were later to get the composer into trouble.

Music For Flute
Stockhausen-Verlag 2 x CD 1996, rec. 1985–91

Music For Flute is a recital of pieces composed in the late 1970s and early 1980s, played by Stockhausen's longterm assistant and partner Kathinka Pasveer. Like *Chöre Für Doris* and *Choral*, it's ideal for playing to people who want to know if modern music composers can write 'proper music' before they will take their more experimental works seriously. The flute pieces are not more personal – because Stockhausen's music is nothing if not personal – but more intimate than the other compositions spotlighted in this survey. Several of them were written as gifts for friends and relations and most have, of course, ended up being incorporated into some part of *Licht*, whatever their original context. Their accessibility and classical elegance will surprise anyone who thinks Stockhausen is only capable of producing harsh, cerebral music.

Helikopter-Quartett
Auvidis Montaigne CD 2000

When asked, in 1991, to write a string quartet to be premiered by The Arditti Quartet in 1994, Stockhausen demurred. He never used stock classical forms. However, not for the first time (*Trans*) a new work came to him, almost whole, in a dream. Most artists would have dismissed the idea as impracticable – or could never have marshalled the resources to make it possible – but this was the man who had managed to get audiences suspended in a globular auditorium a quarter of a century before. In the dream each member of a string quartet was aloft in a helicopter, their sound and image transmitted to each of four towers of screens and speakers on the ground. At each 'station', one member of the quartet could be seen and heard in close-up. The ignition of the helicopter engines and the throbbing of the rotors form part of the music, often blending remarkably well with the string tremolos and the occasional (and, frankly, rather irritating) vocalisations of the musicians, but Stockhausen wanted the helicopters to fly sufficiently high above the audience for their direct sound to be masked by the relayed sound. Since, during the period concerned, Stockhausen expected anyone who commissioned a work to accept that it would be incorporated into the *Licht* cycle, the *Helicopter Quartet* initially became part of *Mittwoch (Wednesday)* from *Licht*.

The involvement of a moderator explaining various elements of the work to the audience, and camera crews following the musicians to and from the helicopters, are crucial aspects of the event. Once airborne, cameras focus in close-up on hands, faces, bows and strings without cuts, fades or changes of angle, and the Earth should be visible behind the musicians. Clearly intended as a multimedia experience, the concept of this music in and from the skies is more impressive than the sounds themselves in the early passages, but as the descent approaches the writing for strings becomes more intense and involving. If that doesn't win you over, surely the vision and sheer theatrical chutzpah will.

Cosmic Pulses
Stockhausen-Verlag CD 2007

One might have thought that, after finally finishing a project like *Licht*, any artist would be reluctant to harness themselves to such a major commitment again, but Stockhausen said that, after completing *Sirius* (which had represented the 12 months of the year), *Tierkreis* (the 12 signs of the zodiac) and *Licht* (the seven days of the week), he wanted to compose for the 24 hours of the day: this project became *Klang (Sound)*. By the time of his death in December 2007, he had completed 21 hours. *Cosmic Pulses* was the 13th hour, which Stockhausen began in December 2006. In this piece he experimented with a new technique for the spatialisation of 24 sound layers in what you might call eight 'choirs' – 192 tracks in all – which might have fazed even Thomas Tallis. Twenty-four melodic loops each contain a different number of pitches between 1 and 24. These rotate in 24 tempi varying from 240 and 1.17 rotations per minute in 24 registers within a range of around seven octaves. These are successively layered on top of one another from low to high and from slowest to fastest, and end

one after another in the same order. Stockhausen compared the piece with the task of trying to synchronise the orbits of 24 planets with individual rotations, tempi and trajectories. In the programme notes for the work's premiere, he admitted, "If it is possible to hear everything, I do not yet know. In any case, the experiment is extremely fascinating!"

Listening to the UK premiere on the BBC Radio 3 relay was a little like watching Kubrick's *2001* on a tiny black and white mono TV, and even the most sophisticated surround sound system is going to be incapable of producing the experience Stockhausen envisaged, so the CD is only an indication of his intentions. Yet *Cosmic Pulses* is such a powerful piece that a good deal of its multilayered intensity comes over in any medium: even listening at home I have been drawn in by its restless vortex of sound. Those who were lucky enough to be present at the Stockhausen Day during the 2008 Proms (held on what would have been the composer's 80th birthday) reported viscera-vibrating bass frequencies welling up from the floor of the arena and head-spinning upper-frequency sounds darting around the dome of the Albert Hall. Reviews were mixed, but in my view it was a triumphant return to form, vividly recapturing the excitement and wonder I had felt when I first encountered Stockhausen's music 41 years earlier.

Since his death in December 2007 there has been a plethora of festivals and seasons celebrating his work but, for years before that, he seemed to have been considered an irrelevance, despite the fact that so much contemporary music in so many genres owes so much to him. However, he did make news in even the tabloid press when he was reported as having praised the destruction of the World Trade Center as a great work of art (his actual words were "What has happened is – now you all have to turn your brains around – the greatest work of art there has ever been"). The somewhat hysterical reaction to this allegation took a while to die down, and Stockhausen was forced to apologise in the face of cancelled concerts and other events.

At a press conference in Hamburg he had been asked if he saw Michael, Eve and Lucifer, the archetypal characters used in *Licht*, as symbols or historical figures: the essence of the journalist's question seemed to be whether Stockhausen saw evil as a real force abroad in the world. The composer answered that he did believe that the forces represented by the three characters exist now, citing Lucifer's "work" in New York. He later clarified, "I have defined Lucifer as the cosmic spirit of rebellion, of anarchy. He uses his high degree of intelligence to destroy creation. He does not know love." His comments seemed to encompass a reluctant acknowledgment that, while an artist can labour for years on a great work of art and not change the world one iota, terrorists changed it irrevocably in a matter of a few minutes. Anyone with the slightest knowledge and understanding of the circumstances of Stockhausen's childhood and youth, let alone the consistent hippy-friendly peace and love stance of his art, could hardly believe that he approved of an act of mass murder.

Iannis Xenakis
by Philip Clark

"The problem is he's an architect, not a musician," British conductor Norman Del Mar reputedly remarked, in a characteristic response from a classical musician to the apocalyptic challenges meted out by Iannis Xenakis (1922–2001). Del Mar was in fact no slouch when it came to contemporary composition, conducting performances of Stockhausen, Peter Maxwell Davies and Olivier Messiaen, but Xenakis let rip with another form of musicality, which pressed non-musical starting points into generating shapes, colours, forms, structures and gestures that urgently demonstrated alternative ways of thinking.

That Xenakis was an architect is exactly what's *right* with his music. His deep roots in the sciences, mathematics, architecture and ancient mythologies gave him tools to stretch definitions of what music can be. Putting his early orchestral works *Metastasis* or *Pithoprakta* next to pieces even as magnificently punk as Stockhausen's *Gruppen* or Ligeti's *Atmospheres* emphasises how, on a subconscious level at least, these works remain immensely 'musical' in a traditional way. "Let us resolve the duality 'mortal-eternal': the future is in the past and vice-versa; the evanescence of the present is abolished, it is everywhere at the same time; the 'here' is also two billion light-years away," Xenakis wrote in his groundbreaking 1968 volume *Towards A Philosophy Of Music*, and his work embodied ancient ideals of a fusion between the arts and sciences, perching itself between stylised antiquity and the modernism of a profoundly visionary oracle.

Born in Romania in 1922 of Greek parentage, Xenakis personified the political and social struggles of post-war Europe more intensely than any other composer. He had immersed himself in the arts and philosophy at boarding school in Greece, later becoming a leader of the resistance movement to the fascist occupation of his country while studying engineering at Athens University. He was left for dead in the unrest that followed, as British troops attempted to suppress the communist resistance, and survived only after his resourceful father bribed a policeman to find him. Xenakis was imprisoned and threatened with deportation to a concentration camp as the new government established itself in Athens, persecuting those with left-wing sympathies. The regime condemned him to death in his absence when he fled to exile in Paris on a false passport, a sentence not revoked until 1974.

The abstract schemata and professorial calculus that characterise his music might appear contrary to this reputation as a firebrand political freedom fighter, and the relationship between the art and the life is an inscrutable paradox lying at the heart of Xenakis's aesthetic. His status as an outsider within the post-Darmstadt avant garde initially made itself felt with a passionate rejection of serial dogma, published in a provocatively titled 1954 article, *The Crisis Of Serial Music*, which pitched his ideas directly against Stockhausen and Boulez. Now in Paris, Xenakis landed a plum job with the modernist architect Le Corbusier. His most famous design was for the Philips Pavilion at the Brussels World's Fair in 1958, and deployed so-called 'hyperbolic paraboloids' to twist self-supporting concrete into dramatic airborne spirals. This radically fresh vision of how to fill empty space with abstract structures had its starting point in the structure of Xenakis's first orchestral piece, *Metastasis*. To be more precise, this orchestral score *was* the starting point, as manuscript paper transmuted into architectural plan and the shapes of what became his trademark string glissandi found their equivalent in space as hyperbolic paraboloids. Through uniquely creative use of electronics in works like *Concret PH* (1958) and *Bohor* (1962), combining sound with light in a series of installations he called "Polytopes", and by cutting across the grain of each instrument he wrote for with untrammelled physical power, Xenakis persistently questioned where the listener's auditory responses ended and their physical instincts began.

The thick skin that he had acquired in Athens made the in-fighting of the 1950s avant garde seem petty in comparison, but the credo of his music is subliminally political: its unique difficulties place arduous responsibilities on performers and listeners to transcend comfortable, received definitions of 'music'. It's consequently revolutionary music in the purest sense of the word, stressing the emotional energy that surges outwards from thinking and ideas. Xenakis's music demands you open up bits of your brain you didn't realise were there.

It's little surprise that as Xenakis was pilloried by both classical reactionaries and the avant garde establishment, he found a supporter in Edgard Varèse. His music – like Varèse's – used technique only as a starting point to look into some-

thing deeper. The fact that he was able to boil all his ideas into music is nothing short of a miracle. "The preliminary calculations are completely forgotten," wrote his onetime teacher Olivier Messiaen. "There is no sign of intellectualism, no mental frenzy. The result in sound is a delicately poetic or violently brutal agitation." Music cut from the stuff of existence itself.

Iannis Xenakis
Metastasis/Pithoprakta/Eonta
Le Chant Du Monde CD 2001, rec. 1965
Anastenaria/Troorkh/Aïs
Col Legno CD 2003, rec. 1981–2000

Concepts of architecture, cubism and Einstein's theories of space-time stimulated Xenakis's mind as he worked on his first acknowledged work, the orchestral piece *Metastasis* (1953–54). Architectural plans led to structures that existed in space and could be appreciated from multiple viewpoints; musical scores were diagrammatic information that guided performers how to move forwards against unfolding time, but in one direction and with a set series of events. Cubism taught Xenakis how a single object on a flat canvas could be viewed from simultaneous perspectives, and he now strove to create the illusion of a multi-temporal experience in sound.

Two key techniques emerged in *Metastasis* that Xenakis would obsessively hone for the rest of his life: string glissandi and the movement of a vast number of instruments locked into a 'sound mass'. The work opens with the whole string section gradually sliding upwards and downwards from a unison G as a heckling woodblock outlines a more persistent sensation of pulse – Xenakis sets up an expectation from the outset that he's dealing with time across dimensions. The glissandi disorientate the angle with which our ear perceives the imposing sound mass created by the strings, and an aural illusion is created of an object twisting around itself in the air, rather like Francis Bacon's painting of a dog chasing its tail.

Metastasis was originally intended as the third panel in a trilogy of works under the collective title *Anastenaria*. Xenakis realised that *Metastasis* made a considerable technical advance on the opening two parts and withdrew them, leaving *Metastasis* as a standalone work. Hearing the Col Legno disc confirms his instinct to be correct, but the earlier sections do highlight that his creative vocation was fully formed from the start. The opening section, *Procession Aux Eaux Claires*, hints at the pungent evocation of ageless folk music that he would achieve in later works like *Oresteïa*. *Metastasis* itself receives its most detailed and secure performance here, from The Bavarian Radio Symphony Orchestra led by Charles Zachary Bornstein, while *Troorkh* (1991) is an incisive late work for solo trombone and orchestra.

The archival 1965 performance of *Metastasis* on Chant Du Monde by Maurice le Roux and The Orchestre National De L'ORTF is a bit frayed round the edges but retains its pioneer spirit, and the disc remains essential because of Le Roux's dazzling performance of *Pithoprakta* (1955–56). Literally translating as *Actions Through Possibilities*, *Pithoprakta* amplified the nascent potential for multidimensional time that *Metastasis* had exposed. Xenakis began exploring the ideas he would eventually label "stochastic music" in *Pithoprakta*; that is to say, musical events that derive from probability theory. In her classic 1981 biography of Xenakis, Nouritza Matossian suggests the image of millions of independent blood cells moving in aggregate as an analogy for how Xenakis applied probability theory to a symphony orchestra; although the model of a massed flock of birds all adhering to the same shape as they fly is also often given. Certainly *Pithoprakta* establishes unprecedented musical syntax: the continuity and discontinuity implied by string glissandi and the woodblock in *Metastasis* are exploded onto a grander scale, as nervy tapping by the string players against the body of their instruments is heard in counterpoint against glissandi. A brutally whacked woodblock suddenly splinters the strings and they erupt into heckling pizzicato interruptions before dropping back into the fold: major orchestral insurgency.

Aïs/Tracés/Empreintes/Noomena/Roaï
Timpani CD 2000
Jonchaies/Shaar/Lichens/Antokhton
Timpani CD 2001
Synaphaï/Horos/Eridanos/Kyania
Timpani CD 2002
Erikhthon/Ata/Akrata/Krihoïdi
Timpani CD 2004

Although nothing can prepare you for the experience of hearing his orchestral music in the flesh, this magnificent four CD survey of Xenakis's orchestral work played by The Orchestre Philharmonique Du Luxembourg under Arturo Tamayo is a Primer all by itself. The orchestral playing is abandoned and unusually tactile, and Tamayo uncorks the dramatic heart of each piece with prodigious insight. The highlight of the cycle is *Jonchaies* (1977), originally composed for The Orchestre National De France, an ensemble renowned for their sonorous possibilities and technical brilliance. A spectacular opening few bars featuring the strings in a dramatic upward glissando from the bowels of the orchestra into the highest register tells you Xenakis is damned if he's going to let go of your ears for the next 15 minutes. The glissando morphs into a keening modal theme in the upper strings that's ethereally beautiful, and just as it seems Xenakis can't push this material any further it flows into fresh vistas. With an abrupt thud from the percussion puncturing the soundscape, he unleashes music of appalling violence, and dramatic surges of energy ritualistically play themselves out.

Pianist Hiroaki Ooï joins the orchestra for *Erikhthon* (1974), and the trickledown effect of Xenakis's microtonal writing in the orchestra cunningly makes it seem as if the piano has been subjected to an exotic tuning system. *Akrata* (1965) for 16 wind instruments dissects hectic momentum with busy silences, and even the late *Krinoïdi* (1991) demonstrates that the composer never lost faith with the orchestra, this time with a sunny score founded on his fascination with the movement of marine life.

Dox-Orkh
Bis CD 1996
Dämmerschein/Persephassa/La Déesse Athéna
Mode CD 1997

Violinist Irvine Arditti has long been a major Xenakis interpreter, both as soloist and in his day job leading The Arditti Quartet. Xenakis's 1991 piece for violin and orchestra, *Dox-Orkh*, was designed to exploit Arditti's reckless virtuosity, and belongs to the same cycle of soloist/orchestra pieces as *Troorkh*. Xenakis describes the work as a struggle between David and Goliath – a typical invocation of an ancient archetype – with 'Dox' (the string instrument) in combat with 'Orkh' (the orchestra). The violinist plays with short and nervy glissandi throughout as the orchestra taunts him with obstreperous clusters. This is a characteristic Xenakis strategy for structuring a piece (think of the string glissandi versus the woodblock in *Metastasis*), and here he weaves typical magic. It could be argued that he is merely setting up a rather obvious clash of opposites, but the writing is full of subtle subclauses, like a brief reconciliation between the violin and the horn section. This is an authoritative performance from Arditti and The Moscow Philharmonic under the British conductor Jonathan Nott, and the disc also contains music by Berio and Rafael Mira.

The Mode disc places another late Xenakis orchestra piece from 1994 alongside a crack performance of Varèse's *Amériques*. With its German title, *Dämmerschein* (*Rays Of Twilight*) making explicit reference to Wagner's *Die Götterdämmerung* (*Twilight Of The Gods*), this is a one-off Xenakis piece with a harmonic language that sails as close to tonality as he ever dared. The high energy level and dramatic sweep is, however, absolutely characteristic. The disc also contains *Persephassa* (1969) – a curtly constructed 26 minute piece for percussion ensemble – and *La Déesse Athéna* (1992) for baritone voice singing in the stylised falsetto Xenakis created for his theatre piece *Oresteïa*, discussed below.

Electronic Music
Electronic Music Foundation CD 1997, rec. 1957–92

A quick count demonstrates that Xenakis's electronic music formed a tiny percentage of his output, but his status as a pioneer in the field is unmatched. He had the best model a young composer interested in electronics could have, namely Edgard Varèse, with whom he became close friends when the expat composer returned to Paris for the French premiere of his part-electronic, part-orchestral *Déserts* (1954). And the inspiring thing about Xenakis's electronic vision is that it doesn't sound like electronic music; at least, the 'anoraky' and dispassionate sounds that too often pass for electronic music in university departments and at festivals – Xenakis's rigorous intellectual poetry remains intact. This EMF disc is the best introduction to his electronics, documenting his early experiments, then coming up to date with *S.709* from 1992. *Diamorphoses* (1957) and *Concret PH* (1958) are both impressive in the seamless way they investigate the same preoccupations as Xenakis's acoustic music of the era.

The recordings of earthquakes, bells, doors slamming and aeroplanes taking off that he sources for *Diamorphoses* are mulched into a vivid sound mass, which climaxes with a feral glissando that bursts the sound barrier. *Concret PH* was originally designed to sit alongside Varèse's *Poème Électronique* in the Philips Pavilion at the Brussels World's Fair (the 'PH' of the title represents 'hyperbolic paraboloids'), and there's pathos in the air as Xenakis makes the sound of burning charcoal punch above its expressive weight. Burning charcoal is, of course, the sort of natural sound phenomenon that he explored in *Pithoprakta*, and it's an intriguing paradox that his treatment reveals the inner mechanisms of smouldering charcoal more clearly than the raw sounds could muster for themselves. *Bohor* (1962) amplifies *Concret PH*'s soundscape onto a larger scale, while *Hibiki-Hana-Ma* (1970) represents the only time Xenakis made electronic hay with acoustic orchestral sounds.

La Légende D'Eer

Mode CD + DVD 2005, rec. 1978

Various

CCMIX: New Electroacoustic Music From Paris

Mode 2 x CD 2001, rec. 1978–94

The music assembled for *La Légende D'Eer* was designed for the Polytope that Xenakis exhibited outside the Pompidou Centre in 1978. Mode's DVD version attempts an interpretation of the visual and architectural material he intended to accompany the sounds, but the original structures themselves are now missing, presumed lost. His title is borrowed from Plato and the music itself conflates a typically diverse selection of sounds – various African and Japanese instruments, the sounds of bricks being hit together – into wildly vibrant sonic matter. The static opening places simple melodic lines against extended durations, curiously Feldman-like in spirit, until Xenakis injects structural shocks into the unfolding argument.

CCMIX: New Electroacoustic Music From Paris documents the history of the UPIC computer-based drawing tablet that Xenakis designed as a composition tool for both professional and amateur composers. The ideal of the system is that any shape made on the computer monitor can find its equivalent as a living sound object, therefore, users don't need to be fluent with conventional notation. His first work for the UPIC, *Mycenae Alpha* (1978), is heard alongside another Polytope, *Polytope De Cluny*. Music by Jean Claude-Risset, Julio Estrada, Curtis Roads and others demonstrates UPIC's multifarious possibilities.

Iannis Xenakis

Chamber Music

Montaigne 2 x CD 2000, rec. 1991

Works For Piano

Mode CD 1999

Xenakis's music oozes outwards from centrifugal tonal centres, dancing around the usual certainties of equal temperament, making his relationship to the stubbornly rigid piano a real challenge. Instead of being cowed, however, he often chose to write these limitations into the construction of a piece. "The

basic question of *Evryali*," he wrote about his 1973 solo piano work, "was how to achieve continuity on an instrument which has an opposite nature." His solution was to use diagrams of trees as his basis, rotating the patterns to generate new shapes. Pianist Claude Helffer lumberjacks his way through Xenakis's piano music on the Montaigne disc like a man with a mission, and he's joined by The Arditti Quartet, who create definitive performances of all the string quartet and solo string music.

Helffer manages to inject a red-blooded physicality into Xenakis's piano music that's scarce within classical performance. The spiky branches of *Evryali* coagulate into a forest of linear movement that's so thick and fast the keyboard buckles under the weight of fanatical activity. Xenakis's last major piano work, *Mists* (1980), begins with imposing ascents up the piano before stochastic processes fling the material to the far ends of the keyboard. His first piano work, *Herma* (1960–61), is one of the most fiercely abstract pieces he composed, combining probability and set theory principles into a structure that's all brain and brawn. Helffer's ability to judge the composer's ever increasing speeds and intensities outruns mere technique, and the final outburst is like being hit over the head.

There's a touching spiritual link back to *Herma*'s roots on Aki Takahashi's Mode disc. The piece was composed for her father Yuji Takahashi, but Aki herself can't match Helffer's near-superhuman grandeur. However there's a fine performance of *Palimpsest*, Xenakis's 1979 work for piano and ensemble, with punchy playing from The Society Of New Music under Charles Peltz.

Violinist Jane Peters joins Takahashi for a performance of the violin/piano duo *Dikhthas* (1979), but where Peters tickles, Arditti stabs – and The Arditti Quartet were born to play Xenakis. His two major quartets, *Tetras* (1983) and *Tetora* (1990), are noticeably distinct works, the earlier piece crafting a belligerently fragmentary soundscape and the later work gelling into one of the most sustained structures Xenakis ever created. The Ardittis' attack and the tightness with which they negotiate the structural minefields of *Tetras*, traversing its abrupt switches between glissandi, gunshot pizzicato and instrumental white noise, breaks new ground in string quartet playing, while the other sides of their brains expertly navigate the cumulative structure of *Tetora*. This slowly evolving music encroaches into territory explored by Bruckner in his vast orchestral adagios, and Xenakis pushes the chamber music aesthetic towards symphonic aspirations.

Siegfried Palm
Intercomunicazione
Deutsche Grammophon CD 2002, rec. 1974
Bjørn Ianke
The Contemporary Solo Double Bass Volume 3
Simax Classics CD 2003

Another highlight of the Arditti set above sees cellist Rohan de Saram untangling the notorious solo cello *Nomos Alpha* (1966), but let's not forget the pioneering version by German cellist Siegfried Palm. His recital disc *Intercomunicazione* was one of the great New Music documents of the LP era, putting Xenakis into the context of Webern, Kagel, Zimmermann, Penderecki, Earle Brown and Isang Yun; this recent reissue has been beautifully remastered and the power of Palm's playing will never be diminished. *Nomos Alpha* made a decisive move away from stochastic music and into a complex series of calculations based around pouring pitch and durational material into 'sieves' with strict parameters, and then manipulating the resultant residue compositionally. It's consequently a breakthrough piece and whatever the processes, the cello gets dissected forensically, with each seemingly incidental sound thrown under the microscope and amplified many times over. Palm's achievement in realising the intensely supple gradations of textural detail while actually making musical sense of it all is phenomenal.

Theraps (1976) transfers comparable principles to the double bass, making telling use of glissandi that suddenly change direction. Norwegian bassist Bjørn Ianke keeps a level head under considerable duress.

Iannis Xenakis
Psappha/Rebonds/Okho Pour Trois Djembés
Mécénat Musical CD + DVD 2005

Pléïades
Harmonia Mundi CD 1996, rec. 1987

The solo percussion pieces on the Mécénat Musical disc, *Psappha* (1975) and *Rebonds* (1987–88), both set up rhythmic patterns that regenerate by elongation and acceleration. Spreading the rhythmic cells over sets of bongos, tom-toms and bass drums has the effect of giving the music a part-frustrating, part-tenacious melodic obstinacy, but these are undeniably charismatic performances by percussionist Pedro Carneiro of works that come as standard within the contemporary percussion repertoire. A bonus DVD explores the challenges.

Pléïades for six percussionists (1987) was conceived for Les Percussions De Strasbourg and involves a self-invented instrument, the "Six-Xen", which Xenakis's sieve calculations formulated into a non-standardised 19 note cell to be struck on metal bars. Its 44 minute construct shifts from pure rhythm in the opening sections towards more pitch-specific material in the middle and then back again. Again, I'm wondering if his processes become too transparent when rhythm is the only parameter on the menu. Certainly there's not the spell that springs from Steve Reich's ease with similar forces in *Drumming*.

A Colone/Nuits/Serment/Knephas/Medea
Hyperion CD 1998
Various
Pupils Of Messiaen
Chandos CD 1999

Xenakis's vocal writing retained the essential physicality of his electronic and instrumental music, but his love of the Greek language and for Greek theatre gave his choral pieces a feeling of being rooted in ancient tradition. His setting of *Medea* (1967) is a case in point: a deeply ritualistic score with intoned choral writing hinting at primordial ceremonies, as rude microtonal trombones and string writing borrowed from *Nomos Alpha* make the point that all radicals plunder tradition. *Nuits* – written in the same year – is justifiably his most celebrated choral work, and carries an unusually explicit political agenda. While he composed, Greece was falling under the rule of a military junta, and Xenakis dedicated his piece to political prisoners the world over, presumably mindful of his own wartime experiences. It opens with a web of glissandi that converts vocalising into the noise of human distress, with microtonal melodic writing making individual voices sound vulnerable and disorientated. Notated tongue clicks and whistling add to the intensity by evoking human sounds normally omitted from choral protocol; brooding, suffocated harmonies produce an apocalyptic atmosphere. Conductor James Wood and The New London Chamber Choir are Xenakis specialists, and their performances are technically and spiritually authentic. The Danish National Radio Choir on Chandos are pretty good too, performing *Nuits* with the gentler *À Hélène* and Xenakis's setting of the Hippocratic Oath, *Serment*. Works by Messiaen and Stockhausen provide context.

Iannis Xenakis
Oresteïa
Montaigne CD 2002, rec. 1987
Kraanerg
Col Legno CD 2003

Like *Medea*, *Oresteïa* fuses ancient ritual with contemporary technique. It originally consisted of two hours' worth of incidental music for a 1966 production in Michigan of the ancient Greek tragedy, but Xenakis distilled and sculpted the highlights into a 50 minute concert suite of vivid intensity. For this 1987 recording made at the Strasbourg Music Festival, he added a new scene, *Kassandra*, scored for baritone Spiros Sakkas and percussionist Sylvio Gualda, and created a new vocal technique. Sakkas half-screams and half-sings his part in an expressive falsetto that packs a dramatic punch by complementing the raw hysteria with cool control. Gualda's drums add demented undercurrents to the relentless flow of Sakkas's vocalising, and the frenzied energy of the woodwind dominates the ecstatic conclusion as the chorus chants its invented folk music.

Earlier, Xenakis created the ballet *Kraanerg* (1969) for the opening of the Ottawa Arts Centre. At a massive 75 minutes, it's one of his most extended pieces – one reason, perhaps, why it lacks the iron surefootedness that ordinarily distinguishes his structures. Another problem facing musicians mounting performances is that, apparently, coordinating the ensemble with the four-track tape is a near impossibility. When New York's ST-X Ensemble (Ensemble Xenakis USA, conducted by Charles Zachary Bornstein) revived the work in the late 1990s, DJ Spooky was co-opted for the task, but The Basel Symphony Orchestra's in-house team manage perfectly well on this meaty performance. Despite reservations about the totality, there are moments of pure genius. Long passages reminiscent of *Concret PH*, where orchestra and tape form a darkly brittle continuum, give way to dangerously unhinged orchestral outbursts placing considerable pressure on orchestral players to act like primed chamber soloists. A discernible energy is derived from this high-risk strategy. But I've no idea how you would dance to it.

Plektó/Eonta/Akanthos/N'Shima
Mode CD 1996
Échange/Okho/Akrata
Mode CD 1996
Échange/Palimpsest/Waarg/Eonta
Attacca CD no date, rec. 1987–89

The two Mode discs feature performances by the excellent ST-X Ensemble; the Attacca disc is by the Dutch ASKO Ensemble. *Eonta* (1962–64) for piano and brass quintet is stochastic music elevated to the sublime. The model Xenakis utilised for the piece was that of light refracted through water, with the piano representing water and the brass portraying near-blinding light, but this is no picture postcard representation. Splashy piano writing trickles everywhere with the power of 1000 simultaneous waterfalls. Underneath, muted brass enter imperceptibly until their reflection becomes a resonant reality; tidal waves of brass later overwhelm the piano as the two battle for supremacy. Another significant masterpiece is the Hebrew-based *N'Shima* (1975) for two voices and instruments. The microtonal vocal writing is kept determinedly untamed for the niceties of the trained voice, and the clustery brass and amplified cello accompaniment equals their raw expressivity.

Échange (1989) for bass clarinet and ensemble remains a deeply elusive work. Originally written for Dutch bass clarinet master Harry Sparnaay, who performs it on the Attacca disc, it's an unremittingly dark work that keeps any 'inner' meaning at arm's length. The bass clarinet obsessively shadows the linear movement of the ensemble, breaking off into dramatic solo cadenzas that explore straining multiphonics. Then – rare in Xenakis – a joke, as a naked tonal fanfare in the ensemble appears without reason. *Plektó* (1993) is oddball again, featuring the pianist ricocheting clusters against a web of counterpoint from flute, clarinet, violin and cello. Xenakis usually locks counterpoint into his familiar sound masses, but here lines jut out provocatively. A mediating percussion part glues the whole raggedy enterprise together.

Ata/N'Shima/Metastasis/Ioolkos/Charisma/Jonchaies
Col Legno CD 2000, rec. 1955–91
Thallein/Jalons/Phlegra/Keren/Harpsichord Works
Erato CD 2000, rec. 1990–92
**ST 48/Polytope De Montréal/Nomos
Gamma/Terretektorh/Syrmos/Achorripsis/
Persepolis/Polytope De Cluny**
Edition RZ 2 x CD 2003, rec. 1969–74

Xenakis stuffs a vast amount of information into relatively brief durations, making his works ideal for anthologising. The Col Legno compilation is a useful budget price introduction to some key pieces, while Erato double up on classy performances of large ensemble works by the Ensemble Inter-Contemporain under Pierre Boulez with a survey of Xenakis's music for avant garde harpsichordist Elisabeth Chojnacka.

The Edition RZ set is, however, much more than a convenient compilation, and dredges some very rare performances from the archives, including a welcome recording of the legendary *Terretektorh* (1965–66) for an orchestra whose members are scattered through the audience. This requires audience and musicians to reconsider their relationship to each other, and Xenakis gives his percussionists giant steel whistles that carry the spiralling ascents of the woodwind surging into infinity.

The second disc concentrates on the Polytopes, including the rarely heard *Persepolis*, originally composed for a music festival in Iran. This is another example of Xenakis blurring the distinction between the white heat of his technology and a sense of the arcane, as his Iranian folk sources are distilled into an imagined ancient electronica. Music from two billion light years away, here and now.